Read the Reviews

"This book on Scaleable Six Sigma is for the rest of us — who know the power Six Sigma can bring our organizations but cannot fund the heavy start-up costs required by most Six Sigma approaches. Finally, small and mid-sized organizations can get a faster return — often within the first year — on their investments in Six Sigma and other continuous improvement methodologies."

> **—Leo B. Walker**, Vice President, Composition
> NEBS, Inc. (A Subsidiary of Deluxe, Inc.)

"If you manage or work in a small to mid-size company, this book is a must-read! The authors provide a common sense approach to Six Sigma recognizing the differences in small to mid-size company deployments. The Scaleable Six Sigma deployment model in this book will help any small to mid-size company implement Six Sigma successfully."

> **—David Porter**, Director, Engineering & Quality
> New Standard Corporation

"Full of practical advice and real-world examples, this book sorts through the clutter of Six Sigma myths and misconceptions and gives small to medium enterprises a doable, affordable path to Six Sigma. Burton and Sams dispel the myth that Six Sigma can be implemented only by large companies with a ton of dedicated resources. This excellent book is chock-full of valuable implementation guidance and tools to use throughout the enterprise, while at the same time remaining accessible to the average, nonstatistician reader. It is a first-rate contribution to Six Sigma thinking."

> **—Sherry Gordon**, VP Supplier Performance Intelligence
> Emptoris

SIX SIGMA FOR SMALL AND MID-SIZED ORGANIZATIONS

Success Through
Scaleable Deployment

Terence T. Burton & Jeff L. Sams

ISBN 1-932159-21-5

Printed and bound in the U.S.A. Printed on acid-free paper
10 9 8 7 6 5 4 3 2 1

Library of Congress Cataloging-in-Publication Data

Burton, Terence T., 1950–
   Six sigma for small and mid-sized organizations : success through
scaleable deployment / by Terence T. Burton and Jeff L. Sams.
      p. cm.
   Includes index.
   ISBN 1-932159-21-5 (hardback : alk. paper)
   1. Total quality management. 2. Six sigma (Quality control standard). 3.
Small business—Management. I. Sams, Jeff L., 1963–. II. Title.
   HD62.15.B8673 2004
   658.4′013—dc22   2004018023

   Direct all inquiries to J. Ross Publishing, Inc., 6501 Park of Commerce Blvd., Suite 200,
Boca Raton, Florida 33487.

Phone: (561) 869-3900
Fax: (561) 892-0700
Web: www.jrosspub.com

TABLE OF CONTENTS

PREFACE

Why does the world need another Six Sigma book and what is unique about this one? The fact is, while there are many great textbooks that cover the statistical theory and methodology of Six Sigma, there are limited resources for successful Six Sigma deployments in small and mid-sized organizations. These organizations *want* and *need* the same improvements as larger corporations, but they do not have the financial and human resources to support a full-scale GE-type Six Sigma initiative. They need a different deployment model that fits their operating environment, and this is the *voice of the customer* for whom this book is written. *Six Sigma for Small and Mid-Sized Organizations* is a practical, quick read that solves the mystery of implementing Six Sigma for these markets. It is written by professionals who work with and understand the realities of small and mid-sized organizations. We have put our best effort forward to make this a *"show me how to"* approach to Six Sigma, particularly in the nonstatistical areas of leadership, strategy, deployment, execution, and measurement. The approaches presented in this book are based on many successful Six Sigma deployments in small and mid-sized organizations.

It is no secret that Six Sigma is the new metaphor shift and world standard for customer satisfaction and profitability improvement in today's industrial society. Almost every organization is either implementing, contemplating, or busy learning more about Six Sigma. Most of the textbooks, industry trade articles, seminars, and other media present Six Sigma as a strategic improvement initiative for large corporations. The deployment approaches are replicated around the successful deployment experiences at companies such as GE, Motorola, Honeywell, Bombardier, and hundreds of other large organizations. Unfortunately, the deployments of these large organizations have left small and mid-sized organizations scratching their heads in confusion about how to implement Six Sigma.

Many of these larger organizations have now dropped the gauntlet and are requiring their supply base to implement Six Sigma as a condition of future business. The market and the opportunity for Six Sigma in small and mid-sized organizations are huge because these organizations represent the other 80 percent of the total value stream. Extending Six Sigma into the total supply chain presents tremendous opportunities for improvement, and most of the small and mid-sized organizations we talk to have a genuine interest in implementing these same improvements in their organizations. The problem is that the entry barriers, as they have been defined and accepted as the standard Six Sigma deployment protocol, are way beyond the reach of small and mid-sized organizations. Therein lies the deployment dilemma for these companies and the reason for this book.

Organizations are bombarded with advice about Six Sigma from consultants, trade publications, web sites, and assorted gurus. A lot of this advice is valuable, but much of it is an inconsistent, ambiguous generalization of what it takes to be successful in your own environment, especially a small and mid-sized company environment. In fact, some of this advice serves the Six Sigma training consultants more than it does their clients. Some even hype it up and suggest ratios of how many *black belts* per million dollars in revenue, how many *green belts* per *black belt*, and minimum savings goals per project. Without knowing anything about their client's strategic and operating issues, the prescription for Six Sigma success is presented as a laundry list of *belt* (and, of course, *training/ consulting*) requirements. Six Sigma has evolved to a game of epidemic proportions about belts, and everyone wants one — like some mad belt disease. Successful organizations realize that Six Sigma is about results, not belts.

Others have turned their offerings toward public and web-based Six Sigma offerings in an attempt to address the needs of small and mid-sized organizations. Individuals may go off to learn the methodology and tools, but then return to an organization missing the strategy, deployment, and implementation infrastructure. Unfortunately, a $150 million company with a few lonely black and green belts scattered around the organization while everyone else is running in different directions does not cut it. For those who understand statistics, the belts, the statistical engineering tools, and the statistical software are the *trivial many* side of the Six Sigma Pareto chart. Six Sigma, or any strategic initiative, requires a serious commitment, unwavering leadership, a well-defined strategy, and a formal deployment and implementation infrastructure. These are the *vital few* elements of the Six Sigma Pareto chart — the elements that allow organizations to either deliver unbelievable financial results or create another short-lived fad improvement program. Organizations cannot buy cultural transformation and breakthroughs in performance from a university or a web site.

As large organizations work their way down the food chain and integrate their supply base into their Six Sigma initiatives, a "one-size-fits-all" approach to Six Sigma is a prescription for failure, especially in small and mid-sized organizations. Having had similar experiences with TQM, reengineering, ERP, and lean over the years, we observed Six Sigma being sold as another Yellow Brick Road improvement program focused on large organizations, too focused on the mechanics and tools, and too focused on *belts* (developing armies of black belts, green belts, and yellow belts). The bottom line was that a different Six Sigma deployment model was needed for small and mid-sized organizations, one they could implement at a pace where they could actually digest and achieve self-funding benefits quicker and without the significant resource commitment and overhead structure of the large-corporation Six Sigma approach. We developed a more manageable approach to Six Sigma deployment (Scaleable Six Sigma™) and discovered that small and mid-sized organizations can, in fact, achieve faster and more impressive results than their larger, more complex customers. This scaleable approach makes implementation user friendly and affordable enough so that these organizations can now tap into Six Sigma and benefit from it. Scaleable Six Sigma™ is about less training and more results. A similar analogy is the personal computer and Internet evolution. Fifteen years ago, the only PCs were in the workplace. It was not until everyone could afford to have a PC and Internet access that we became a *digitally fluent* society.

WHY THIS BOOK IS A MUST-READ

Six Sigma for Small and Mid-Sized Organizations presents an overview of the Six Sigma methodology and tools and many new and practical approaches to Six Sigma deployment aimed at small and mid-sized organizations. If you are a Six Sigma purist in a large organization, you may not agree with some of these different approaches, but they work for these small and mid-sized organizations. This book also includes many new lessons about Six Sigma deployment that are equally applicable to large organizations and small divisions of large organizations as well. Our aim is to provide a practical implementation roadmap of the most important aspects of Six Sigma and, at the same time, include knowledge about the most critical success factors such as leadership, strategy and implementation planning, deployment and execution, and closed-loop performance that are universal to all organizations. These are the things that really matter...things that are not included with belts.

We are extremely pleased with the final product of this book because it is not just another Six Sigma book. *Six Sigma for Small and Mid-Sized Organi-*

zations incorporates many new concepts, practices, and principles of Six Sigma deployment for small and mid-sized companies. These organizations experience a high degree of frustration when they contemplate how to implement Six Sigma without spending millions of dollars and dedicating 30 percent of their workforce full time to the program. The objectives of this book are to:

- Provide a new framework (*Scaleable Six Sigma*™) for deploying Six Sigma in small and mid-sized organizations that takes into consideration their operating constraints and need for faster return on investment
- Build awareness and importance of soft-side improvement issues (*The Sixteen Key Requirements for Six Sigma Success*) to help organizations and individuals avoid the most common pitfalls of Six Sigma or any other strategic improvement and steer clear of flavor-of-the-month fad programs
- Present a detailed discussion of the *Define, Measure, Analyze, Improve, Control (DMAIC)* methodology with practical applications to small and mid-sized organizations
- Discuss the importance of *Transactional Six Sigma* and the benefits of including the administrative and support functions in the Six Sigma deployment
- Understand the strategic journey from *Operational Excellence* to *Enterprise Excellence* to *Extended Enterprise Excellence* to *Adaptive Enterprise Excellence*
- Provide a *Strategy Deployment and Project Selection* model to help launch and target Six Sigma efforts on the highest impact opportunities and to maintain real-time alignment to the business plan
- Develop Six Sigma cohesion via the concepts of *Mentoring and Individual Project Management,* while learning how to lead and mentor project teams and manage projects to a successful outcome — success, one project at a time
- Provide a deployment (*Plan-Deploy-Execute*) and performance measurement approach for Six Sigma (*Six Sigma Assessment Process or SSAP*)
- Learn about the strategic compatibility of *kaizen, lean, Six Sigma, ERP, and enabling IT* and how to integrate these methodologies into a unified powerhouse improvement initiative

We are confident that you will find many new and interesting concepts in *Six Sigma for Small and Mid-Sized Organizations*. Our mission was to provide a book that delineates how to implement Six Sigma successfully in small-scale environments. This book provides the leadership, strategy, implementation planning, deployment, execution, integration, alignment, soft-side Six Sigma, and performance measurement issues that are universal to all organizations and shows how these can be applied successfully in small and mid-size organizations. It is a practical Six Sigma cookbook and "give me the answers quick" guide that provides a structured roadmap to success. We have made every attempt to make our work a hands-on, no-nonsense approach for executives and practitioners seeking to achieve the benefits of Six Sigma without leveraging the whole farm. Supplying models, hands-on techniques, and a framework for small-organization Six Sigma success, this book provides a collection of new skill sets needed to retrofit Six Sigma to the realities of small and mid-sized organizations.

> *Terence T. Burton, President*
> *The Center for Excellence in Operations, Inc.*
>
> *Jeff L. Sams, Director of North American Operations*
> *Casco Products, a Unit of Sequa Corporation*

THE AUTHORS

Terence T. Burton is Founder and President of The Center for Excellence in Operations, Inc. (CEO). He has over thirty years of experience in manufacturing, quality assurance, engineering, materials management, purchasing, distribution, and management consulting. Terry holds a B.S. and M.S. in Industrial Engineering from the University of New Haven and an M.B.A. from Boston University. He is a certified Six Sigma Black Belt, National LEAN SIG Chairman, and CPIM certified member of APICS. He is a frequent instructor/educator, speaker, and author at various industry association events and writes for numerous trade publications. Terry has written hundreds of articles on lean, Six Sigma, supply chain, and accelerated product development and is the author of five books published by Prentice-Hall, Harcourt Brace, and J. Ross Publishing.

Jeff L. Sams is Director of North American Operations for Casco Products, a Unit of Sequa Corporation. He has over sixteen years of experience in manufacturing, quality, operations, and customer engineering. Jeff has extensive implementation experience in lean and Six Sigma, having previously worked for Allied Signal, Johnson Controls, Toyota Gosei, and Bosch. He holds a B.S. and M.S. in Organizational Development from Southern Illinois University, an M.B.A. from the University of Tennessee, and is a certified Six Sigma Master Black

Belt and Certified Quality Engineer. Jeff is a member of APICS, the American Society for Quality, the American Society for Training and Development, and the International Society of Six Sigma Professionals.

ACKNOWLEDGMENTS

If we could mention the names of everyone who has influenced our work, this section would be as long as the book itself. Even if we tried, we would inadvertently omit a few individuals. At the top of our list are our families, friends, and close professional colleagues who provided constant encouragement to write this book. They knew that what we were doing with small and mid-sized organizations was a very entrepreneurial and groundbreaking Six Sigma activity. Much of this book is about what we do on a day-to-day basis, but it takes a phenomenal amount of time, commitment, and sacrifice to communicate this in a professional way. For the past year, our families and friends tolerated the many weekends, holidays, and late nights to create this book, and we are fully appreciative of their patience and understanding.

The next group of people we wish to acknowledge are the hundreds of companies and clients, thousands of executives, and hundreds of thousands of people with whom we have worked collectively over the years. We developed the content of this book together, working through the universe of business challenges and discovering successes together. That is the best kind of success, the kind where you make a positive difference in thousands of employees' lives. This book would not be possible without the experiences, education, and knowledge gained by our affiliations with you.

Another group we wish to acknowledge is our favorite professional societies: the American Society for Quality, the American Production and Inventory Control Society, the Association for Manufacturing Excellence, the Society of Manufacturing Engineers, the Product Development Management Association, and the Supply Chain Institute. We have crossed paths with thousands of fellow professionals over the years, and our affiliations have allowed us to grow along many paths. We also thank the universities, educators, and authors for the thousands of textbooks, trade publications and articles, web sites, webinars, workshops and seminars, and other learning opportunities that are available to all of us. Writing this book creates a new level of appreciation for the commitment and efforts of fellow authors who also keep the knowledge pipeline full for all of us. It also makes one appreciate the great education/professional development infrastructure we all have available to us throughout our entire lives.

Many executives and professional colleagues provided their time, invaluable insights, feedback, and thought leadership ideas for our *Six Sigma for Small and Mid-Sized Organizations* mission: Bill Garrison, Don Blake, and Kurt Robertson of Boeing; Gary Cone of Global Productivity Solutions; Frank Colantuono, Bill McDermott, Paul Barden, George Loo, Marty Mrugal, Sudipta Bhattacharya, and Eddie Whitfield of SAP America; Steve Schaus of Sequa Corp.; Charles Annette and Peter Kornhaas of Belimo Air Controls; Art Dirik of Demantra Systems; Tom Shaw of the Government Electronics and Information Technology Association of the Electronic Industries Alliance (GEIA); Mary Driscoll, Vin Capasso, and Eric Simeonidis of W.R. Grace; Bob McDonald and Jeff Kleiber of Fox River Paper; Oddie Leopando and Terry Bell of Maxima Technologies; Darrell Taylor of MKS Instruments; Steve Boeder of Libbey Corporation; John Tallis of Thomas and Betts; Mike Curtis and Frank Milne of Symmetry Medical; Leo Walker and Jen Morrissey of New England Business Services (NEBS); Bob Watson of the Juran Institute; Joanne Kalp and Dave Gronewald of Tyco Healthcare; Bob McInturff of McInturff & Associates; Chris Christensen of the University of Wisconsin Madison; Douglas McGill of Lockheed Martin; Eric Lussier of Atlantic Research Corp.; Dennis Grahn of Menasha Corp.; Alfonso Navarro of Stewart Warner Performance; Mort Zifferer, Dave Porter, and Bob Lefeber of New Standard Corporation; Dave Delmonico and Peter Horton of Teradyne; Sherry Gordon of Emptoris; Dan Marconi of Hubbell, Inc.; Mike Gastonguay of GE; and Mike Cyger and everyone at the best Six Sigma web site in the world, iSixSigma.com.

Special thanks to Drew Gierman and Barbara Caras of J. Ross Publishing. Without the entrepreneurial and publishing competencies of these individuals, our book would not have been possible.

Through the professional collaboration of everyone we have mentioned, this book was born. This was a professionally rewarding experience for us, especially now that we can share the results of our efforts with you.

Web Added Value

Free value-added materials available from
the Download Resource Center at www.jrosspub.com

At J. Ross Publishing we are committed to providing today's professional with practical, hands-on tools that enhance the learning experience and give readers an opportunity to apply what they have learned. That is why we offer free ancillary materials available for download on this book and all participating Web Added Value™ publications. These online resources may include interactive versions of material that appears in the book or supplemental templates, worksheets, models, plans, case studies, proposals, spreadsheets and assessment tools, among other things. Whenever you see the WAV™ symbol in any of our publications, it means bonus materials accompany the book and are available from the Web Added Value Download Resource Center at www.jrosspub.com.

Downloads available for *Six Sigma for Small and Mid-Sized Organizations: Success Through Scaleable Deployment* consist of value-added Six Sigma implementation tools, templates, worksheets, and assessment guides.

1

SIX SIGMA
TAKES HOLD

Six Sigma or 6σ — If you have not heard of it, you have probably been living under a rock! If you have heard of it and are not deploying Six Sigma as a strategic initiative, you are either in denial or suffering from sticker shock from the implementation costs. Six Sigma has been presented as a strategic improvement initiative for large corporations. There are many success stories out there about Six Sigma at GE, Motorola, Honeywell, Bombardier, 3M, American Express, Sears Roebuck, Ford, and Toshiba, to name a few. Most large organizations have been deploying Six Sigma for years now and have posted megabucks in their annual reports to show for it. Granted, they have invested millions of dollars in human and financial capital costs for their Six Sigma implementations, but they have impressive returns on investment for their efforts. In a recent quarterly report, Caterpillar attributed $150 million of its profits to its Six Sigma success. Motorola claims to have saved $15 billion over the past eleven years. GE reports a $2.5 billion savings from Six Sigma from its combined operating units. Honeywell reports about $1 billion per year savings. Although these numbers are fact, pulling the numbers out of these organizations' annual reports does nothing to help a small or mid-sized organization figure out if Six Sigma is the right strategy for it to implement. Make no mistake about it, Six Sigma is here to stay because its success is in the numbers. Many of these larger organizations have now dropped the gauntlet and are requiring their supply base to implement Six Sigma as a condition of future business. This presents a serious gap and a serious challenge for small and mid-sized organizations. Large company deployments have included a few key suppliers in each wave of their black belt or green belt training. However, this approach is

1

not creating enough critical mass fast enough to bring the entire supply chain on board.

THE PROBLEM: ONE SIZE *DOES NOT* FIT ALL

The market and the opportunity for Six Sigma in small and mid-sized organizations are huge because these organizations represent the other 80 percent of the total value stream. The benefits of Six Sigma are both internal to these organizations and residual to upstream suppliers and downstream customers. The problem is that the entry barriers, as they have been defined and accepted as the standard Six Sigma deployment protocol, are way beyond the reach of smaller and mid-sized organizations.

An all-too-familiar story line from large corporations and their large consulting firms is that Six Sigma requires millions of dollars in investment, dedication of full-time resources, and training of the masses. There is a lot of truth to this statement if you are a $10 billion company with 14,000 employees scattered around the globe. Face it, it is difficult to get 14,000 people on the same page of any improvement strategy. The remote organizations and cultural differences, the hundreds of executives and managers who feel a need to influence the direction of their program, the political agendas, and communication issues make deployment and implementation a very complex process. Another complexity is the number of layers and links in the total supply chains of these organizations. Fortunately, these factors are much simpler to deal with in smaller and mid-sized organizations. Those who have experienced this dilemma will agree that this Six Sigma deployment structure and approach is not only inappropriate, but totally unrealistic for smaller and mid-sized organizations.

About four years ago, I (TB) was meeting with a CEO from a $100 million company. During this meeting, my firm presented an executive overview of Six Sigma and how to deploy the methodology for success. The CEO, an ex-automotive industry executive and engineer, commented, "I understand what large organizations must do to make Six Sigma stick. I used to work for one. Our business is much simpler and our company can't afford this traditional approach. There's no question that we can benefit from Six Sigma. Further, I believe that we can achieve Six Sigma success without all of that overhead and start-up investment. Would you be willing to pursue a more entrepreneurial approach that fits our requirements?" Being familiar with the realities and constraints of smaller and mid-sized organizations, I could not agree more with his comment and it turned my lights on. The real question was: "Can an organization achieve significant benefits from Six Sigma without spending millions of dollars up front, without educating the masses and going through the traditional top-down black belt thing?" That discussion made me realize that Six Sigma is not about belts or how many black and green belts an organization needs. It is all about business improvement and whatever it takes to make it happen. We shook hands and went to work collaborating and experimenting with an alternative implementation model for Six Sigma. For nine months, their deployment was an entrepreneurial adventure. To make a long story short, we achieved great success with a different Six Sigma deployment model focused on the realities and constraints of these organizations. We also organized our kaizen, lean, Six Sigma, supply chain, and new product development offerings into an integrated powerhouse improvement effort for these organizations; hence, a quiet expansion of our Six Sigma practice to the low-end marketplace and the essence of this book.

As large organizations work their way down the food chain and integrate their supply base into their Six Sigma initiatives, a "one-size-fits-all" approach to Six Sigma is a prescription for failure, especially in small and mid-sized organizations. Having had similar experiences with total quality management (TQM), reengineering, enterprise resource planning (ERP), and lean over the years, we were feeling that Six Sigma was being sold as another Yellow Brick Road improvement program focused on large organizations, too focused on the mechanics and tools, and too focused on developing armies of champions, black belts, green belts, and yellow belts. We will discuss these topics in more detail in subsequent chapters, but the bottom line was that a different Six Sigma deployment model was needed for smaller and mid-sized organizations, one that they could implement at a pace where they can actually digest and achieve self-funding benefits quicker and without the significant resource commitment and overhead structure of the large-corporation Six Sigma approach. We developed a more scaleable approach to Six Sigma deployment and discovered that smaller and mid-sized organizations can, in fact, achieve faster and more impressive results than their larger, more complex customers. This scaleable approach makes implementation user friendly and affordable enough so that these organizations can now tap into Six Sigma and benefit from it. A similar analogy is the personal computer and Internet evolution. Fifteen years ago, the only PCs were in the workplace. It was not until everyone could afford to have a PC and Internet access that we became a *digitally fluent* society. The remainder of this book presents an overview of the Six Sigma methodology and tools and many new and practical approaches to Six Sigma deployment aimed at smaller and mid-sized organizations. If you are a Six Sigma purist in a large organization, you may not agree with some of these different approaches, but it works for smaller and mid-sized organizations. Our aim is to provide a practical implementation roadmap of the most important aspects of Six Sigma and, at the same time, include knowledge about the most critical success factors such as leadership, strategy and implementation planning, execution, and closed-loop performance that are universal to all organizations.

THE EVOLUTION OF SIX SIGMA

One of the most interesting aspects of this book project was chasing down the roots of Six Sigma. One of our conclusions was that process variation has been around as long as Neanderthal man, swinging his club at saber-toothed tigers and understanding the true consequences of variation. We were enlightened with so many interesting history lessons about variation and decided to share a few of the more relevant ones with you.

The original roots of Six Sigma can be traced back to Carl Frederick Gauss (1777–1885), who introduced the concept of the normal curve. Around that same era, Eli Whitney (1765–1825) designed the cotton gin that standardized the separation of cottonseed from the short-staple cotton fiber. Whitney's greatest contribution, however, was his "uniformity system" of manufacturing interchangeable components by demonstrating that randomly selected parts could be fitted together into a complete, working musket lock. In his factory in New Haven, Connecticut, Whitney proved that standardized machine tools, used by workers who were not skilled gunsmiths, could produce standardized parts to exact specifications and that any part could be used as a component of any musket. This factory was probably the first mass-production facility with standard work and spawned the machine tool industry throughout the southern and central Connecticut region.

Uniform measurement systems evolved in the early to mid 1800s with the introduction of patterns, templates, no-go gages, and a few other methods. These measurement systems eventually evolved into specifications. One such company of this era was Downings and Abbotts Company, a Concord, New Hampshire manufacturer of stagecoaches for Wells Fargo and many other customers across the country. Downings and Abbotts had a lean, progressive assembly operation where patterns were used to cut white oak and ash wood for body parts and spokes, patterns were used for the millwork parts and leather upholstery, and templates were used to paint fancy designs on the exterior. This was not a mass-production line, but a mass-customization line where coaches were built to a customer's carefully drawn-up specifications. Many of the components were standardized, and Downings and Abbotts would also provide standard options or one-of-a-kind options often requiring hand forging. The company prided itself on quality and later developed stylebooks for its stagecoach, pie wagon, hearse, buggy, and omnibus product lines.

One of the most famous examples is Henry Ford's 1913 automobile assembly line, where the need was for consistent, good parts to be available for production. Variation caused the assembly workers to slow down or stop the process while they sifted through parts bins for a good part. The auto industry and its suppliers drove a new Industrial Revolution that demanded new levels of quality and consistency of parts. Skilled craftsmen with no-go gages who could make parts fit together were replaced with assembly line equipment with a limited process capability. This also drove the evolution of new methods to define and monitor process quality.

Six Sigma as a measurement standard in product variation was used in the 1920s when Walter Shewhart showed that three sigma from the mean is the point where a process requires correction. Shewhart was really focusing more on product quality, not process quality. In the early part of the twentieth century, he was viewing quality from the goalpost perspective where anything inside the specification was acceptable.

Of the World War II era, we are all familiar with gurus such as Juran and Deming, who were commissioned to share U.S. manufacturing management practices with Japan in an effort to rebuild its economy. Deming promoted his famous Plan-Do-Check-Act (PDCA) cycle, and statistical quality methods grew rapidly. For over twenty years, companies like Toyota mastered these powerful quality improvement methodologies before anyone knew it. Another related driver of change at that time was the modern globalization movement, which had begun in the White Mountains of New Hampshire. At the Mount Washington Hotel in 1944, the soon-to-be winners of the war met and conceived several multinational institutions like the World Bank, the International Monetary Fund, and the General Agreement of Tariffs and Trade. Their hope was to inoculate the world from the economic influenza and rabid nationalism that had started World War II. In the process, they seeded a change to the global economy forever.

The 1973 oil embargo was an enormous wake-up call to the rest of the world. Most organizations spent the rest of that decade becoming painfully aware of the importance of quality, and by 1980 we were all scratching our heads as we watched the documentary "If Japan Can, Why Can't We?" The 1980s became the era of field-of-dreams improvement and team-based problem solving. Although Nashua Corporation was featured in that 1980 documentary, there were rumors of a major organizational shake-up because state inspection stickers that used its adhesive products began to fall off windshields. Organizations were losing world market share rapidly and they needed quick fixes. Many organizations spent millions on training the masses about methodologies being touted by gurus such as Juran, Crosby, Deming, Feigenbaum, and a few others. They were all driven by the belief that if you preach quality, the results will come. These gurus were right; however, execution by most organizations was poor and Total Quality Improvement (TQM) became a fad program. In this era, companies like Motorola, Texas Instruments, and Polaroid began to investigate statistical engineering, and Ford Motor Company also began to explore Taguchi experiments to improve car designs and quality.

We refer to the methodologies of this era as *sufficient cause thinking,* where quality circle teams used brainstorming, graphical techniques, the PDCA cycle, and other basic problem-solving tools. People met and, for the most part, speculated on the cause and effect relationships, voted out the priorities, and then took short-term actions. It was better than individual hip shooting, but was often far from data- and fact-driven change. Those who dabbled in more sophisticated statistical engineering techniques were totally misunderstood, and many of these individuals were accused of having "a solution looking for a problem" mentality. The concept of working in teams and involving employees was in its infancy for most organizations that forgot that when you hire a pair of hands, you also get a brain. Many of these improvements were impressive because these teams were able to pick off a lot of low-hanging fruit, and America certainly had a lot of low-hanging fruit as far as quality goes. Some of these actions were permanent, but the majority of these actions were symptomatic fixes because they were based on opinions, not facts. In all fairness, time pressures and the need for quick answers drove people and organizations to these approaches. Some of these organizations celebrated that 90 percent of their workforce was on quality improvement teams and that 80 percent of their teams had been together for over a year. While *sufficient cause thinking* is a step in the right direction, Six Sigma takes the organization to the next level of *fact-driven root cause analysis.*

The real credit for Six Sigma as we know it today goes to Motorola in the late 1970s and specifically to an engineer and lead Six Sigma architect named Bill Smith. Motorola developed the Six Sigma methodology and documented over $16 billion in savings. More recently, hundreds of organizations around the globe are pursuing Six Sigma as a critical component of their business strategy. More recent pioneers such as Mikel Harry, Richard Schroeder, Bill Ross, Gary Cone, Steve Zinkgraf, John Lupienski, and several others deserve honorable mention for further thought leadership and development of the Six Sigma methodology at companies like GE, Honeywell, 3M, Whirlpool, and other highly publicized successes.

As a sidebar, we want to share a funny aspect of our research. Figure 1.1 provides a comical perspective on specifications. This text actually arrived as an e-mail joke from a colleague who knew we were conducting this research,

The U.S. standard railroad gauge (the width between the 2 rails) is 4', 8.5", which is an exceedingly odd number. Why was that gauge used? Because that's the way railroads were built in England, and the U.S. railroads were built by English expatriates. Why did the English build them like that? Because the first rail lines were built by the same people who built the pre-railroad tramways, and that's the gauge they used. Why, then, did "they" use that gauge? Because the people who built the tramways used the same tools that they used for building wagons, and the wagons themselves used that wheel spacing.

Okay! Now we're getting somewhere. Why did the wagons have that particular odd wheel spacing? Well, if they tried to use any other spacing, the wagon wheels would break on some of the old, long-distance roads in England...Because that's the spacing of the wheel ruts. So who built those old rutted roads? The first long-distance roads in Europe and England were built by Imperial Rome for its legions. The roads have been used ever since. And what about the ruts in the roads? Roman war chariots first formed the initial ruts, which everyone else had to match for fear of destroying the chariots' wagon wheels. Since the chariots were made for Imperial Rome...they were all alike in the manner of wheel spacing.

The U.S. standard railroad gauge derives from the original specifications for an Imperial Roman war chariot. Specifications and bureaucracies live forever. So the next time you are handed a specification and wonder what horse's backside came up with it — you may be exactly right, because the Imperial Roman war chariots were made just wide enough to accommodate the backsides of two war horses. Thus, we have the answer to the original question.

Expanding on this idea, when we see a space shuttle sitting on its launch pad, there are two big booster rockets attached to the sides of the main fuel tank. These are solid rocket boosters, which are made by Thiokol Corp. at its factory in Utah. The engineers who designed these boosters might have preferred to make them a bit fatter, but the boosters had to be shipped by train from the factory to the launch site. OK, now you might have figured out where this is going. The railroad line from the factory had to run through a tunnel in the mountains. The boosters had to fit through that tunnel. The tunnel is slightly wider than the railroad track, and the railroad track is about as wide as two horses' backsides.

So, the next time you are handed a specification, remember this story about a major design of what is arguably the world's most advanced transportation system that was determined over 2000 years ago by a horse's backside!

Figure 1.1   A lesson in specifications and the 5 Whys.

and we are not sure where it came from. Anyone who has spent his or her career dealing with specification issues should appreciate it as much as we did.

Specifications are a topic unto their own. Many designers overspecify tolerance limits beyond form/fit/function requirements or the physical limitations of process capability because they believe that this will improve manufacturing quality. In many cases, specifications are cut and pasted from previous CAD drawings to save time. There is never time for detailed tolerance studies. Often, there are too many critical dimensions specified; if everything is important, the chances of design for manufacturability drop significantly. Manufacturing responds by staying on the high side of the specification in case there is need for rework. Everyone spends all of their time pointing fingers at each other and everyone loses. Companies such as Motorola and many others have made great strides by rationalizing product and process specifications. As a precaution, we wish to state here that rationalizing and relaxing specifications is not the total answer. It often helps, but it is typically the engineer's solution to the problem.

Six Sigma is rapidly becoming the new metaphor shift in today's industrial society and the new world standard for customer satisfaction and profitability improvement. Almost every organization is implementing, contemplating, or busy learning more about Six Sigma. Notwithstanding its twenty-plus-year history beginning at Motorola and the usual hype of any new management concept that promises huge bottom-line benefits, Six Sigma is paying off in a big way. Benchmarking information obtained from industry sources such as the American Society for Quality, iSixSigma.com, consultants, and many others indicates that organizations are saving millions from their Six Sigma efforts. But beyond the initial savings, organizations are building a solid foundation for growth and cash generation through common analysis tools and a global improvement language.

WHY YOU NEED SIX SIGMA

Does your business have problems? Do your business and operations processes have variation within them? We will give you the answer: a resounding YES! YES! Many businesses have different versions of the same chronic, repeat problems. Listen to the voice of the internal as well as external customers and this often becomes clear. You may hear phrases like, "This is similar to the (X) problem we had on the (Y) program" or "Customer B is experiencing the same interface problems with our system as Customer A did last year" or "We've already made a lot of progress on this issue." These types of phrases are indicative of chronic, systemic problems. Furthermore, how many times has your organization supposedly fixed, or attempted to fix, these problems? Two great examples are returns and allowances and excess/obsolete inventory. How do we fix these problems? We allocate reserves to cover the anticipated expenses, but does that ever fix the problem? If you really had a Six Sigma process, you would have just $3.40 in returns and allowance expenses per million dollars of revenue, or $3.40 in obsolete write-downs per million dollars of inventory!

The solutions to these types of chronic or systemic problems are unknown to your organization. This is not as bold an assumption as one might initially presume, as it seems intuitive that if you had the solutions, you would have already implemented them. Therefore, whether the problems are old or brand new, the variation is unknown, the root causes of variation are unexplainable, and the permanent solutions are unknown. Current thinking brought about current problems and is not sufficient to solve them. Some organizations really believe that this variation is black magic or an art form, but the reality is that it is not. This reminds us of a large advertising agency we visited which believed that Six Sigma was not applicable to its environment because it did not have business processes like other organizations; it provided 100 percent creative services to its clients. This is also a familiar argument in many R&D, engineering, and marketing organizations. If you believe that this variation is an art form, then you will accept and institutionalize variation — and it will be reflected in the cost of running your business in this manner. If you believe that much of this variation is explainable and the root causes of variation can be reduced/eliminated, you will reduce your operating costs and improve customer satisfaction significantly. But you need a new way of thinking about these challenges: Six Sigma.

It is the approach of Six Sigma that makes it unique. The statistical tools used in the Six Sigma process are not new. However, these tools have only recently gained widespread practical application due to the advance of computer software and hardware in order to put the tools into the hands of the masses. One of the key components of Six Sigma is the methodology of Define, Measure, Analyze, Improve, and Control (or DMAIC), which we will cover in more detail in Chapter 4.

BASIC STATISTICS AND RELEVANCE OF SIGMA

Sigma is a Greek term used to describe variation. As we mentioned earlier, the Gaussian or normal distribution (Figure 1.2), commonly known as the bell curve, was developed by Carl Frederick Gauss. This distribution was defined as having a mean or average, plus and minus three standard deviations. For a better understanding, let's take a closer look at the concept of the normal

68.26%	of the data will fall within + / − 1σ from the mean
95.46%	of the data will fall within + / − 2σ from the mean
99.73%	of the data will fall within + / − 3σ from the mean
99.9937%	of the data will fall within + / − 4σ from the mean
99.999943%	of the data will fall within + / − 5σ from the mean
99.9999998%	of the data will fall within + / − 6σ from the mean

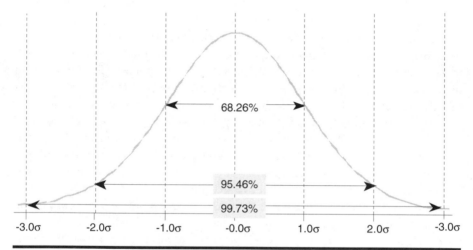

Figure 1.2   The normal distribution.

distribution and its implications. The mean is the statistical equivalent to average. Sigma is a term used to describe variation in terms of standard deviation. Simplified, standard deviation is defined as a space equal to the average of the sum of distances each data point is from the grand average of all the data. An example would be taking a group of people and defining their average height, then going back and asking each person how far his or her height is from the group's average height, and then taking the average of the sum of those distances. This would yield the average distance away from the overall average height of the group. Standard deviation, therefore, is loosely translated as average distance away from the overall average.

The overall (or grand) average of a normal group of data, plus and minus three standard deviations, makes up the "normal" distribution. This means that the data are centered about the mean and move away from it in a symmetric fashion. Therefore, if you randomly selected data from a population that was normally distributed, such as height in a randomly selected group, you would see that as more data are collected, the record of the data (such as Xs or tick marks) begins to form a bell shape. This is quite logical if you stop to think about it. Most of the data will be in the middle, centered about the average, as this is what creates the average. The further you move away from the average, whether higher or lower, the less data you would expect to see. This "stacking" of the data toward the middle and tapering toward the ends forms the bell-shaped curve or normal distribution.

The normal distribution states that 99.73 percent of the data in a normally distributed environment will be between the mean (average) plus and minus three standard deviations. To return to our earlier example, let's assume the average height of the group is five feet, eight inches and the average distance away from the five-feet, eight-inch mean is two inches. In this example, we would conclude that if this group was randomly selected, 99.73 percent of the people would be between five feet, two inches and six feet, two inches tall. This comes from subtracting three standard deviations of two inches each from the average and adding three standard deviations of two inches each to it as well:

$$5'8'' - (3 * 2'') = 5'2'', \ 5'8'' + (3 * 2'') = 6'2''$$

This information has a powerful impact on the ability to apply statistics to probabilities of occurrence. For example, if we were planning to continue to select from this population, we could predict that 95 percent of the people would be between five feet, four inches and six feet tall. The reason for this is that the normal distribution states that 95 percent of the data will fall within two standard deviations of the mean:

$$5'8'' \pm (2 * 2'') = 6' \text{ and } 5'4'', \text{ respectively}$$

Finally, in a normal distribution, 68 percent of the data will be within plus and minus one standard deviation of the mean.

Think of the power of this information! If we have one thousand people being hired for a factory and we need to purchase uniforms, lab coats, safety shoes, etc., we know after our initial hires of, say, thirty people, how many of each size to order. For example, we would be able to predict the following patterns for purchasing: 2 percent of the people will be five feet, two inches to five feet, four inches; 13 percent will be between five feet, four inches and five feet, six inches; and 34 percent will be between five feet, six inches and five feet, eight inches. In addition, 34 percent would be also be between five feet, eight inches and five feet, ten inches; 13 percent would be between five feet, ten inches and six feet; and 2 percent would be between six feet and six feet, two inches. We simply need to multiply the percentages by the number of people we plan to hire.

We arrive at the percentages discussed above by applying the rules of the normal distribution. Again, roughly speaking, 68 percent of the data fall within plus and minus one standard deviation of the mean. Since the bell is symmetric from the mean, 34 percent of the data are one standard deviation larger and 34 percent one standard deviation smaller. The plus and minus three standard deviations number of 99 percent includes the two 95 percent and one 68 percent numbers, so we know that 2 percent (99 percent – 95 percent or 4 percent divided by two; half for each equal side) will be in the area of the third standard deviation(s). Using the same logic, [(95 percent – 68 percent)/2], we get the 13 percent number for the amount of data in the area of the second standard deviation(s). It should not take long for the dollar signs of benefit to become apparent when one considers all the areas to which this type of information could be applied.

Performance capability is also predicted using this information coupled with specification limits. We can use the "hard" specification limits and the actual performance demonstrated from sample data to predict what percentage of the production will fall outside the specification limits. We can use a sample from the production line to predict what the scrap cost for each workstation will be, as well as the number of "extra" component inventory we must carry on hand to meet the customer demand given the "scrap" that will fall beyond the specification limits by workstation.

If the special cause variation has been eliminated, one can easily establish appropriate work-in-process inventory levels to carry by workstation based on demonstrated mean time between failure and mean time to repair data. This is critical information to maintain productivity in a serialized work environment. One can also make more accurate budget analyses by knowing what the scrap and uptime will be. This would promote better planning for scheduling. In addition, this type of information is also quite helpful for cost justification of process improvements.

Six Sigma (Figure 1.3) uses the normally distributed bell curve concept mentioned earlier. The difference is that instead of using the average plus and minus three standard deviations, it uses the average plus and minus six standard deviations. Using this method, in order to have Six Sigma capability, one must either decrease the variation by becoming more consistent or increase the specification limits to accommodate the variation inherent to the process.

WHAT IS SIX SIGMA?

Put simply, Six Sigma is a data-driven methodology that strives for perfection in the organization's entire value chain. The Six Sigma methodology goes well

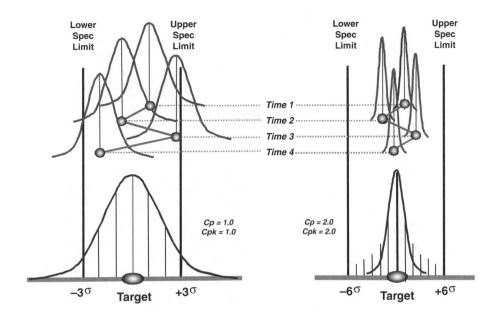

Processes shift by 1.5σ over time due to the inherent variation.
A 3σ process generates a long-term defect rate of about 66,807 ppm.
By contrast, a 6σ process generates only 3.4 ppm.

Figure 1.3   Variation and effect on process capability.

beyond the qualitative eradication of customer-perceptible defects and is deeply rooted in statistical engineering techniques. The statistical objective of Six Sigma is to drive down process variation so that plus or minus six standard deviations (6σ) lie between both the upper and lower specification limits and the target value in a process. The practical explanation equates to just 3.4 defects per million opportunities.

The Six Sigma process is a highly disciplined effort that closely examines variation and root causes of current performance, with a focus on not only the production floor, but on *all* key business processes. Six Sigma puts the entire value stream under the microscope: new product development, manufacturing, engineering, configuration management, quality, sales/order management, customer service, finance, and suppliers.

Six Sigma uses a deliberate structure commonly referred to as DMAIC (Define, Measure, Analyze, Improve, and Control) (Figure 1.4). The DMAIC process is the needle and thread that sews Six Sigma together, and we will cover this methodology in great detail in Chapter 4. Within each phase are specific Six Sigma process

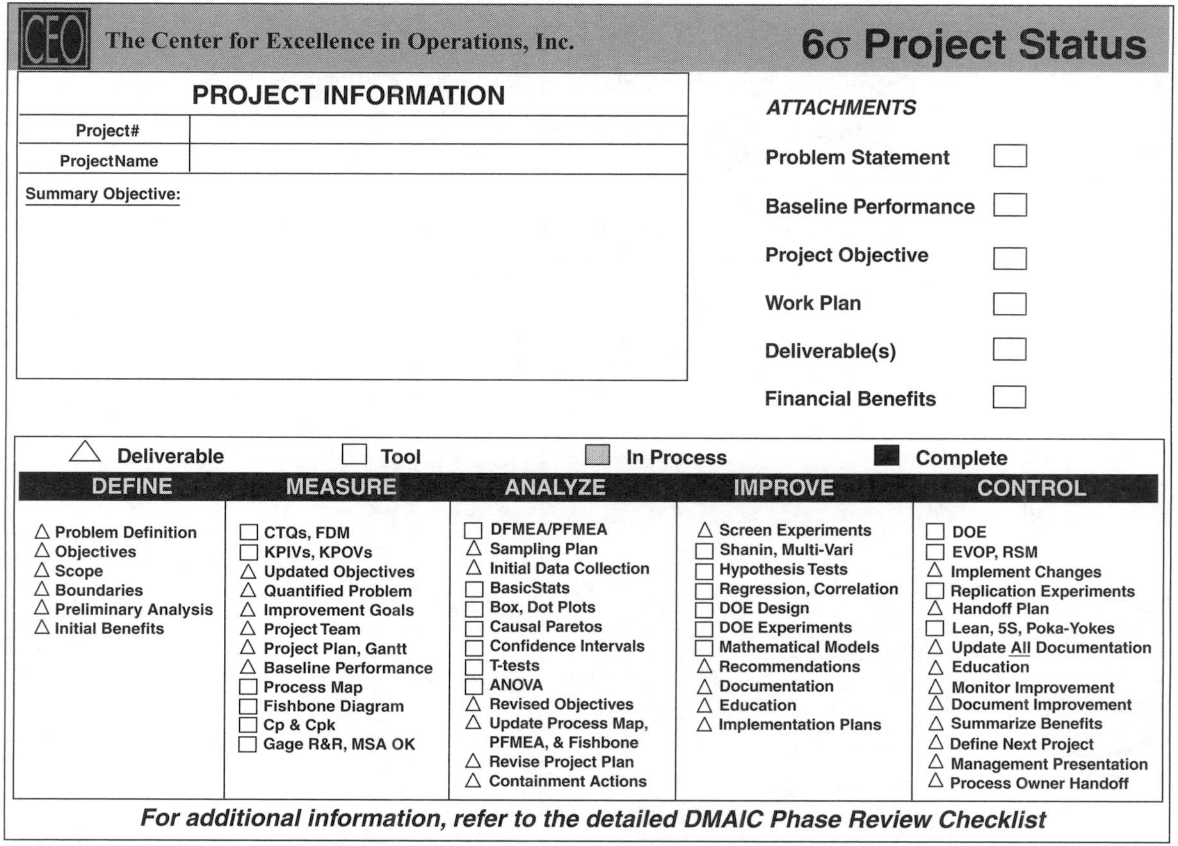

CEO The Center for Excellence in Operations, Inc.

6σ Project Status

PROJECT INFORMATION

Project#

ProjectName

Summary Objective:

ATTACHMENTS

☐ Problem Statement

☐ Baseline Performance

☐ Project Objective

☐ Work Plan

☐ Deliverable(s)

☐ Financial Benefits

△ Deliverable ☐ Tool ▨ In Process ■ Complete

DEFINE	MEASURE	ANALYZE	IMPROVE	CONTROL
△ Problem Definition	☐☐ CTQs, FDM	☐ DFMEA/PFMEA	△ Screen Experiments	☐ DOE
△ Objectives	☐☐ KPIVs, KPOVs	△ Sampling Plan	☐☐ Shanin, Multi-Vari	☐☐ EVOP, RSM
△ Scope	△ Updated Objectives	△ Initial Data Collection	☐☐ Hypothesis Tests	△ Implement Changes
△ Boundaries	△ Quantified Problem	☐☐ BasicStats	☐☐ Regression, Correlation	△ Replication Experiments
△ Preliminary Analysis	△ Improvement Goals	☐☐ Box, Dot Plots	☐☐ DOE Design	△ Handoff Plan
△ Initial Benefits	△ Project Team	☐☐ Causal Paretos	☐☐ DOE Experiments	△ Lean, 5S, Poka-Yokes
	△ Project Plan, Gantt	☐☐ Confidence Intervals	☐☐ Mathematical Models	△ Update All Documentation
	△ Baseline Performance	☐☐ T-tests	△ Recommendations	△ Education
	☐☐ Process Map	☐☐ ANOVA	△ Documentation	△ Monitor Improvement
	☐☐ Fishbone Diagram	△ Revised Objectives	△ Education	△ Document Improvement
	☐☐ Cp & Cpk	△ Update Process Map,	△ Implementation Plans	△ Summarize Benefits
	☐☐ Gage R&R, MSA OK	PFMEA, & Fishbone		△ Define Next Project
		△ Revise Project Plan		△ Management Presentation
		△ Containment Actions		△ Process Owner Handoff

For additional information, refer to the detailed DMAIC Phase Review Checklist

Figure 1.4 Six Sigma project tracker.

requirements and the deployment of various statistical problem-solving techniques. Individuals are educated in how to follow the Six Sigma process, as well as use the appropriate analytical tools at each step of the process. DMAIC is the heart of the Six Sigma process; it provides the structure, discipline, and logical progression for achieving breakthrough improvements.

BENEFITS OF SIX SIGMA

Six Sigma strives for perfection and value added in every aspect of the total value chain. The DMAIC-structured methodology provides the foundation for a more quantitative and surgical approach to problem solving, and the statistical tools provide the means for identifying and reducing process variation. Another major differentiator is that Six Sigma begins and ends with financial performance, one project at a time. The average company spends about 10 to 20 percent of revenues on Cost of Poor Quality (COPQ). A company that has a few years of Six Sigma under its belt can knock this down to 2 to 7 percent of revenues. To be conservative and put this into perspective, consider a $100 million company that saves $5 million per year or a $5 billion company that saves $50 million per year with its Six Sigma initiative. That is probably the equivalent of 30 to 50 percent revenue growth — real money! Beyond the financial savings, imagine the customer satisfaction velocity and other additional market benefits involved in having only 3.4 defects per million products shipped, 3.4 bugs per million lines of code written, 3.4 defects per million drawings released, $3.40 of excess/obsolete inventory per million dollars of total inventory, or 3.4 unhappy customers per million customer service calls received. Now you understand why most organizations are pursuing Six Sigma as a strategic improvement objective.

Unlike many previous quality improvement initiatives, Six Sigma focuses on all aspects of the total value stream. Many organizations are having tremendous success with Six Sigma in the professional and soft process support areas such as product design and development, customer service, purchasing and supplier management, distribution/logistics, accounting, sales and marketing, advertising, and other "soft" transactional processes. Customers take product quality for granted these days. A big differentiator in today's marketplace is total value-added services. Customer satisfaction can be improved significantly by paying attention to the soft processes inside and outside the four walls of the organization. These are the "hidden costs" where prevention and containment up front can improve the bottom line very quickly. Think about how many organizations deal with excess/obsolete inventory and warranty/returns; they create financial reserves to cover it. Next, think about creating a one-page ad for a catalog or trade publication. It probably takes most organizations three to five pages of effort and cost to create this single-page ad. If you could prevent these problems from occurring in the first place, that is instant megabucks to the bottom line.

UNDERSTAND, ASSIGN, AND ELIMINATE PROCESS VARIATION

The key to Six Sigma's success is the extreme focus on process variation. Some of the variation in a process is pure inherent noise and is uncontrollable, but most variation is controllable and comes in many "flavors":

- **Part variation**: Piece to piece, raw material lot to lot, etc.
- **Human variation**: Operator to operator, supervisor to supervisor, differences between setup people, number of tasks performed in a procedure/practice, ergonomic conditions, skill and experience levels, information accuracy, etc.
- **Tool variation**: Tool wear over time, mold cavity to mold cavity, spindle position, tool to tool, etc.
- **Time variation**: Hour to hour, shift to shift, sample time to time, day to day, week to week, month to month, season to season, etc.
- **Location variation**: Plant to plant, state to state, machine to machine, line location to line location, building to building, country to country, etc.

What is Six Sigma all about? The main crux of Six Sigma, therefore, is the passionate pursuit of variation elimination. Variation will always exist, but to seek elimination means continued minimization. Therefore, Six Sigma and lean both have the same goal: elimination of waste; variation from the target is a form of waste and must be eliminated or minimized.

Variation is everywhere and in everything. However, variation in processes (whether they are manufacturing or transactional) reduces predictability and, therefore, reliability. Six Sigma methodology employs terms normally associated with the martial arts to define skill level in the application of statistical tools. Yellow belt, green belt, black belt, and master black belt are used to describe statistical skills from basic to advanced accordingly. Again, the higher the level, the more skilled a person is at defining and reducing variation in product or process performance.

Think of it this way. When you drive a car, you have a general expectation of what will occur when you press on either the accelerator or brake. However, we have all had the experience of driving a vehicle different than the one to which we are accustomed and getting different responses to these same inputs. This is variation.

Sometimes the variation is negligible and we may not even notice it. This is when variation is determined to be insignificant. There is a difference between statistically significant and practically significant. The engineers who design vehicles might be able to measure a difference in the linear acceleration between two vehicles using sophisticated measurement devices in order to prove there is, in fact, a difference. This is what is known as being statistically significant.

A consumer might drive the same two vehicles and never know about the statistical significance. This is when variation is said to have statistical significance, but no practical significance. In other words, this is not a "real" problem and should not command resources to resolve it.

If, however, there were two similar vehicles that had grossly different stopping distances given the same applied braking force, this would be variation with practical significance as well as statistical significance. In this case, the variation could be a priority problem to be solved. We say "could" because not every problem with statistical and practical significance has enough financial impact to warrant resolution. This is the practical side of the business of solving problems.

The secret to success in applying Six Sigma in business is determining which problems have enough impact on the *voice of the customer* that the consumer is willing to pay for minimization of variation. One could spend resources to minimize variation and still miss the market if one does not understand the voice of the customer.

Consider the quartz watch, which has less variation than a mechanical watch and is actually much less expensive. However, if a watch manufacturer is trying to compete in a market filled with customers who are more concerned with prestige than precision, this focus on minimization of variation would prove to be a poor business decision. Therefore, efforts applied to Six Sigma must begin with a thorough understanding of the voice of the customer, which can be internal as well as external.

Consider another example from the transportation industry. One airline may assign seats, while another does not. For some customers, this variation is too much and they are willing to pay for an assigned seat. Other customers are not bothered by the variation in seating and are not willing to pay for it. From a business standpoint, the airlines must define the vision of their market and the customers they serve and decide if this is a real problem or a competitive advantage.

To improve any process, we need to chase down and understand variation, and the first step is to baseline current capability. Process capability indices (Cp and Cpk) are used to measure the spread and noncentering characteristics of a process. The next step is to understand the components of variation and the associated factors and root causes that create this variation in the first place. Every process includes both common causes (inherent noise) and special causes (explainable variation). The common causes create a 1.5σ shift over time, but the special causes can be categorized and eliminated. With a 3σ-capable process, there is a built-in scrap rate of 6.68 percent at best.

Figure 1.5 provides a graphical representation of process variation. Every time we go out and take a sample from a process and calculate the mean and standard deviation, we obtain different values due to the different types of variation present in the process. As we understand the key process inputs and outputs statistically, we can begin to assign causes and make changes that reduce/eliminate variation. As we reduce variation, we improve process capability by reducing the spread (Cp) and centering (Cpk). The diagram says, "The garage door is equal in width to the car," which is the same as saying that our process is equal to the specification limits. Any shift will produce both a dented fender or defective parts, respectively, about 6.68 percent of the time. That is the best performance we can ever hope for because that is the capability of our

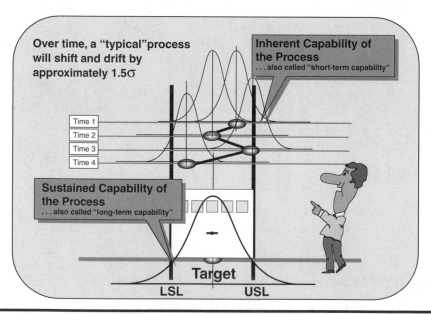

Figure 1.5 Visualizing the dynamics of process variation. Copyright ©2004 by The Center for Excellence in Operations, Inc. (CEO).

process. Now if we could open up the specification limits by a factor of two, or squeeze the distribution curve to be narrower by eliminating some of the variation (or both would even be better), we have a different situation. Now, "The garage door is twice as wide as the car," which is the same as saying that our process capability is twice the specification limits. A process shift will still produce good parts. Hence, we improve quality exponentially. Even better, we reduce the COPQ exponentially. This is a dynamic process. If we begin storing garden tools, bicycles, and other things in the free space (if we do not have the right metrics in place to identify and eliminate creeping variation), we lose some of that capability.

Table 1.1 shows defects per million opportunities. Using this table, an organization can quickly plug in the defects per million for the entire organization or for a particular process and quickly determine the current process capability and σ level of performance.

Table 1.1 Defects per Million Opportunities

DPMO	Sigma Level (with 1.5σ Shift)	Cpk (with 1.5σ Shift)	DPMO	Sigma Level (with 1.5σ Shift)	Cpk (with 1.5σ Shift)
933,200	0	0	52,100	3.125	1.042
915,450	0.125	0.042	40,100	3.25	1.083
894,400	0.25	0.083	30,400	3.375	1.125
869,700	0.375	0.125	22,700	3.5	1.167
841,300	0.5	0.167	16,800	3.625	1.208
809,200	0.625	0.208	12,200	3.75	1.25
773,400	0.75	0.25	8,800	3.875	1.292
734,050	0.875	0.292	6,200	4	1.333
691,500	1	0.333	4,350	4.125	1.375
645,650	1.125	0.375	3,000	4.25	1.417
598,700	1.25	0.417	2,050	4.375	1.458
549,750	1.375	0.458	1,300	4.5	1.5
500,000	1.5	0.5	900	4.625	1.542
450,250	1.625	0.542	600	4.75	1.583
401,300	1.75	0.583	400	4.875	1.625
354,350	1.875	0.625	230	5	1.667
308,500	2	0.667	100	5.125	1.700
265,950	2.125	0.708	130	5.25	1.75
226,600	2.25	0.75	80	5.375	1.792
190,800	2.375	0.792	30	5.5	1.833
158,700	2.5	0.833	23.4	5.625	1.875
130,300	2.625	0.875	16.7	5.75	1.917
105,600	2.75	0.917	10.1	5.875	1.958
84,550	2.875	0.958	3.4	6	2
66,800	3	1			

Source: iSixsigma.com

STATISTICAL ENGINEERING MEETS COMMON SENSE

Considering its history, Six Sigma has seen a slow adoption in organizations. Companies have been using bits and pieces of Six Sigma since its initial evolution at Motorola in 1978. Like many strategic improvement programs, the only thing that is new is the execution. The Six Sigma statistical techniques have existed for decades, some dating as far back as the 1930s at Western Electric and Pareto's 80/20 rule in the nineteenth century. The *new* element is the structured Six Sigma process and methodology.

Over 30 percent of organizations today either have a formal Six Sigma program implemented and in place or are pursuing Six Sigma as a strategic improvement program. It is our opinion that this slow adoption over the past twenty years is due largely to four major factors:

1. The approaches of previous TQM programs placed much of the emphasis on education about the philosophy and individual tools, but little on implementation, application, and results. As we mentioned earlier, it was "field-of-dreams" quality at its best; if you keep up the activity, the results will come: people equipped with a bag of religion and tools looking for a problem — quality for quality's sake. Hence, organizations saw little return on investment for their TQM efforts.

2. Many of our previous quality improvement initiatives focused on process control with statistical tools as a first step without understanding process variation. Quality gurus such as Deming, Crosby, and Juran professed their views about quality, but many initiatives in organizations fizzled after the training. The programs that survived were often limited to measuring defects on the shop floor. Many organizations relied on statistical process control charts and symptomatic fixes and took all the underlying process variation for granted. Finally, many statistical engineering efforts were not much more than exercises in "techniques looking for data." The underlying root causes were left unsolved and the anticipated benefits never arrived to the bottom line. In contrast, Six Sigma is a highly structured problem-solving methodology that focuses first on understanding explainable process variation and root causes, followed by reengineering the process, preventing future defects, and then controlling the process.

3. The availability of user-friendly statistical applications software such as Minitab did not exist. Twenty years ago, it took a statistician three months to conduct a Design of Experiments (DOE) manually. When it was done, nobody could understand the analysis, so many improvements

were never implemented. In today's Six Sigma environments, engineers, maintenance techs, and team leaders can perform several DOEs in a day. Minitab automates the analysis and simplifies the intimidating statistics. More emphasis is placed on fact-driven interpretation of the results versus statistical theory and derivations.

4. The Six Sigma process and methodology are very new. The main missing ingredient up to now was an application roadmap for a complex set of statistical tools. Six Sigma also has a much stronger leadership, project, and measurement focus. The Six Sigma methodology provides a highly disciplined and structured DMAIC approach. The methodology is powerful because it strings together the application of appropriate Six Sigma problem-solving tools to use for different stages of the structured DMAIC problem-solving process.

TURNING SKEPTICS INTO BELIEVERS

Everything new has its skeptics, and Six Sigma is no exception. In fact, skepticism is healthy, particularly as one reflects on the experiences of previous continuous improvement programs. A four-month experience through black belt training removes the skepticism very quickly. For many candidates, Six Sigma is almost a religious experience where they see their previous thinking shattered and replaced by a whole new set of feature-rich methodologies and tools. For four months, candidates are placed in a Six Sigma boot camp–like experience. They receive intensive training on the Six Sigma methodology/tools and statistical software, and then they apply this new knowledge to a real business problem. This mandatory project (usually with a mandatory savings goal) is *success measured by achievement, not attendance* at its very best. Sometimes the pressure and emotions are as much as preparing for a bar exam.

For some, that project might be analyzing vacuum pump weld leaks that every engineer in the place has failed to fix (often these folks stick to their *"You don't understand, it's black magic...We've looked at this a dozen times before...It's a secret process"* mind-sets). But those *"it-can't-be-done"* projects really make a candidate appreciate the power of Six Sigma and become a strong advocate of the methodology. The skeptics snicker as the inexperienced candidate deploys the DMAIC process and tools religiously. Then one day, the root causes of variation are understood using facts and real data, and the technical experts become very nervous. The right process changes/adjustments are recommended and implemented, and it works! The skeptics fight to readjust the parameters back to the 70 percent yield areas they are familiar with, and replication experiments prove the candidate's recommendations correct and the expert's recommendations wrong. The candidate demonstrates with data and facts that the secret process is not a secret process at all and the variation that the so-called process experts have chosen to live with can be eliminated. Strong Six Sigma leadership supports the candidate, and finally the candidate's recommendations are fully implemented (often at $0 capital investment). Yields improve to a steady-state 94 percent! The company saves $500,000 to $1 million per year from that one project alone. The skeptics stand around and think about their misguided energies as an inexperienced black belt candidate fixes their problem. Both the black belt candidate and the experts learn a solid lesson about managing process variation. The black belt candidate realizes his "Eureka!" moment and begins to tell everyone how great Six Sigma works; management suggests that the so-called experts be included in the next black belt wave.

These black belts lead the charge by completing and/or supporting dozens of other projects, making Six Sigma a way of life in their organizations. They convert many skeptics by putting them through their own Six Sigma experience. They recognize that Six Sigma is very powerful, impressionable stuff. They begin to use the Six Sigma process and methodologies without even thinking about it. They develop others on Six Sigma tools and methodologies and expand their own knowledge and beliefs. They become very intolerant of those who insist on "winging it" and creating even more problems for the organization.

One of the common dilemmas we observe about Six Sigma is that some organizations are reluctant to jump in until they have seen other successes. For some, they go to extremes by trying to benchmark organizations exactly like themselves or look for the exact project success that replicates their environment to a tee. They try to justify that Six Sigma is not a whole lot different than what they are already doing. They place too much confidence in the experiences and opinions of their own people and accept the notion that "We've already looked at these things a dozen times" or "We're doing okay." These actions are all a huge waste of time — valuable time in the new economy. If you are unsuccessful at finding a competitor or other organization exactly like yours, this is not a good reason to postpone action. In fact, it is all the more reason to jump in and be the first to leverage Six Sigma as a competitive weapon.

One of the most effective approaches that we have used in these situations is a Six Sigma Pilot. This is typically two to three projects in targeted areas to demonstrate the power of the DMAIC methodology and statistical tools. When you can demonstrate a big improvement in just four to six weeks in an area that people have attempted to fix several times in the past, you usually get people's attention. Data, facts, and savings talk very loudly and clearly. We will discuss how to organize a Six Sigma Pilot in more detail in Chapter 6.

THE FUTURE OF SIX SIGMA

Is Six Sigma worth the effort? The answer is a resounding "yes." Like any new management technique, there is much debate about the newness or mechanics, but benchmarking data speak for themselves. TQM proponents say that TQM would have accomplished the same results if management supported it. Others call it a slick marketing ploy and a new twist on an old topic. One vice president of quality who completed black belt certification commented, *"I've been in quality for twenty-five years and I thought I knew it all. Six Sigma certification was a real eye-opener. It makes you realize all the hidden opportunities you've been missing."*

Six Sigma is not the silver bullet, nor is it the panacea for all of management's challenges. But make no mistake about it — Six Sigma is here to stay because its demonstrated success is proven in the numbers. Six Sigma is a highly "customer-centric" improvement process that focuses on tangible results, one project at a time. Many organizations are well into Six Sigma and are migrating the methodology upstream to new product development and suppliers. Many smaller and mid-sized companies that are suppliers to these larger organizations recognize this trend and are proactively implementing Six Sigma before they are told to do so. These organizations are the early beneficiaries of Six Sigma.

If you are implementing Six Sigma, there is a good chance that you will see millions of dollars added to your company's bottom line this year. Congratulations to you, your employees, and your stakeholders! If you are not currently implementing Six Sigma or have not heard about it yet, chances are that you will — especially if you do business with any Fortune 1000 company. If you wait until one of these organizations mandates Six Sigma as a condition for doing business with it in the future, you have given away a lot of ground to your competition.

For many organizations, Six Sigma is an arduous task, but not a totally overwhelming one. In fact, the heart of the Six Sigma process is a lot closer to arithmetic than integral calculus, particularly through the user-friendly Minitab software application. For practitioners, Six Sigma is about perfection, deep core drilling to root causes, logical reduction of variation, and driving significant cost reductions out of all processes. It is about deploying indignant people who become upset about bad processes with the right technical and people skills to make a big difference. It is about developing "relentless hunters" versus becoming a hunted organization.

CHAPTER 1 TAKE-AWAYS

- The Six Sigma entry barriers, as they have been defined and accepted as the standard "top-down, train-the-masses" deployment protocol, are way beyond the reach of smaller and mid-sized organizations.
- A "one-size-fits-all" approach to Six Sigma is a prescription for failure, especially in small and mid-sized organizations. A more scaleable implementation whereby these organizations can digest and achieve quicker benefits from Six Sigma is a more feasible approach.
- Six Sigma is about understanding and chasing down variation in processes. When variation is unknown and not understood, the root causes of variation are unknown and the permanent solutions remain unknown. If you believe that this variation is an art form, then you will accept and institutionalize variation, and it will be reflected in the cost of running your business.
- The statistical tools used in the Six Sigma process are not new. The Six Sigma statistical techniques have existed for decades, some dating as far back as the 1930s at Western Electric and Pareto's 80/20 rule in the nineteenth century. However, these tools have only recently gained widespread practical application due to the advance of computer software and hardware in order to put the tools into the hands of the masses.
- One of the key components of Six Sigma is the structured methodology of Define, Measure, Analyze, Improve, and Control (or DMAIC).
- Six Sigma begins and ends with financial performance, one project at a time. The average company spends about 10 to 20 percent of revenues on Cost of Poor Quality (COPQ). A company that has a few years of Six Sigma under its belt can knock this down to 2 to 7 percent of revenues.
- The secret to success in applying Six Sigma in business is determining which problems have enough impact on the *voice of the customer* that the consumer is willing to pay for minimization of variation. One could spend resources to minimize variation and still miss the market if one does not understand the voice of the customer.
- Six Sigma is not the panacea for all of management's challenges, but it is here to stay because its demonstrated success is proven in the numbers. Six Sigma is a highly "customer-centric" improvement process that focuses on tangible results, one project at a time.

SUGGESTED FURTHER READING

Breyfogle, Forrest, *Managing Six Sigma,* John Wiley & Sons, 2000.
Brue, Greg, *Six Sigma for Managers,* McGraw-Hill, 2002.

SIX SIGMA FOR SMALL AND MID-SIZED ORGANIZATIONS

One of the more familiar dilemmas in business today is how to implement Six Sigma in smaller and mid-sized organizations. This is a serious issue because larger organizations are beginning to mandate Six Sigma to their supply base as a condition of doing future business. Let's be honest about the typical response. Smaller and mid-sized organizations go out and talk to the typical Six Sigma consulting firm about a program only to find out that it requires millions of dollars in investment, dedication of their best full-time resources, and training of the masses. Those who have experienced this dilemma will agree that this approach to Six Sigma is not only inappropriate, but also totally unrealistic for smaller and mid-sized organizations. But beyond sheer magnitude and cost, there is a real need to bring smaller and mid-sized suppliers into the Six Sigma fold because collectively they might represent as much as 75 to 80 percent of total value stream activity.

There are definite differences between large and small organizations. Although we could dedicate a chapter to this topic alone, let's consider the critical few differences that impact a Six Sigma deployment. First, large organizations have more resources and more specialized resources than smaller organizations. The depth, breadth, and sheer number of available resources are much higher than one finds in smaller organizations that typically run much leaner and meaner. The resources in smaller organizations tend to wear more hats and do not have the opportunity or the luxury to become specialized in a particular narrow area. For example, large organizations may have an army of resources conducting competitive benchmarking surveys or tracking Cost of Poor Quality (COPQ). Most small organizations do not have any idea about their COPQ. Large organizations may have multiple sites around the world and must deal with the complexities and political realities of getting thousands of employees to embrace a common goal. Small companies have much simpler organizations and political environments. Larger organizations can out-resource, out-spend, out-invest, out-source, and out-invest their smaller counterparts. When a decision is made in a small or mid-sized organization, it is much easier to implement and does not require review by committee after committee. The list goes on and on, but the important thing is that there are distinct differences. These distinct differences require different approaches to Six Sigma and many other improvement initiatives.

We have experimented with alternative Six Sigma deployment models that allow smaller and mid-sized organizations to implement at a pace at which they can actually digest the methodology and achieve benefits without the significant resource commitment and overhead structure of the traditional top-down Six Sigma implementation approach. A few years ago, we modified our Six Sigma deployment and execution process to accommodate the realities of our small and mid-sized client environments and operating styles. As a result, these organizations are able to achieve faster and more impressive benefits than their larger customers. Regardless of the supposed benefits of Six Sigma, the traditional top-down implementation approach is a major barrier to entry for smaller and mid-sized organizations. This chapter will present new options for deploying Six Sigma in these environments.

TEN SIX SIGMA MYTHS

In order to accept a different deployment option, we need to expose you to several myths. Like everything else, trade publications and speakers tend to tell you about the more positive side of their experiences and sugarcoat the very tough side. If you are a small or mid-sized organization, you need to be aware of some of the myths of Six Sigma. This section presents some of these myths and how to accommodate breaking the rules while still achieving success. While these are norms in larger deployments, they are barriers to entry for small and mid-sized organizations.

Myth #1: Six Sigma Is a Business Strategy

Six Sigma is not a business strategy; it is a powerful *enabler* of business strategy. However, people in some organizations believe that Six Sigma is a business strategy and say things like, "We want to become a Six Sigma organization." What does that mean? Six Sigma is a very powerful methodology and tool set to help organizations execute strategy flawlessly. We have also been involved in many transactional Six Sigma strategy projects where the analysis resulted in a change or enhancement in business strategy. By itself, Six Sigma is not a strategy, nor is it the cure-all and end-all for an organization's strategic and operational issues.

Sometimes we use the tool chest analogy to discuss kaizen, lean, Six Sigma, enterprise resource planning, and other enabling IT applications. All of these methodologies are very powerful improvement tools when deployed correctly to the right opportunities. But that is all that they are — tools in a tool chest. It is very possible to misuse these tools, and a single tool is not universal for every task at hand.

Myth #2: An Organization Must Follow the Top-Down Six Sigma Approach to Be Successful

The most difficult thing to accept about a scaleable Six Sigma approach is that small and mid-sized organizations can use a different deployment approach and still achieve significant benefits. With all the written literature, textbooks, and case studies about GE, Honeywell, DuPont, 3M, and many others, it is easy to be convinced that their approach is the best approach and the only approach. Why not? It was very successful for them, so it must be the right approach for you, right? Most small and mid-sized organizations have postponed Six Sigma because this top-down model puts Six Sigma out of their financial reach. However, many other organizations have used a little imagination and innovation and have figured out how to tap into Six Sigma and benefit without creating a financial hardship. The scaleable approach to Six Sigma produces more affordable, better, and faster results for small and mid-sized organizations.

Myth #3: An Organization Requires One Master Black Belt for Every Ten Black Belts and One Black Belt for Every Million in Revenues

If you buy this myth, then you have just accepted a huge price tag for your deployment. If you are a $100 million company, this means that you will need to dedicate one hundred people full time to Six Sigma at some point. Based on industry rates, you can expect to spend $2 to 3 million for black belt training. Does this make sense? It might for GE, but it is a prescription for financial disaster in smaller and mid-sized organizations. First of all, how can an organization commit to these guidelines before it has revisited its business strategy and understands gaps between current and desired performance? Further, how can we accept these ratios until we have determined the organization's specific improvement requirements, develop a business improvement strategy, and factor in the barriers and constraints?

Myth #4: An Organization Requires Six to Eight Green Belts for Every Black Belt

Returning to the $100 million company example, this means that you need to think about developing six hundred additional resources at a typical cost of $10,000 each or an additional $6 million. This is off the wall! Recognize that these ratios have served the large Six Sigma firms that provide the training and consulting more than their clients. But large organizations have deep pockets and this is a small fraction of their annual $80 million consulting budget. We are not being cynical on purpose. We have just demonstrated how to spend millions on a Six Sigma deployment before your requirements are understood. This approach is totally unacceptable to smaller and mid-sized organizations.

Myth #5: Black Belts Save $250,000 per Project and Green Belts Save $50,000 to $100,000 per Project

If you accept this myth, then you accept that the millions in Six Sigma deployment costs are not a big deal. Many organizations generate significant savings from Six Sigma. Some of these projects are worth $1 million and some are worth $15,000. On average, the numbers are substantially less than $250,000 per project in smaller and mid-sized organizations, but on a scale of magnitude they are huge positive hits to profitability. You may see these savings on some of your projects, but you will not see them 100 percent of the time. The more projects an organization completes, the more difficult it becomes to mine those golden egg projects. The most important success factor is not about the artificial $250,000 per project thresholds; it is about people learning how to think differently about their jobs every minute of every day. The $15,000 and $30,000 projects add up very quickly in a $75 million company. A preferred approach in our opinion, especially for small and mid-sized organizations, is to micromanage every Six Sigma project to financial success, one project at a time. Manage the deployment in a manner that achieves a speedier, self-funding, return-on-investment (ROI) mode.

Myth #6: Individuals Must Have Previous Statistical Education to Understand Six Sigma

There are two factors that make Six Sigma user friendly. First, the structured DMAIC (Define, Measure, Analyze, Improve, Control) methodology provides a common problem-solving language for the organization. If you follow this process diligently, it will take you to the answer to your problem. We have shared many "Eureka!" moments with thousands of people who were not subject matter experts on their projects. Second, Minitab removes much of the statistical theory that has intimidated people in the past. People can become very proficient at the basics of Minitab quickly, and the focus is more on interpretation of what the data are telling us. Minitab has many applications beyond Six Sigma, such as kaizen and lean or pure analysis. Whether it is kaizen, lean, or Six Sigma, there is nothing like teams that make improvements based on data and facts.

Some of our worst candidates have been a few engineers who already *knew it all* and did their own thing, rather than following the DMAIC methodology. One particular example was a candidate who had been trying to get a $50,000 capital requisition approved. He started his project with the answer and attempted (unsuccessfully) to use Six Sigma as a way to justify what he had already decided to do. (He used Minitab's Random Number function to generate his samples, but we nailed him during replication.) Some of our best green belt candidates have been hourly employees and nontechnical people. One hourly candidate who worked in the safety area solved a leak problem that the engineers had been working on for years. Another individual from human resources with *zilch* production experience showed a crew of experienced screw machine operators how to save $400,000 in tool changes and downtime. An hourly shop mechanic saved his organization over $700,000 in oil, fuel, and fluids consumption. After several years in this Six Sigma business, we believe that previous statistical experience can be very helpful, but it can also get in the way of fresh thinking. Commitment and willingness to follow the DMAIC methodology and see the project through to the end are much more important. When individuals go through Six Sigma training, they are not being exposed to anything that they are not capable of learning. The greatest learning comes from applying Six Sigma to a real business problem and experiencing how well it works.

Myth #7: Six Sigma Is Geared More Toward Manufacturing

Most improvement programs including Six Sigma begin in the manufacturing area. The product is tangible and the key process input variables (KPIVs) (e.g., speed, feed, raw material dimensions, etc.) and key process output variables (KPOVs) (e.g., pieces per hour, yield, rework, dimensional characteristics, etc.) are more tangible than soft transactional processes. We have beat the shop floor to death with previous improvement programs, and that is not where the large opportunities exist. In many cases, manufacturing groups are ahead of the improvement power curve, and we can learn several good lessons from their experiences. The largest opportunities in most organizations, therefore, lie in their transactional process areas. Many of these transactional processes are untouched territory and ripe for improvement, and organizations can make dramatic improvements rapidly. Furthermore, the root causes of process performance are not understood. Opportunities in the warranty/returns, invoicing, quotations, customer service, purchasing, sales and marketing, new product development, and human resource areas are in the millions of dollars. If you are beginning to understand root cause problem solving, ask yourself two simple questions: (1) What are the root causes of manufacturing issues? (2) What are the root causes of customer issues? Many of the answers to these questions lie outside of manufacturing, waiting to be cultivated.

Myth #8: Organizations Must Decide Between Kaizen, Lean, and Six Sigma

Every organization has a continuum of improvement opportunities, and the Six Sigma tools are not the cure-all and end-all to these opportunities. We discuss the integration of these improvement methodologies in detail in Chapter 9, but no single set of improvement tools will make an organization world class. However, the DMAIC methodology and the thoughtware, in particular, are universal. On one end of the spectrum are kaizen or quick-strike opportunities that require limited analysis. Next are the lean opportunities aimed at waste and cycle time reduction, standardization, and highly disciplined processes. Finally, there are the complex issues that lend themselves to the more complex Six Sigma tools. Again, Six Sigma is not the cure-all and end-all, but it is powerful stuff when applied to the right improvement opportunities, and kaizen and lean are just as powerful for the right applications. The key is to understand the nature of the specific improvement opportunity and apply the right methodologies and tools to the right opportunities.

Myth #9: Six Sigma Is Not Needed for Our Business

We often hear several interesting comments about this topic. People in some organizations say things like: "Our customers are not asking us to do Six Sigma" or "Our business is different" or "We're already using the Six Sigma tools sporadically." An advertising agency executive from a creative organization commented that "Six Sigma is not applicable to us because we do not have processes." That is their fundamental problem. They have a process and they might have a dozen different processes, all of which are broken. Every organization on the planet has processes, and these processes have variation within them. Some of this variation is assignable and manageable, but much of it is totally misunderstood. If an organization is content with its current performance and the associated costs, then Six Sigma is probably not the right choice at this time. Sometimes a quick Six Sigma assessment or Six Sigma pilot is a great eye-opener for these organizations. Most organizations these days know and recognize the need to get better, and this is what Six Sigma is really all about. It is not about statistical tools — it is about a common, data- and fact-driven methodology to improve all aspects of the business. Any organization that thinks it either cannot or does not need to improve its business is falling behind.

Over the years, we have heard people in denial about variation in their processes. Figure 2.1 provides some of our favorite "brainfog" (opposite of brainstorm) statements about process variation. These are telltale signs that a new approach is needed — same people, same process, same thinking, same results.

Myth #10: Six Sigma Does Not Apply to Variation in Magic, Craft Processes

For years, organizations lived with this myth that variation in their processes is a function of their business and therefore an institutionalized component of their business. Some organizations call it the mystery of their operations, and others insist that their processes are part art form and rely heavily on the experience, touch, and feel of their operators and engineers. When a problem arises, these people tinker and make adjustments to the process until it appears to be corrected. Everyone cheers, but the same problems always return. A seasoned Six Sigma professional sees right through this mode of operation and can become very indignant of those who choose to wing it. Without an understanding of variation and root causes, the tinkerers often claim to solve a problem; however it might be process shifts. Worse yet, they may improve performance temporarily on one KPOV and create problems with other KPOVs. When several people are making adjustments to a process throughout the day and from shift to shift, there is usually a lot of process variation, downtime, poor yields, and customer service issues. The correct application of Six Sigma to these types of situations can really nail variation and the subsequent problems it causes.

One company had a bank of screw machine operations. The operators ran their machines at whatever speed they wanted and changed tools whenever they felt they needed to. Although a machine was running fine, the first thing operators on different shifts would do is reset the machine to *their* settings. Was the operator on the previous shift making scrap? Of course not, but standardization did not exist. One setup required a chuck change that needed to be tightened. If the chuck was too tight, it would cause jams. If it was too loose,

- "This only becomes a problem when our sales go down. That's the biggest problem in the company."
- "This sounds great, but we don't have time to improve and do our regular jobs."
- "When this comes up, only Joe can fix it."
- "We have these problems because the customer's expectations are unreasonable."
- "This is an art...It takes years of experience to learn this."
- "I think it's set on the value I vaguely remember it to be set on a few months ago."
- "I don't need data...I know because I've been here for 16 years."
- "No, I don't have any data. But I know there's something wrong with your data."
- "We've always done Six Sigma. We just don't call it that."
- "That's a good idea. You're probably right, but we can't afford to work on it because there's nothing in the budget."
- "If you think it's bad now, you should have seen where it was before."
- "I already know what needs to be done. We need to make sure these green belts don't go off and focus on something else."
- "I've watched many of these improvement programs fail with my previous employers."
- "It's intuitive, can't you see this?"
- "We improved it by paying more attention to it."
- "I think...In my opinion..."
- "Let's talk to Ken. He has all the answers."
- "We've already fixed that problem dozens of times."
- "If it ain't worth doing twice, it ain't worth doing."
- "We don't have time for that analysis...We have real problems to solve."
- "You don't understand...This is unique, it's different here."
- "Although we were producing scrap, our settings were somewhat in the ballpark of your DOE."
- "This is not like any organization you have ever worked in before."
- "It's not variation, it's a craft."
- "It's not a problem, it's just part of the cost of doing business in this industry."
- "How do I know? I just know because I know."
- "We tried that one already. It worked for a while, but then it stopped working."
- "I know because I feel it. Some of this stuff you just need to get a feel for."
- "You can't measure it. You just know when it's right."

Figure 2.1 Brainfog statements about process variation.

it would cause a crash. This was the number one cause of unplanned downtime cost and time. The company was spending hundreds of thousands of dollars on unplanned downtime due to this chuck problem and a Six Sigma project was launched to reduce costs. Data and facts isolated the problem to deciding *how tight is tight?* Everyone had the answer based on their opinion, but were missing the facts. Some people are stronger than others, not everyone used the same tools, and some people claimed "you can feel it when it's tight enough." Some people claimed that two or three whacks with a mallet would snug it up properly. Some people even wrapped a rag around their wrench and slammed their palm into it. (We discovered coincidentally that three operators were out on medical leave for hand fractures.) The Six Sigma analysis helped to pin down and define "tight" based on data and facts. A simple torque device was designed by a team member and the correct torque was defined. Instantly, downtime was reduced by 20 percent and saved over $320,000 per year. Better yet, disability claims dropped as people were no longer hurting themselves trying to do their job. Believe us, this stuff is not magic!

Another company began its Six Sigma journey with a pilot effort aimed at building a successful case. The company had a secret room — a clean room where a proprietary process was located and where access was limited to only a few key employees. This was a complex, high-tech assembly area and had 60 percent yields. In addition, there was a belief that "that is the best we can do because of the design; we've been at this level for years." We were looking at a perfect Six Sigma pilot candidate. This process was supported by Tom Tweaker, a senior engineer who everyone in the organization relied on. He could outtalk anyone in the organization about the details of the process, but unfortunately it was all based on his perceptions, opinions, and experiences. Since access to the process was limited, how could anyone argue with his opinions? Neither he nor anyone else in the organization understood the true process variation. Why was this a perfect Six Sigma candidate? Because this is the type of situation where everyone walks around congratulating and telling each other how technical and smart they are, and pretty soon it becomes fact. A Six Sigma team was established, but only two members were allowed clearance into the area. Tom Tweaker told these individuals that they were wasting their time because all problems were due to lower cost suppliers that could not provide parts as good as the previous suppliers. Tom never paid much attention to supplier quality data, which validated that the company had the same problems with the previous suppliers. The initial analysis identified most of the fallout to a TIG welding operation, a technology around fifty years old. Tom replied, "No way! There's something wrong with your data!" The team conducted web searches and learned a lot about the process and its KPIVs and

KPOVs without even looking in the window of the secret room. The team also found several Six Sigma TIG welding project references on the web. A Design of Experiments (DOE) was planned on the operation in a remote conference room. The two authorized team members and the operator ran the trials and collected data. Within three weeks, the team developed, implemented, and replicated process setting changes on the TIG weld operation that improved yield to 75 percent (about a $480,000 per year savings). Tom Tweaker was furious with the study results and put up a last-ditch fight to implement the recommendations. He even went to the president and told him that the company's security in the secret room had been breached. But the facts are the facts, and the team won out in the end. There is no secret to Six Sigma's success, just persistence, chasing down and reducing variation and root causes, and then starting all over throughout the entire process.

ONE SIZE FITS ALL? NOT!

Time and cost are large entry barriers to smaller and mid-sized organizations. Typically, a Six Sigma effort begins by developing executives at the champion level. By the time the events are scheduled and delivered, four to eight weeks may have elapsed. This is followed up with a wave of black belt training that might include approximately twenty individuals over a five-month period. Each of these individuals is required to complete a mandatory project, and the savings bogie varies from company to company. Then a wave of green belt training occurs. This might include another twenty individuals who complete five days of training plus a mandatory project. Finally, organizations develop additional resources at a basic yellow belt level. This is usually four to eight hours of training and provides individuals with an understanding of the Six Sigma methodology and basic tools. Granted, in large organizations these efforts do not happen serially. There could be several champion, black belt, green belt, and yellow belt waves going on concurrently. Over time, much of the Six Sigma training and project mentoring can also be handled by internal resources. Nevertheless, these large deployments require a significant investment up front and may realistically take two years to generate a return on that front-loaded investment. For a smaller organization, this level of resource development is too costly, requires too much rollout time, and provides an overkill approach for what is actually needed. The challenge becomes how to structure a Six Sigma deployment for these organizations that provides faster time-to-ROI and is within the reach of their spending capability. Figure 2.2 provides an accelerated Six Sigma deployment model that fits conceptually with the requirements of smaller and mid-sized organizations.

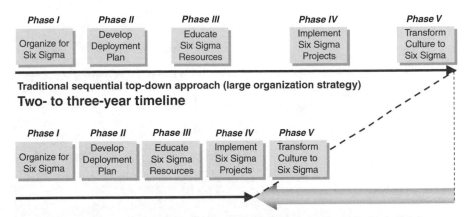

Figure 2.2   An accelerated Six Sigma model geared to small and mid-sized organizations.

One of the facts about Six Sigma's implementation life cycle is that the majority of benefits are not derived from black belts; they are generated at the green and yellow belt level, especially when the Six Sigma process becomes institutionalized. Another observation is that black and green belts are interchangeable for about 80 percent of the organization's Six Sigma opportunities. Accordingly, we have developed a more "middle-out," bootstrap implementation approach to Six Sigma, which is really *Scaleable Six Sigma*™. It is not rocket science, but it does address the constraints of smaller and mid-sized companies and allows them to implement at a more manageable pace. Regardless of the name, one fact is certain: These organizations become just as technically skilled as their larger-company counterparts, and in fact, many are outperforming their larger customers in terms of both financial results and cultural transformation.

SCALEABLE SIX SIGMA™

Figure 2.3 provides a brief overview of our Six Sigma deployment and execution process for smaller and mid-sized organizations.

This scaleable approach is modified to fit a particular organization's requirements and operating constraints. On a company-by-company basis, the deployment details, scope, focus, and timing are different; however, in general the approach works like this:

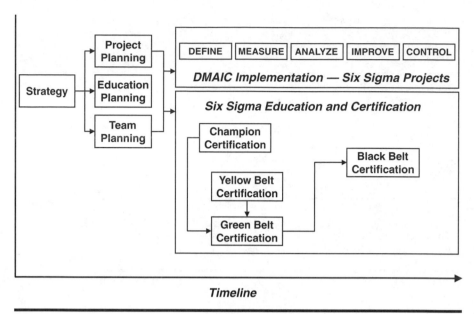

Figure 2.3   Scaleable Six Sigma™ implementation.

1. A Six Sigma pilot project is initiated to demonstrate the applicability of Six Sigma, to build awareness and support for the methodology and approach through early successes, and to learn more about the company's operating environment and challenges so that subsequent phases can be tailored to specific strategic requirements.
2. A Six Sigma strategy and deployment plan is developed and a recommended implementation infrastructure is designed. The strategy, implementation approach, and initial projects are directly aligned to the organization's strategic plan and customer requirements. This step also includes well-organized communication and awareness building for Six Sigma.
3. Implementation planning is completed. Beyond the overall program, this includes defining objectives, scope, goals, priorities, work plans, deliverables, baseline performance, and expected performance/financial improvements for a pool of high-impact Six Sigma projects.
4. Team formation and the education plan begin concurrently. The up-front groundwork provides background and focus for the teams and prevents wasted time and resources debating what needs to be done. In addition, the education is customized to the client's business and includes sample issues, data, and examples from its actual processes.

5. Executives complete a two-day champion education where they learn about the Six Sigma process, methodology, and tools. Executives also focus on how to lead, structure, and mentor a successful Six Sigma effort through several exercises.

6. Individuals complete green belt certification (e.g., a group of twenty-five individuals over a two- to three-month period). This education focuses on Six Sigma, but includes and integrates kaizen and lean. This program also stresses deployment of the right tools to the right opportunities because not all problems require a complex, statistical approach. Green belt training is expanded to seven days and makes these resources interchangeable with black belts about 80 percent of the time.

7. Team members complete two-day yellow belt certification (e.g., twenty-five to fifty individuals over a two- to four-week period). This education focuses on the basic "blocking and tackling" tools of Six Sigma as well as kaizen and lean. Yellow belt training is also expanded to two days to develop more capable Six Sigma team participants.

8. Later in the life cycle, individuals are transitioned to the next level of Six Sigma achievement. Some selected green belts are developed into black belts and some yellow belts are developed into green belts. Other new resources are developed into green and yellow belts based on need. The goal is to ramp up in a manner where the tangible savings are funding the Six Sigma program.

9. In all cases, certification is by achievement, not attendance. Beyond the classroom time, all certification candidates must complete a mandatory project that demonstrates the correct deployment of Six Sigma, solves a real business problem, and achieves a targeted savings.

This is a gross oversimplification of what happens on a case-by-case basis. One fact is very clear: It is different from organization to organization and is driven by needs and constraints. The strategy and deployment plan, scope, and focus of Six Sigma are designed around the organization's requirements, learning/digestion capabilities, financial constraints, and timing with other critical business events. We wish to emphasize a few points made earlier. First, green belt resource development always precedes black belt development in these smaller organizations. Often, a wave of green belt training is stretched out over a three- to six-month period (including implementation and validation of results). This makes it easier to schedule with other activities and prevents these smaller organizations from having to make full-time resource commitments (usually it ends up as a one- to two-day per week commitment, but varies from week to week). Why is this approach successful? Because you get to ROI faster with twenty-five projects over a three-month period than you do with two to three projects over a five-month period. Besides, everything gets done: certification, successful project completions, and all of the other normal business activities. The executives of many clients have also gone through green belt training, and this actually makes them about three to five times as technically skilled as other executives who only go through champion training. Some organizations eventually develop their own internal black belt resources, and others continue in an *outsourced black belt* mode by continuing their relationship with us. Some never require their own in-house black belts, and some allow their green belts to grow for more professional development reasons. Another unique twist in this approach is collaboration, where two or more clients may participate in black belt training and share the costs. This is an interim approach somewhere between in-house and public training.

We have also expanded the green belt training to seven days. Candidates learn about Six Sigma tools all the way through DOE (full and fractional factorials). The topics are obviously not covered in the same depth as black belt training, but candidates have no trouble conducting their own DOEs. In addition, candidates learn lean, kaizen, and Design for Six Sigma basics and how to integrate all of these methodologies into a unified powerhouse improvement initiative. Green belts also have a mandatory project with a savings bogie of $50,000. Yellow belts spend two days in training and learn the Six Sigma methodology and basic tools through process capability (Cp and Cpk) and Gage R&R analysis. These individuals do not have a mandatory project, but they have a mandatory checklist of applications to demonstrate their Six Sigma proficiency. These individuals are well equipped to serve as Six Sigma team members and complete some of the analytical work on their own or with others.

This program and building-block approach is modularized so that the organization can quickly transition its Six Sigma resources to the next highest level of achievement. Additionally, it can accomplish its Six Sigma implementation at a more manageable pace and scope. The number of projects, the levels of education, and the whole deployment and execution approach occur at a digestible pace, with a direct link to strategy and results. Unlike the traditional top-down deployment, black belts are, in effect, outsourced resources. This scaleable Six Sigma approach is much more practical for our smaller and mid-sized clients because it becomes self-funding much more quickly.

SPOON FEED AND IMPLEMENT: THE BEST TEACHER

Another activity that we have adopted as part of our Six Sigma certifications is periodic two- to four-hour implementation field trips. First, candidates are provided with a refresher and additional technical aspects of a particular selected tool(s). Prior to this education, actual client needs are identified and *teed up* for analysis by the candidates, and the education is focused on their assignments. At the conclusion of this instruction module, candidates are teamed up and perform real analysis in their organization. For example, the education might include a refresher of Gage R&R or capability studies followed by five to six real team assignments in the plant. Individuals really see the benefit of Six Sigma when you can get them into implementation as soon as possible. Besides reinforcing the tools and building confidence through repetition on real problem situations, the organization makes many improvements external to the assigned projects in the formal Six Sigma wave.

THERE IS ALWAYS A BETTER WAY

Although the Six Sigma approach is different in smaller and mid-sized organizations, success still requires leadership and commitment. In these organizations, we have developed many executives beyond the champion level and put their entire executive team through green belt certification. These individuals become *super-booster* Six Sigma leaders because they understand the power of Six Sigma through both philosophy and the mandatory hands-on project experiences. This sends a strong message to the rest of the organization that Six Sigma is serious business.

There are many ways that small and mid-sized organizations can benefit from Six Sigma, and it does not require that quantum leap of commitment and spending up front. Figure 2.4 provides one such approach. Many of our Six Sigma deployments in these organizations begin small and ramp up at a manageable rate. At one end of the spectrum may be a few days of Six Sigma Support to a particular problem. Next this may grow into a more structured Six Sigma Pilot effort, where the organization commits to two or three relevant, high-impact projects to prove the methodology and establish initial successes quickly. The next phase is Partial Deployment and may include a formal green belt/yellow belt wave, where the organization commits to fifteen to twenty-five Six Sigma projects, while relying on master black belt/black belt expertise externally. This eventually becomes a Full-Scale Deployment of additional green belt/yellow belt waves, where the deployment speed and timing are based on specific client needs. At this point, organizations commit to developing their own internal black belts.

Throughout this chapter, we have presented Six Sigma deployment options that are quite different from the ones you may have read about in other books. Some of our colleagues in industry have stated their opinions very strongly: "This approach will never work" or "There's only one proven path to Six Sigma

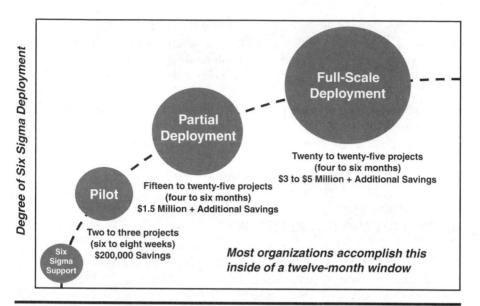

Figure 2.4   Scaleable Six Sigma™ for small and mid-sized organizations.

success." But for small and mid-sized organizations, Scaleable Six Sigma™ *is* working well and "one size fits all" does not work. On a scale of magnitude, the scaleable approach to Six Sigma enables smaller and mid-sized organizations to achieve results at a more digestible pace, and they achieve results much quicker. These organizations are much more resource constrained than larger companies, they have less funding for Six Sigma, and they need to see their ROIs quicker. Usually, "one size fits all" of anything eventually gets organizations into trouble, especially with this mid-market Six Sigma environment. Finally there is a way for smaller organizations to respond to the Six Sigma requests from their larger customers without jeopardizing customer service or financial results. The Scaleable Six Sigma™ implementation model works well with smaller and mid-sized companies.

CHAPTER 2 TAKE-AWAYS

■   There are definite differences between large and small organizations, differences that significantly impact a Six Sigma deployment. Regardless of the supposed benefits of Six Sigma, the traditional top-down implementation approach (i.e., time and cost) is a major barrier to entry for smaller and mid-sized organizations. There are many ways that small and mid-sized organizations can benefit from Six Sigma, and they do not require that quantum leap of commitment and spending up front.

■ The written literature, textbooks, and case studies about GE, Honeywell, DuPont, 3M, and many others present a top-down approach to Six Sigma; however, most small and mid-sized organizations have postponed Six Sigma because this top-down model puts it out of their financial reach. The scaleable approach to Six Sigma produces more affordable, higher, and faster results for small and mid-sized organizations.

■ The Scaleable Six Sigma™ approach works well because it is not a black-and-white, one-size-fits-all approach. Scaleable Six Sigma™ modifies the deployment approach to fit a particular organization's requirements and operating constraints. On a company-by-company basis, the deployment details, scope, focus, and timing are different.

■ Scaleable Six Sigma™ is a building-block approach that enables organizations to quickly transition their Six Sigma resources to the next highest level of achievement. Deployment occurs at a rate at which these organizations can benefit quickly from their efforts. The number of projects, the levels of education, and the whole deployment and execution approach occur at a digestible pace, with a direct link to strategy and results.

SIX SIGMA LEADERSHIP AND DEPLOYMENT

Here we go again…another spin on fad improvement programs. Whether it is lean, Six Sigma, lean Sigma, or lean/Six Sigma, strategic improvement initiatives are now the norm for most organizations throughout the world today. Unfortunately, strategic results are less commonplace. Most organizations recognize the need to reinvent themselves as superior competitors, dial in more precisely to customer and supplier needs, and adopt to ever-changing business conditions. The heart of these programs is improving strategic and operating performance by fundamentally changing the way organizations think, behave, and conduct their business. In spite of the never-ending stream of improvement methodologies offering clear and consistent promises of improvement and returns on investment (ROIs), different organizations have achieved varying degrees of implementation success. In many cases, the real benefits have been part fact, part illusion.

STRATEGIC IMPROVEMENT IS A CORE COMPETENCY

The ideas presented in this chapter are critical to ultimate success because they represent about 80 percent of your improvement journey. Before we jump to conclusions about Six Sigma or strategic improvement in general, this chapter will reflect on the critical leadership, deployment, and *soft-side* infrastructure aspects of improvement. We need to stand in front of the mirror and answer some very tough questions about improvement programs before we go any further. Why is there variation in success among organizations implementing kaizen, lean, Six Sigma, enterprise resource planning (ERP), and other strategic improvement programs? What are the root causes of their successes and failures? How can we get beyond all the excuses and the enigma of these various situations and deal with the real facts about successful improvement? We do not hold a monopoly on all the answers to these questions, but we do know from all of our experiences that strategic improvement is a core competency. What exactly do we mean by this core competency statement? It is a skill that most organizations do not have internally by osmosis and they underestimate the difficulty of strategic improvement. Organizations must learn how to define, lead, and execute strategic improvement. You do not get there by developing a grand strategy and then delegating it to a powerless organization. You do not go to a Six Sigma seminar and become an instant change master. You do not wake up one day, flip a switch, and have these competencies in place throughout your organization. It takes a huge, long-term commitment to define and organize a strategic improvement initiative and then integrate strategy, leadership, execution, the right methodologies, and permanent culture change. Those organizations that have achieved impressive results from their improvement programs do so because they understand this fact. Although most improvement methodologies such as Six Sigma offer steps and tools that are necessary to achieve success, they are neither sufficient nor exhaustive. Further, improvement methodologies are ineffective without the right improvement strategy and infrastructure bundled around them. Six Sigma methodologies, tools, and enabling technologies are only the *means*, not the *ends*.

We talked about the Six Sigma superstars in Chapter 1, but there have also been failures. The folks at GE, Honeywell, Motorola, Johnson Controls, and Bank of America are successful because they have been living Six Sigma every day for years. They also have more resources to dedicate to these programs than smaller and mid-sized organizations. Why, then, do other organizations fail miserably? The Six Sigma methodology and tools work, but the human drama of deployment can kill you. Lack of a well-defined strategy, leadership and commitment, communication and awareness, looking for the quick magic pill, or just plain succumbing to the pressures of short-term results are a few reasons totally unrelated to the Six Sigma methodology and tools. But if we think about this question in more detail, we can increase our success by learning from the lessons of others. This is the essence of this chapter: to discuss many of these successful leadership and deployment factors in greater detail. Every executive knows about these factors, but *know how to* is much more prevalent than *doing*. There is a big difference between *knowing how to do* something and *doing it*. When we hear "We're already doing A" or "We know how to do B," more often than not there is not much happening. Our objective in this chapter is to reinforce the importance of these factors in the success of your Six Sigma journey. Six Sigma is not about collecting the right ratios of belts; it is about cultural transformation and financial results.

We were recently invited to a company to discuss Six Sigma. The CEO told us that a premier Fortune 100 customer was mandating that the company become involved with Six Sigma. We went through the normal discussions about how to implement Six Sigma as a business philosophy and the commitment and process required to get there. Near the end of the meeting, the CEO said, "We're not ready for all of that. We just want you to give our management team a four-hour course on Six Sigma, and then maybe you can certify our company, kind of like an ISO certification. Then we can put a Six Sigma plaque in the lobby and the 6σ logo on our web site and be able to talk about it with our customers." He doesn't get it. He wishes to become a Six Sigma organization with a Two Sigma approach!

Executives who view strategic improvement as a punch list usually skip the most critical elements of change, and their results unfortunately show it. There is a common pattern of practices that result in performance above or below expectations. We have worked with hundreds of organizations, and regardless of the industry, there are a lot more similarities than differences in their successes. We have been benchmarking and studying these patterns for years and have summarized them into Sixteen Key Requirements for Six Sigma Success (Figure 3.1), and they apply to Six Sigma or any major strategic improvement initiative. These patterns allow us to reflect and learn from our mistakes and throw us back into the battle with renewed knowledge and skills. Mistakes and

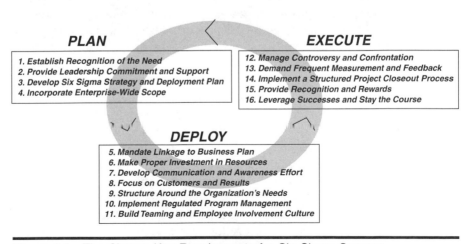

PLAN

1. Establish Recognition of the Need
2. Provide Leadership Commitment and Support
3. Develop Six Sigma Strategy and Deployment Plan
4. Incorporate Enterprise-Wide Scope

EXECUTE

12. Manage Controversy and Confrontation
13. Demand Frequent Measurement and Feedback
14. Implement a Structured Project Closeout Process
15. Provide Recognition and Rewards
16. Leverage Successes and Stay the Course

DEPLOY

5. Mandate Linkage to Business Plan
6. Make Proper Investment in Resources
7. Develop Communication and Awareness Effort
8. Focus on Customers and Results
9. Structure Around the Organization's Needs
10. Implement Regulated Program Management
11. Build Teaming and Employee Involvement Culture

Figure 3.1   The Sixteen Key Requirements for Six Sigma Success.

learning are a part of any improvement effort, especially in your own organization. They provide us with valuable insights about what went wrong with our previous improvement efforts. Skipping ahead with a Six Sigma implementation without a solid foundation in the prerequisite activities usually makes the improvement effort crumble, hit the wall, or fade away over time.

SIXTEEN KEY REQUIREMENTS FOR SIX SIGMA SUCCESS

The Sixteen Key Requirements for Six Sigma Success are more important than the methodologies and tools. Remember that DMAIC (Define, Measure, Analyze, Improve, Control), Minitab, and statistics are only the means, not the ends. On a good day, they are only 20 to 30 percent of the success criteria. The Sixteen Key Requirements for Six Sigma Success are the other 70 to 80 percent of the success criteria. These are the factors that result in a very positive and profitable Six Sigma experience.

1. Establish Recognition of the Need

One of the greatest leadership challenges is to keep executives and the entire organization focused. Many executives have a full plate of priorities, and often strategic improvement is lower on their list than other more pressing needs. Some organizations postpone change and hope the economy will take care of things. Change is a reactive event rather than a proactive living event. Sometimes executives begin a strategic initiative like Six Sigma and unintentionally break the momentum for change by hitting the remote control improvement button, celebrating initial successes too long, or simply moving on to other priorities (which sends a strong message that something else is more important). It is very difficult to look reality in the face, and the first reaction is a string of denial thoughts and opinions or to blame suppliers, customers, or someone else. Another common occurrence is the continued debate about what needs to be done, which creates total confusion and conflicting directions about change.

The fact is, no matter where your current performance lies, it simply is not good enough beyond today. Just think about the hundreds or thousands of organizations that have been market leaders only to relinquish that position to a competitor within twelve to twenty-four months. The global economy is moving at clock speed, technology and product life cycles are very short, and everyone is involved in business improvement. Customers are continuously sourcing faster, better, cheaper suppliers around the globe. The bar is rising at a much faster speed than many organizations can keep up with. However, this also provides the opportunity to leapfrog and surprise the competition with the right strategy. The best time to change is now, but it is unfortunate that it often requires a catastrophic event to prime the organizational pump for change. It is a lot easier to create urgency with catastrophe rather than leadership, but it often makes you late for the party. Catastrophe-driven improvement is also intermittent. The ratio of organizations that change due to proactive leadership is much lower than organizations that change due to a catastrophic event. Without a solid recognition of the need to change, improvement programs are typically reactionary and short-lived, and the results are also disappointing.

Another part of this is getting the organization to "think big and stay hungry." This includes stretch goals and quicker celebrations followed by stirring up awareness that the organization can do even better. The objective is to find balance between congratulating teams on their successes and throwing down new challenges for them to meet. It is better these days to proactively raise the bar than to have your competition impose it in your organization.

2. Provide Leadership Commitment and Support

When executives fail to lead both intellectually and through daily actions, the organization suffers. They often launch a Six Sigma effort and then disappear or appear weekly to ask, "Are we done yet?" We have worked with several executives who try to justify their commitment by saying, "Sure I'm committed. Look how much money I'm spending on you guys!" We help them to understand the true meaning of commitment, and most then rise to the occasion. Mentoring and leadership are things that people say they *can* and *know how* to do, but they fall down in actual practice. Why does this happen? They want to be effective leaders, but strategic improvement is a core competency that executives need to cultivate and develop because it is new to them. The best leaders have the vision, conviction, confidence, and an amazing emotional resolve to prevail no matter what gets in the way. They live, breathe, and understand the details of lean, kaizen, Six Sigma, or whatever else they are doing. They have a passion to succeed, and their fire-in-the-belly commitment is very real. They make the effort to educate themselves like everyone else. They walk the talk and many even take on a project like everyone else. They have a remarkable concern and interest in change and people. They put it all on the line and make it clear that participation and success are the only options. They superglue their executive team together in unity of purpose with a consistent message of improvement. They calibrate and recalibrate their organizations and create a solid center of gravity. Recognize the difference between *knowing how to do something* and actually *doing it*. When everyone is running around saying they do not need help because they already *know how* to change, usually very little is changing. Recognize the organization's limitations and constraints, and seek outside help to deal with these issues from the get-go. You will achieve greater success.

There is so much power and influence over change when executives send the right message and then align their actions to that message. On the flip side, when they do not, it is just another fad program with discouraging results. Recently, one company decided to pursue Six Sigma as a response to serious customer design, quality, and delivery issues. The executive team was very busy and decided to delegate a feasibility effort to a middle-management committee. This organization had a track record for failed fad programs, and the committee began debating Six Sigma, the applicability, and benefits. The majority of the team members recognized the need to improve the business, but they were all overloaded with other responsibilities. They putzed around in meeting after meeting for months until the leadership group requested a definitive *what should we do* from the team. One skeptical individual wanted to calculate the ROIs and earnings before interest and taxes (EBIT) to five decimal places and then benchmark which competitors had already implemented Six Sigma and what benefits they achieved. Another individual thought the company's low-volume/high-complexity configured products were too unique for Six Sigma and that no improvement program could add to the capabilities of their current engineering organization. Another individual was trying to make sure the team addressed the internal politics of who to include and not include in training. Another acknowledged that even though the organization was doing a lot of the wrong things, Six Sigma would be too disruptive because everyone was already overworked. These people were missing the point; they were in space looking for a planet with a scanning electron microscope. They could not envision the destination because they were too busy studying the particles in front of them at ×2,000 power. They were in denial and were looking for all the reasons why it would not work, and their actions were proportional to their commitment. The committee was assigned an impossible task and the end result was pretty obvious. What were they all thinking? Regardless of the label you assign to these programs, it is pretty ridiculous to debate whether or not an organization should improve its business or resolve serious customer issues. But the bigger point is that great intentions fail when executives fail to create a vision, lead, communicate, and align their actions with the message.

With Six Sigma or any strategic improvement initiative, actions definitely speak louder than words, and the organization always observes the leadership and follows accordingly. Leadership must be visible, consistent, decisive, unwavering, and polarizing to focus the organization on a common theme.

3. Develop Six Sigma Strategy and Deployment Plan

Many organizations live by the improvement myth that the organization must learn as it goes. What is the result of this myth? When you walk through a naive organization that practices this approach, every manager has a white board with his or her own list of Six Sigma projects thought up in support of the program. Each has a personalized checklist code to monitor progress and a little border drawn around it. Sometimes there is so much stuff on their boards you wonder how they even notice it. They all get together once a week to go through their lists. If you interview all the management team and copy their lists, you find strategy disconnects, conflicts, redundancies, disagreement, finger-pointing, and "just going through the motions." There is this huge misconception that the volume of activity and the speed of *perceived* completion are proportional to the end results.

Six Sigma is not a business strategy. It is one of many enablers to achieve the business strategy. However, organizations still must think through the details of how they will improve the business via Six Sigma. Although many of the Six Sigma statistical tools are based on chance, a successful Six Sigma deployment is a matter of choice. Many organizations skip the most important element of improvement: the Six Sigma strategy and deployment plan. Organizations tend to skim over this process and dive into the methodologies and tools. People select and implement tools and techniques in an effort to get quick results. Their intentions are good because they are trying to make a quick impact, but their actions are bad because they end up chasing outcomes and symptoms because they do not have a solid improvement plan. The anxiety of jumping in leaves the rest of the organization in initial confusion and doubt. In the absence of a well-defined Six Sigma strategy and deployment plan, activities are "perception driven" versus "fact driven" and not focused on strategic gaps and root causes of poor performance. Most of the focus is on scheduling wave after wave of Six Sigma training and developing the right number of black belts and green belts, and the mandatory projects are an afterthought. This approach may produce a few short-term benefits, but it never becomes a sustaining process. A closer look usually reveals disconnects between customer requirements and the company's day-to-day improvement activities. The results are eventually very questionable and illusive, and before you know it, they are victims of another "flavor-of-the-month" improvement program. For the employees of these organizations, introducing them to Six Sigma gets about as much enthusiasm as passing a mononucleosis culture around.

Again, we need to ask why. The answer is the same reason as above. Strategic improvement is a core competency that executives need to cultivate and develop because it is new to them. Dealing with change is ambiguous, even on a good day. Nevertheless, a formal Six Sigma strategy is missing in three-quarters of the organizations pursuing Six Sigma. Developing a solid Six Sigma strategy and improvement plan is complicated. It takes a lot of research, thought, and time to put a good workable improvement plan together. Most of the time, there are tremendous pressures to *make things happen now,* so the plan goes out the window because people think they know what needs to be done. Speed can be an extremely harmful diversion, particularly if organizations choose to shortcut the most critical steps of improvement. Good leaders recognize that it took time and current thinking to get into the situation, and it will take time, different thinking, and persistence to change the situation.

Organizations will never realize the results they expect without this well-defined Six Sigma strategy and deployment plan. This becomes the vision, goals, and implementation instrument by which they can communicate why and what needs to change. A good improvement plan also answers many questions and concerns people may have about change and how certain issues will be handled. Granted, it does not have all the answers contained within it, but it becomes a great target to shoot at, embrace, deploy, and execute. Moreover, it provides structure and formality to the Six Sigma initiative and a great litmus test for Six Sigma activities.

4. Incorporate Enterprise-Wide Scope

Every organization has improvement opportunities throughout the entire organization. A closer look at the causal factors of customer issues or substandard performance verifies this fact. Often, the root causes of performance in manufacturing, sales, engineering, finance, or customer service lie outside of these areas. We are not encouraging finger-pointing because many of these root causes are well within the immediate control of these areas; however, business processes are cross-functional, where the performance of the whole is dependent on the process touchpoints throughout the organization. An enterprise-wide approach to Six Sigma achieves much more benefits because it addresses the critical spectrum of process variation. All processes (be it equipment or business processes) have variation and defects, whether a purchasing process, the monthly close process, the order management process, or an injection molding machine. In the total value stream perspective, manufacturing is quickly becoming a smaller link in the chain and the transactional processes are becoming increasingly important in terms of strategic performance.

A few years ago, our Six Sigma consulting engagements were focused almost entirely on manufacturing (e.g., yield and throughput improvement) and supplier quality. Today, it is common for client engagement activity to be in the ranges of 60 percent transactional and 40 percent shop floor. Additionally, many of these transactional projects include suppliers, distributors, and ultimate customers. Organizations have discovered the nonmanufacturing applications of Six Sigma and the tremendous benefits of cash-to-cash cycle time reduction, excess/obsolete inventory, supply chain/logistics cost reduction, and warranty/returns, to name a few. It has been our experience that manufacturing organizations have been involved in operations improvement for a decade. A point of yield on a machine might be worth $50,000 per year, which often gets washed out by other concurrent activities like mix changes or smaller order sizes, but a 20 percent reduction in returns and allowances could be worth millions that are very visible to the bottom line.

5. Mandate Linkage to the Business Plan

Most successful Six Sigma efforts are led by an executive steering group that reconciles strategic needs and Six Sigma activity. This executive steering group typically provides broad Six Sigma direction to the organization on critical areas of improvement. Most also have a formal process of putting potential projects through a litmus test for prioritizing strategic importance. Some even regulate the amount of activity in progress at any given time, so Six Sigma does not take on a life of its own like previous improvement programs. A few even maintain a rolling, project-by-project Six Sigma ROI. Chapter 6 (Strategy Deployment and Project Selection) provides a framework for linking and aligning Six Sigma activities to the business plan.

This approach prevents the *project for project's sake* syndrome and minimizes nonvalue-added Six Sigma activity. Many organizations are guilty of this, but may not be willing to admit it. For example, we have observed several instances in organizations where their original Six Sigma goals are replaced by the mechanics of the process itself. They view deployment as selecting candidates, assigning projects, scheduling waves of training, and reporting meaningless statistics. Often, candidates are assigned Six Sigma projects that really are not Six Sigma projects at all. We wish we had $10 for every person who has mentioned that they think Six Sigma is a big waste of time because they were assigned a certification project they knew the answer to on the first day, but were told they had to go through the motions for the next five months. Activity does not always translate into improvement. A formal linkage to the business plan is very beneficial, but it needs to be balanced by the effort required to achieve this linkage. It definitely makes people do their homework before embarking on a project because they know the steering committee has its finger on the pulse of Six Sigma.

6. Make Proper Investment in Resources

This is a common stumbling block for many organizations pursuing Six Sigma. First, people must be provided with new skills through training and their mandatory Six Sigma projects. Second, commitment of resources is measured by actions, not words. It is a lot easier to complain about allocating resources than managing them, but successful organizations take a hard line on this topic. If you have Six Sigma candidates and their managers are not allowing time for training and project work, it is time to intervene and reset the expectation. Otherwise, the wrong message is sent to the rest of the organization. Once resources are committed to a Six Sigma effort, participation is no longer a choice. Do not let managers get away with threatening that their subordinate's participation in Six Sigma means something else will not get done. Do not be fooled by the cries of "They don't have time to do Six Sigma and their regular job." There is a big difference between managing proactively and moderating the way things have always been done. Deal with the facts and manage it! There are always options for fitting everything in, but it requires getting out of the *same people, same process, same thinking, same results* routine.

A deep dive into what managers have their people doing is often controversial because it questions the value-add of current activity versus improvement activity. For these people, their statistics are usually made up on the spot to justify their actions. Most claims can easily be offset with facts such as value-add ratios, dollarizing lost opportunities, and Cost of Poor Quality. The point here is that once the commitment is made, there is no turning back. You are *in*, and you *will* complete that $150,000 cost-reduction project. And management will create the environment for success, not nonparticipation and excuses. Will a catastrophic customer event ever come up in the middle of green belt training? Sure, but most of these things can be handled. One of the tasks of leadership in this area is to rid the organization of binary thinking — "If I do A, I can't do B" — and get people thinking out of the box.

7. Develop Communication and Awareness Effort

A well-executed Six Sigma effort communicates the vision and need to change, builds employee awareness and commitment, and states the consequences of not changing. It addresses people's expectations and fears right up front and uses facts to win over people's hearts and minds. Remember that nothing changes until people are ready to change. Awareness and communication keep the interest level and momentum at a peak level. The Six Sigma strategy and deployment plan, town meeting updates, and visual storyboarding are common approaches to facilitate communication and awareness. Crystal-clear, vivid communication and awareness are needed over and over because people are human and need constant reinforcement of the message.

Leadership behavior and actions must be consistent with the communication and awareness message. When leaders live the vision, people will follow. Similarly, when executives deliver one message and then act inconsistently with that message, it sends the wrong vision about change. Leadership behavior takes people forward or backward at an exponential rate. One company CEO required that he and his entire executive staff go through green belt certification with others in the organization. All training sessions were mandatory, and they each completed their mandatory projects. This sent a very strong message about commitment. As a side note, these executives became so good at "Six Sigma-think" that it quickly became the kiss of death to show up at meetings with opinions instead of facts. Consequently, others decided that they better enroll in future Six Sigma waves without even being told to do so. Today, Six Sigma is no longer a program — it has evolved into the way this organization thinks and conducts business. Executives must be very conscious about their selection of words and then match their actions and behavior to the words. The right words followed by the right actions create the right enabling behaviors for success.

8. Focus on Customers and Results

There are two aspects to this requirement. First, all Six Sigma activities must have a distinct customer focus, whether it is the ultimate customer or the many touchpoint customer/supplier relationships in a business process. This focus is achieved by understanding the customer/supplier value proposition (i.e., what the customer requirements are, spoken and unspoken) and gaps between current and desired performance. Further, this is best defined by data and facts, baseline and goal performance criteria. There are other Six Sigma tools, such as Function Deployment, Kano, KJ Analysis, etc., that enable us to quantify these criteria. Without a formal understanding of customer and market needs, and the key drivers of their (and your) success, a Six Sigma effort can quickly become a set of disheveled improvement activities.

Second, all strategic improvement initiatives require some semblance of balance. Many years ago, we heard someone say, "The customer is not always right, but the customer is always the customer." In our fast-paced global society, businesspeople have the best intentions, but they are not always the best intentions for everyone involved. A blind "yes" to every customer requirement is a prescription for disaster. Many suppliers in the automotive industry have said yes to every customer demand only to find themselves filing for Chapter 11.

Collaboration is the key to success. Proactive problem solving between customers and suppliers results in win-win value stream improvements.

9. Structure Around the Organization's Needs

This is particularly important for smaller and mid-sized organizations and organizations with unique industry characteristics. First, avoid the boilerplate Six Sigma programs, implementation processes, and timelines. It is very possible to implement Six Sigma in several ways, structured around key strategic issues and the organization's ability to digest and benefit from the effort. Chapter 2 provided several options and thoughts about a more scaleable approach. Second, the emphasis of Six Sigma must be matched to the industry characteristics of the organization. Implementing Six Sigma in discrete consumer products is much different than in the paper, pharmaceutical, aerospace, automotive, food, insurance, healthcare, or financial services industries. Third, use industry-specific examples and data for the Six Sigma statistical exercises. Nothing makes a better connection than seeing these methodologies and tools applied to a process that people work with every day. Retrofitting the Six Sigma approach, methodology, and statistical tools to the types of issues in these particular industries is a necessary success factor.

10. Implement Regulated Program Management

One of the mistakes executives make with Six Sigma and other improvement programs is to allow the effort to get away from them. Left in the absence of a well-defined strategy, program management, and performance feedback, these efforts can take on a life of their own. The first thing you know, there is a proliferation of teams comprised of resources that do not have time to serve on all of them, there are many redundant and/or nonvalue-adding activities, and not much to show for it all in the final analysis. We have witnessed 5S activities in a men's room, kanbans for office coffee cups, visual management for a copy machine and paper cutter, the same people on many different teams, and use of Six Sigma tools to justify what an individual had already decided to do. Six Sigma is only as good as the strategy, deployment, and execution process. By itself, it is just a structured problem-solving process, Minitab software, and a menu of statistical tools. Earlier versions of Six Sigma in the 1980s were just that — a gang of statistical intellectuals with a bag of tools running around the organization looking for a problem. They faded away quickly.

Organizations need a structure and discipline around Six Sigma to ensure alignment between strategy and effort. In our experience, organizations beginning Six Sigma have a limited capacity level where they can pursue improvements and maintain daily business requirements. Further, it makes sense to focus limited resources and time on the highest impact opportunities. Many of our clients have a formal management process to regulate projects and activity and measure ROIs project by project. Many also have a structured project closeout process, adding a high degree of formality to project completion and results.

11. Build a Teaming and Employee Involvement Culture

This one is self-explanatory. There are two sides to this value proposition. This type of culture is characterized by "empowerment," which means "giving power away." Management must be willing to give up power because there is a level of trust in their people's ability to perform. People must be given the correct education and skills to accept power. They also need to act responsibly with that new power and have the authority to act as process owners. They must have access to information and feedback so they can measure progress. Organizations have come a long way with teaming and employee involvement, but there are still many untapped opportunities in this area.

Organizations need to grow employees who are willing to go beyond their normal job expectations. Although most organizations are involved in teaming and employee involvement at some level, there are a few common dilemmas with the mechanics of teaming. Sometimes, the right people who can make a big difference are not involved in the right places or they are spread too thin across teams. Another dilemma is the launching of teams and assignments before there is a solid improvement plan. This is not directly a teaming issue, but the point here is that we want to do everything in our power to set the teams up for success.

A final thought about teaming: Should participation be mandatory? We have had great success establishing the baseline that the need for the organization to change is mandatory and the need for employees who are willing to help implement change is mandatory. We encourage good citizen employees to set the example for others. Eventually, other employees get the message via peer pressure and observing success after success and fall in. Some may never join in and self-destruct their careers. The end of this chapter provides a more descriptive overview of this process.

12. Manage Controversy and Confrontation

Organizations that are not experiencing anxiety and controversy with change are having too much fun and, in fact, are probably not changing at all. Major strategic improvement creates a lot of emotions. We need to remove all the emotions and do a better job of managing change with data, facts, and analysis. Controversy and confrontation are extremely healthy when managed correctly and in a timely manner. When an organization begins its improvement journey, there is no answer to many of these issues. That is the challenge of improvement. Great leaders have a magic perseverance, faith, and confidence that the organization will figure out how to put it all together and succeed together.

Confrontation is a little stronger. When a candidate's project recommendations are correct, supported by facts, and supported by the majority, then organizations need to recognize and knock down the barriers and remove the prima donnas. Failure to do this sends a very strong message that it is okay not to change, plain and simple. Nothing undermines a major change process more than allowing the nay-sayers to function against the tide of improvement.

Some people will never get it no matter what you do; it is not in their psyche to change or to be part of a Six Sigma or team improvement effort. Sometimes, there is a place in the organization for these individuals, and sometimes the lights go on and these individuals grow to be your champions. Occasionally, some of these individuals become hostile and attempt to undermine and sabotage change. When organizations encounter this situation, looking the other way is not the answer. You cannot make believe that bad performance is good performance. Leadership gets organizations through these barriers and sends a clear message to the rest of the organization. Failure to deal strongly with inappropriate behavior derails commitment and support.

13. Demand Frequent Measurement and Feedback

This is a real strong point of Six Sigma. Inherently, Six Sigma promotes financial success, one project at a time. Everything begins and ends with financial performance. There is a focus in Six Sigma that if every project is successful, then the entire effort will be successful. There is no waiting or *pie-in-the-sky* hopes of results showing up someday.

In the DMAIC structure, there are several measurement points. In the Measure phase, there are measurement criteria for project selection, qualification, and benefits. In the Analyze phase, candidates define baseline performance and financial expectations for every project. In the Analyze and Improve phases, the tools themselves provide measures of causals, severity, and focus. Finally, in the Control phase, candidates implement, monitor, and track financial performance until the initial goal is reached. The mechanics are in place. It is up to the Six Sigma steering committee, the champions, and process managers/sponsors to establish a formal routine to monitor and track progress.

14. Implement a Structured Project Closeout Process

One of the most frequent Six Sigma questions we are asked is: "When is a project complete?" This is a great question. Many people celebrate success prematurely after DMAI, before the tough work of implementation in the C or Control phase is finished. Many organizations hold project fairs or executive reviews at the Improve phase, where the recommendations and benefits have been defined and there is agreement to go forward. We have established a Structured Project Closeout Process (Figure 3.2) within our Six Sigma practice to clarify this issue. This process requires Six Sigma team leaders to monitor and report progress frequently until the initial goal has been achieved. Then there is a formal postaudit and validation process with the team and a financial representative. A secondary goal of this closeout process is to peg operational improvements to the profit-and-loss statement.

15. Provide Recognition and Rewards

In a major improvement effort, recognition and rewards are often afterthoughts for most organizations. In the planning stages of Six Sigma, recognition and rewards are typically viewed as way out there in the scheme of things. We agree that there are many higher priority issues in the initial innovation stage of Six Sigma, but eventually this is a topic that requires definition and thought.

Recognition is something that we view as a continuous process and nonfinancial in nature. Some companies showcase their top performers in town meetings or in featured articles on storyboards or in corporate newsletters. A key point of recognition is its genuineness. Recognition criteria should be somewhat formalized so people understand why a particular individual was recognized in the first place. We want to recognize our good Six Sigma citizens, but if we begin patting everyone on the back, then real recognition disappears. Rewards, on the other hand, tend to be financial in nature.

Many organizations conclude a wave of Six Sigma certification with a corporate project fair. Usually the corporate officers and vice presidents attend, and each candidate has an opportunity to present his or her projects and results to the group, followed by a dinner and formal certification ceremony. Some organizations go a step further and reward candidates with stock certificates or bonus checks for their effort and contribution. Others might provide a jacket or dress shirt or another gift that sets candidates apart from those who have not yet earned their Six Sigma stripes. The point here is that eventually we need to think about a standard recognition and rewards process for all waves of Six Sigma certification.

16. Leverage Successes and Stay the Course

Cultural change and transformation occurs far at the end of a strategic improvement program, at the point where there is a transition from a program to a new operating philosophy. This happens when organizations are successful at behav-

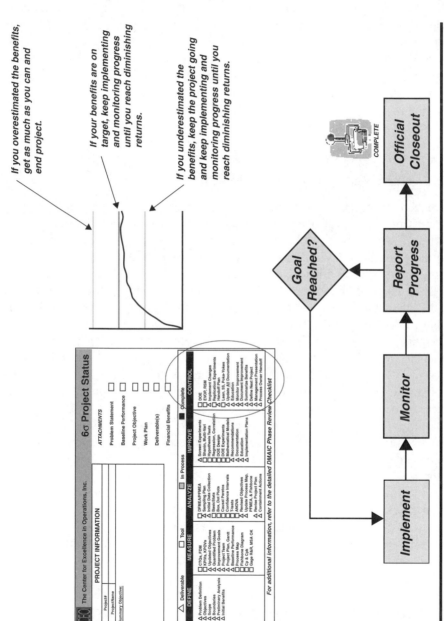

Figure 3.2 Structured project closeout process.

ioral change and they have internalized and institutionalized the improvement process. Culture change occurs only when a new way of operating takes place without being constantly shored up by management and for a reasonable period of time. It is the time when people no longer say, "I don't have time to do Six Sigma and my regular job." Change is now viewed as *part of* their job, instead of *in addition to* their job. It is the point where people identify and solve problems without giving a second thought to whether it is a kaizen, lean, or Six Sigma problem. It is a fascinating phenomenon when organizations cross over this magic line, where strategic improvement is embedded in their cultural DNA. It is very rewarding to observe people seeking out and implementing improvements without giving a second thought to whether they are dealing with a kaizen, lean, ERP, or Six Sigma problem.

Let's be realistic. Ideally, improvement never ends once the transition from program to operating philosophy takes place and it becomes embedded into the culture. Picture a force-field diagram of your strategic improvement program with its driving forces and restraining forces defined. For driving forces, you have all of these great improvement efforts in place. We are improving financial performance and competitiveness, and we might have been awarded a new chunk of business. People are enthusiastic, individual behaviors have changed, the culture is changing, and it is just a lot more fun to come to work every day. Now let's visit the restraining forces. First, there is a very gray area between behavioral change and cultural change, and you experience backslides occasionally. Second, people do not remain in their same positions forever. Sometimes new management comes in with a different twist on improvement. Sometimes people are promoted and their motivation/reward system changes. Critical resources may be on sick leave, retire, and/or new people are hired. Third, people have human frailties. We get tired, we need reinforcement, we become complacent, our company relationships change, we drift and become unfocused, etc. Fourth, there are always dozens of other human dramas tugging at us in the company, in our personal lives, and in the world that impact our continued progress. All of these factors add to the complexity of staying the course, but there is no other option these days. Either we implement and benefit from change or we become victims of our competitors.

RECOGNIZE THE ORGANIZATIONAL REALITIES

During the launch stage of a Six Sigma effort, organizations need all of the passion and innovation that they can find. We have found that staffing the initial efforts with the right people is a key attribute of early successes. Figure 3.3 provides a conceptual model for thinking about organizational resources.

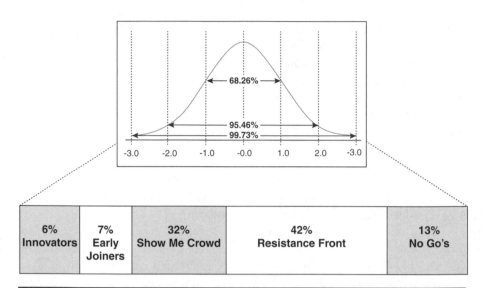

Figure 3.3 Organizational reference spectrum.

On the left side are the Innovators, who represent about 6 percent of the organization. These are your go-to, make-it-happen people who are always up on current management topics. You will find these people reading and talking about Six Sigma long before it happens. Many of these individuals may have advanced education like an MBA or professional society certifications and are always in tune with what is going on through industry and trade publications. For the most part, these people sometimes act like hyperactive children, always questioning what else can be done to improve the business. Besides being intellectually open-minded, they are great at getting things done.

The next segment is the Early Joiners, who represent about 7 percent of the organization. These individuals become oriented to Six Sigma and their first response is, "What a great idea. Why didn't I think of this?" As soon as they are exposed to Six Sigma, they are ready to roll. Moving to the next segment, we find the Show Me Crowd, which represents about 32 percent of the organization. These individuals are initially slow and cautious, but join in enthusiastically as soon as they see a few successes.

The Resistance Front represents about 42 percent of the organization. This is a tougher segment that either ignores Six Sigma because they are too busy with other duties or resists change because they are nonbelievers. It becomes increasingly difficult in this segment because you cannot win these people over with logic. Approximately half of these people join in when the risk of resistance becomes greater than the risk of participation. Finally, we have the No-

Go's that represent the remaining 13 percent of the organization. These are the problem employees who just don't get it. They might demand a raise for serving on a team or remain inattentive to change. Some of these individuals pursue other employment and some of them hang around and talk a good game.

Should you front-load your initial Six Sigma effort with all of your best resources? Ideally yes, but not necessarily from a practical point of view. There is no cut-and-dried way of deploying the right resources, but eventually you cannot place the burden for success on a small segment of the organization. Six Sigma requires broad organizational involvement, so there is no sense in postponing what needs to be accomplished anyway. Sometimes resources to the right of the spectrum are emotionally stuck in their jobs and may develop an attitude over time. Some of these people are chomping at the bit for a new opportunity and grow to become your Six Sigma superstars. Some of the nontechnical people bring a fresh perspective to a problem that technical people have been unable to solve. Some people are literally dying for someone to listen to them and to make a new contribution to the business. Pairing achievers and low performers on a team can often result in growth for everyone. Sometimes you take risks with people and it ends up being a bad decision that drags the whole team down. The key here is to recognize the dynamics of the deployment and implementation process and act quickly if things become derailed.

A FINAL AXIOM ON LEADERSHIP

The horrific tragedy of September 11, 2001 had its impact on every business, including ours. Proposals were put on hold, several projects were postponed or canceled, and the interest level for our services fell drastically. It seemed like almost every organization plunged into a huge industrial coma. A few months later, I (TB) was having dinner with the CEO of one of our clients. I asked him why he did not cancel or postpone our Six Sigma project after 9/11. His response: "Honestly, I thought about it. But I realize that 9/11 has nothing to do with our problems. And if the economy gets better tomorrow, we will have worse problems if we do nothing. This is actually the best time to make changes. The risks are low and we have breathing room. Believe me, we will be much stronger than those who are doing nothing right now when things turn around." Today, this client is a market leader in its industry.

Think about this and then think about what your organization has been doing relative to strategic improvement. This is a great nugget of wisdom. If you are honest with yourself, you will admit that your delivery performance has nothing to do with bulls or bears. The design robustness of your new products has nothing to do with elephants or donkeys. Terrorism did not cause your billing errors, excess and obsolete inventory, or warranty/return problems. Those problems existed in 2001, and they will be much larger problems in 2005 if you do not take action. It is always easier to think of reasons to postpone Six Sigma, but it is a lot more painful for those who wait for the wrong reasons. Think about it, then lead others to do the right things for your stakeholders, the economy, and society as a whole. Organizations that are heavily into strategic improvement are now accelerating in the economic upturn, gaining significant market share from those that have done nothing and are wondering what happened.

CHAPTER 3 TAKE-AWAYS

■ Strategic improvement is a core competency. Organizations must learn how to define and organize a Six Sigma initiative and then integrate strategy, leadership, execution, the right methodologies, and permanent culture change. This skill is not automatically derived by osmosis or stature in the organization.

■ DMAIC, Minitab, and statistics are only the means, not the ends. On a good day, they are only 20 to 30 percent of the success criteria. The Sixteen Key Requirements for Six Sigma Success are the other 70 to 80 percent of the success criteria. These are the factors that result in a very positive and profitable Six Sigma experience.

■ The fact is, no matter where your current performance lies, it simply is not good enough beyond today. The global economy is moving at clock speed, technology and product life cycles are very short, and everyone is involved in business improvement. Customers are continuously sourcing faster, better, and cheaper suppliers around the globe. The bar is rising at a much faster speed than many organizations can keep up with. However, this also provides the opportunity to leapfrog and surprise the competition with the right strategy.

■ The best time to change is now, but it is unfortunate that it often requires a catastrophic event to prime the organizational pump for change. It is a lot easier to create urgency with catastrophe rather than leadership, but it often makes you late for the party. Without a solid recognition of the need to change, improvement programs are typically reactionary and short-lived, and the results are also disappointing.

■ With Six Sigma or any strategic improvement initiative, actions definitely speak louder than words, and the organization always observes the leadership and follows accordingly. Leadership must be consistent, decisive, unwavering, and polarizing to focus the organization on a common theme.

- Organizations never realize the results they expect without a well-defined Six Sigma strategy and deployment plan. This becomes the vision, goals, and implementation instrument by which they can communicate why and what needs to change. A good improvement plan also answers many questions and concerns people may have about change and how certain issues will be handled.

- A well-executed Six Sigma effort communicates the vision and need to change, builds employee awareness and commitment, and states the consequences of not changing. It addresses people's expectations and fears right up front and uses facts to win over people's hearts and minds. Crystal-clear, vivid communication and awareness are needed over and over because people are human and need constant reinforcement of the message.

- All Six Sigma activities must have a distinct customer focus, whether it is the ultimate customer or the many touchpoint customer/supplier relationships in a business process. This focus is achieved by understanding the customer/supplier value proposition (i.e., what the customer requirements are, spoken and unspoken) and gaps between current and desired performance. Further, this is best defined by data and facts, baseline and goal performance criteria.

- Implement Six Sigma in a manner that is structured around key strategic issues and the organization's ability to digest and benefit from the effort. The emphasis of Six Sigma must be matched to the industry characteristics of the organization. Retrofitting the Six Sigma approach, methodology, and statistical tools to the types of issues in a particular industry enables the organization to see how these methodologies and tools can be applied to its environment.

SUGGESTED FURTHER READING

Burton, Terence and Moran, John, *The Future-Focused Organization,* Prentice-Hall, 1995.

Collins, James, *Good to Great: Why Some Companies Make the Leap...And Others Don't,* HarperCollins, 2001.

Cotter, John, *The Heart of Change,* Harvard Business School Press, 2002.

Harris, Michael, *Value Leadership: Winning Competitive Advantage in the Information Age,* ASQ Press, 1998.

Naumann, Earl and Hoisington, Steven, *Customer Centered Six Sigma: Linking Customers, Process Improvement, and Financial Results,* ASQ Press, 2001.

Snee, Ronald and Hoerl, Roger, *Leading Six Sigma,* Prentice-Hall, 2003.

VonOech, Roger, *Expect the Unexpected or You Won't Find It,* Berrett-Koehler Publishers, 2002.

IMPLEMENTING SIX SIGMA: THE REALITIES OF DMAIC

Six Sigma is successful not because of its destination — 3.4 parts per million effective nonconformities — but because of the journey and the lessons learned along the way. One can have the same level of quality by chance if quite a bit of luck is involved. This result has no validity as a process. A process is a specified plan, method, or approach that should be repeatable. Luck fails this test. Many times, we hear people say, "We've made money in spite of ourselves, but now the market has changed and we're in trouble." Does this sound familiar? Depending on luck sounds insane, doesn't it? Do you have a specific plan that yields a repeatable process toward success? Is someone *moving your cheese to China?*

DEFINING THE STRATEGY: WHAT DOES SUCCESS LOOK LIKE?

Linking the Vision to a Critical Few Key Initiatives. In problem solving, there is a phenomenon known as the "Pareto" principle. Pareto was an engineer who actually studied economics and determined that the bulk of the money, 80 percent, in an economy is held by 20 percent of the people. He stated this as Pareto's law: Significant items tend to be distributed disproportionately in any given environment. Today, this is known as the 80/20 rule.

The Pareto principle (or 80/20 rule) affects us all as it helps determine everything from insurance rates to mutual fund investment activities: 20 percent of the people will have 80 percent of the accidents; 80 percent of the investments will only yield 20 percent of the results. However, the other 20 percent of investments in a mutual fund will yield 80 percent of the results and so on.

Businesses must be aware of this principle as they approach problem solving. One must consider the effort and resources required to solve problems against the results that are to be achieved once the problem is solved. From there, the Pareto principle will take over in that 20 percent of the problems, if solved, would yield 80 percent of the results. All businesses must be able to utilize their resources where they will have the biggest impact. By using the Pareto principle to prioritize the problem-solving efforts, the problems with the largest potential for impact are tackled first.

The bottom line is that any organization must define the vision for the future compared to where the business is today, as well as those key targets or inputs to lead it to the desired destination. In addition, businesses must determine how to measure those most significant inputs on a continual basis. It is also impractical to have too many measures of a business, as this would cloud the vision and blur any sense of direction. The Pareto principle enables businesses to focus on the "critical few" versus the "trivial many."

MAPPING THE APPROACH: KEY PROJECTS TO ACHIEVE CRITICAL INITIATIVES

One would never highlight an entire page in an atlas. This is akin to having too many measures of a business. It is efficient, however, to highlight the route to be taken as well as significant landmarks. This is the approach taken by Six Sigma. Define where you want to go, Measure where you are now, Analyze the best route to take, Improve the situation by beginning the journey toward the destination, and Control the process by checking the significant measures (the landmarks) often and making adjustments when necessary.

This Define, Measure, Analyze, Improve, Control (DMAIC) approach is logical, proven, and solid. It does not matter if you are trying to solve a true statistical Six Sigma problem, a lean problem, or working a kaizen blitz. Having a vision of where you want to go, a baseline of where you are, and a logical approach to getting there works. There are few things that are so robust in their design that well-intentioned people cannot mess them up. This is also true with Six Sigma. If one makes the determination that this is a kaizen, value stream mapping, or lean problem and "We don't need all that data and structure," the power will be lost. Therefore, one could surmise that the real power of Six Sigma is simply its structured approach to project management. This would be an accurate observation, as the principles to sound project management do not change with the project being managed. It is the same with Six Sigma when applied to lean, kaizen, value stream, or design projects.

ANALYZING THE BEST ROUTE: PLANNING TO AVOID DELAYS AND DETOURS

The success of Six Sigma will be directly proportional to the consideration that has gone into linking the project selection to the strategic direction of the organization. This is the method used to help ensure that the projects do not give way to "urgent" issues, which is otherwise known as firefighting. Even with careful consideration, it takes proper planning and determination of measurement structure to add to the probability of success for the projects involved with this approach. No matter the type of project, whether lean, value stream, kaizen, etc., the approach should be the same DMAIC.

When one first begins the study of Six Sigma tools, it may seem that there is nothing new. True, the tools used in the Six Sigma process are not new. However, these tools have only recently gained widespread practical application due to the advance of computer software and hardware in order to put the tools into the hands of the masses. The practicality comes from the simplification.

Analysis used to take so long that the results were of little use because they were not current by the time they were available. While the analysis may have been correct, the conditions that created the data that were analyzed had often changed. Therefore, any decisions made based on the analysis stood the possibility of being outdated and unreliable. This phenomenon is where the sayings such as "liars figure and figures lie" and "there are lies, damned lies, and statistics" come from.

One could argue that all this training and technology just made the lies come faster. This is true if the foundations are invalid. However, with user-friendly technology, more and more people are finally beginning to understand the statistics they dredged through in college. Therefore, they can start to speak and, more importantly, *understand* the language. This is part of the power of Six Sigma, as many people have historically reasoned that most people use statistics like a drunkard uses a lamppost, more for support of their position than for illumination.

Okay, so if people understand the statistics, now what? Well, to be sure, you are equipped to challenge data as they are presented as well as to request modeling before making changes in order to assess "what-if" scenarios with minimal cost. While all these are results of Six Sigma training, the real power remains in the DMAIC structure, not the statistics!

The real leverage of DMAIC is the fact that it is a standardized, disciplined approach to problem solving, no matter what type of problem you are facing. The success of DMAIC is in the process of approaching problem solving as much as it is the tools. Again, the tools in and of themselves are not the secret to successful problem solving using Six Sigma. Instead, it is the process of having a structured method to follow, no matter what type of project one is working on or what type of problem is being solved. This is the most important point and warrants repetition.

So how can one approach be applied to different problems? Isn't that like the old adage says: when all you have is a hammer, everything looks like a nail? This is not at all the approach of DMAIC. The difference is that DMAIC is a toolbox that one selects from given the type of problem presented. However, the approach and supporting structure used in solving the problem is always the same, no matter which tools are used.

One can think of this structured process as a roadmap to follow in order to solve problems successfully. Much like using a map, following DMAIC uses a standardized approach to reach a desired result. It has become the uniform standard for solving problems in the world of business.

IMPLEMENTING THE PLAN: BEGINNING THE JOURNEY

Figure 4.1 indicates a macro view of the DMAIC roadmap. The turns on this diagram are phases of the journey toward the destination of problem resolution. Each destination becomes the baseline for continuous improvement or taking the project to the next level. Each of these phases has specific tasks or Six Sigma "tools" that are meant to be used to know when a project is "ready" to move on to the next phase. In other words, the tools are "checkpoints" to be monitored to ensure that the project has not taken a shortcut from definition to resolution.

But what if you already know the solution to your problems? Then the DMAIC roadmap and the checkpoints should take less time to offer a confirmation that the proposed solution is really addressing the root cause of the variation. If you do not have a 100 percent kill rate on the chronic problems your organization has tried to address, you need this structure. Consider the added benefit of being mathematically able to discern critical turning points, successes, and failures — what went right and what went wrong and why. If you knew this information from last year's chronic issues, chances are this year would have been much easier.

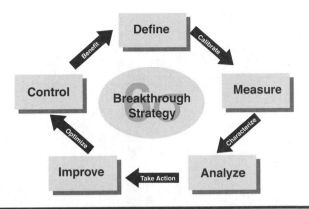

Figure 4.1   The Six Sigma DMAIC roadmap.

If you have a sound mathematical model, it is much easier to create a mathematical solution scientifically. This is true at the top level as well as the project level. For the strategic planning process to be effective, it must be directly linked to the tactical annual plan and accurately measured. The strategic plan must translate into a critical few projects that address chronic issues. For each of these issues, a top-level project status form should be used to outline the linkage between the project(s) that will address the issue and the annual plan attainment. An example of such a project status form is provided in Figure 4.2.

CHECKING THE ROADMAP: STEERING THE PROGRESS BY DRIVING TO THE CHECKPOINTS

The project status form should be maintained by the project leader and reviewed regularly with the champion. If projects are selected appropriately, there will be a direct link between the status form and the attainment of the annual operating plan. The overall roadmap of DMAIC is to take a practical problem, translate this problem into a statistical problem, form and test a hypothesis until a statistically sound solution is discovered, and then translate that statistical solution back into a practical solution for the original problem.

In order to accomplish this, several tools within each phase are employed and a checklist is used to verify the application of the tools for each phase in order to exit that portion of the project and move to the next. The checklist portion of the project status is shown in Figure 4.3 and will be discussed in detail. Again, the bottom line is that this is a method of translating a practical

CEO The Center for Excellence in Operations, Inc.

6σ Project Status

PROJECT INFORMATION	
Project#	
Project Name	
Summary Objective:	
COPQ – Internal:	$
COPQ – External:	$
Annual Cost Savings	**$**

ATTACHMENTS

- **Problem Statement** □
- **Baseline Performance** □
- **Project Objective** □
- **Work Plan** □
- **Deliverable(s)** □
- **Financial Benefits** □

△ **Deliverable** □ **Tool** ▒ **In Process** ■ **Complete**

DEFINE	MEASURE	ANALYZE	IMPROVE	CONTROL
△ Problem Definition	□ CTQs, FDM	□ DFMEA/PFMEA	△ Screen Experiments	□ DOE
△ Objectives	□ KPIVs, KPOVs	△ Sampling Plan	□ Shanin, Multi-Vari	□ EVOP, RSM
△ Scope	△ Updated Objectives	△ Initial Data Collection	□ Hypothesis Tests	△ Implement Changes
△ Boundaries	△ Quantified Problem	□ BasicStats	□ Regression, Correlation	□ Replication Experiments
△ Preliminary Analysis	△ Improvement Goals	□ Box, Dot Plots	□ DOE Design	△ Handoff Plan
△ Initial Benefits	△ Project Team	□ Causal Paretos	□ DOE Experiments	□ Lean, 5S, Poka-Yokes
	△ Project Plan, Gantt	□ Confidence Intervals	□ Mathematical Models	△ Update All Documentation
	△ Baseline Performance	□ T-tests	△ Recommendations	△ Education
	□ Process Map	□ ANOVA	△ Documentation	△ Monitor Improvement
	□ Fishbone Diagram	△ Revised Objectives	△ Education	△ Document Improvement
	□ Cp & Cpk	△ Update Process Map, PFMEA, & Fishbone	△ Implementation Plans	△ Summarize Benefits
	□ Gage R&R, MSA OK	△ Revise Project Plan		△ Define Next Project
		△ Containment Actions		△ Management Presentation
				△ Process Owner Handoff

For additional information, refer to the detailed DMAIC Phase Review Checklist

Figure 4.2 Project status form example. Copyright ©2002 by The Center for Excellence in Operations, Inc. (CEO).

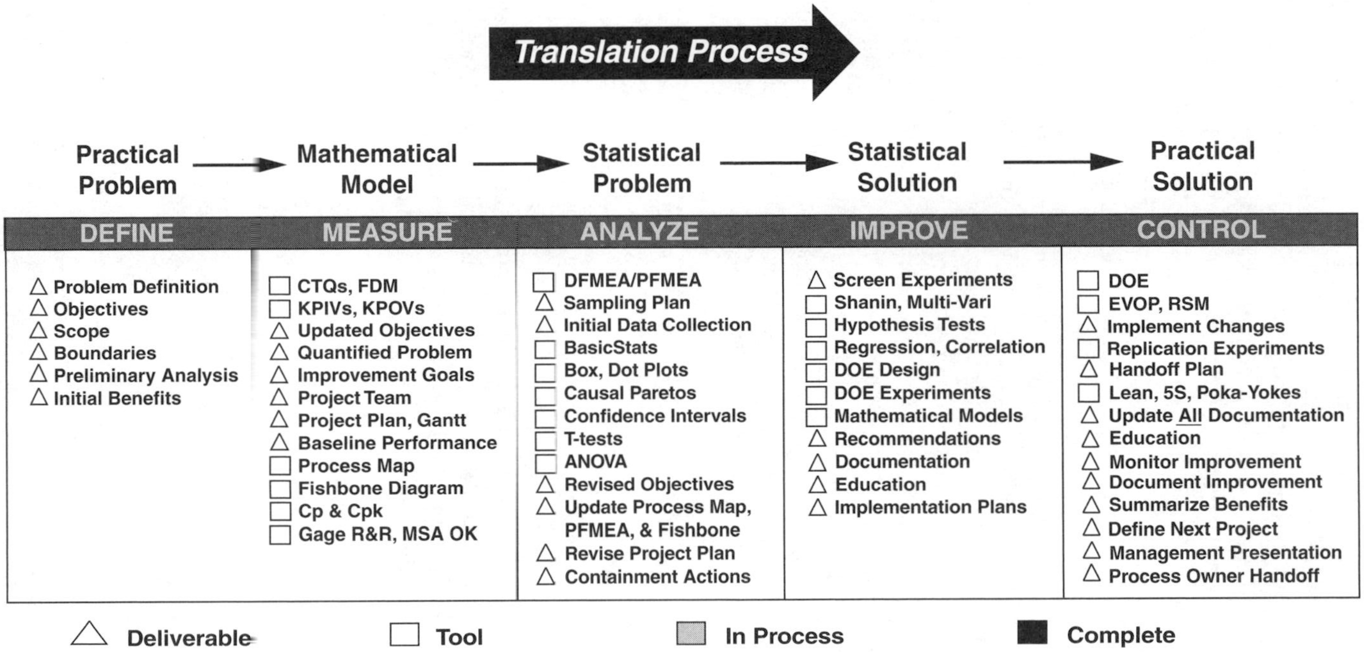

Figure 4.3 Project status checklist. Copyright ©2002 by The Center for Excellence in Operations, Inc. (CEO).

problem into a statistical problem and finding a statistical solution that can be translated back into a practical solution for the original problem.

When one begins to think of this structured approach to problem solving as analogous to a roadmap or atlas, it becomes evident that the true benefit comes from being able to follow a repeatable, proven approach to problem solving. On the surface, this seems quite logical, doesn't it? Why is it, then, that in the world of business, we do not always follow the roadmap? Some companies get confused in trying to use all the tools all the time and abandon the approach in frustration.

It is not very practical to ponder every possible turning point on a map when looking for direction. There are a critical few "checkpoints" that will tell you if you are moving in the desired direction or if correction is required. The DMAIC methodology provides those checkpoints. They are not all used all of the time, but are there for practical application when their use is warranted. Consider the fact that you do not use every page of an atlas every time you want to take a trip. The pages used depend on the destination. Likewise, in problem solving, the tools applied depend on the problem being solved. Additionally, similar to taking a trip, the secret to completing the journey successfully is to first understand where it is you want to go. This is the "Define" phase (see Figure 4.4).

Define Phase

The Define phase is where the project management begins by providing a statement of the problem as observed. The objective must be clearly stated in terms that are known and measurable. Some preliminary Pareto-type analysis should be used to identify scope of the project as well as boundaries. If project selection has been done properly, this should never pose a problem, as this problem should be high profile. During the Define phase, a project charter is completed, which includes a brief description of the project that specifies its business case and the strategic importance. The project charter also names the executive champion who will have overall responsibility for the project.

The project charter serves as a tool for project review as well as a reminder of the criticality of the project by demonstrating the direct linkage to the strategic plan. This is an important phase, as it shows that this project is a "must do" in order to make budget this year and support the longer range strategic performance. The project cannot simply be a "nice to have" or "in support of," as these get killed as soon as a crisis comes up. These projects have to be the "we're betting the company on this" or "if we don't do this, it's impossible to make the strategic plan." For these reasons, the expected results and benefits must be stated up front as part of the project charter.

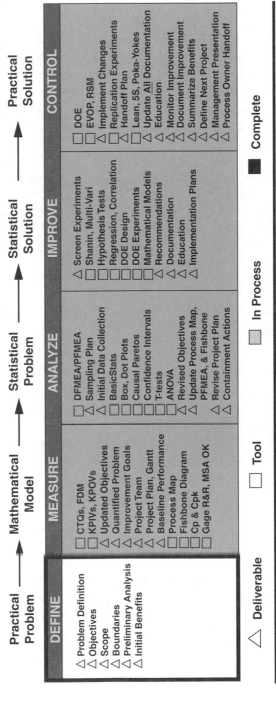

Figure 4.4 Tools used in the Define phase. Copyright ©2002 by The Center for Excellence in Operations, Inc. (CEO).

First, the projects should be selected based on a Pareto principle view of all the requirements to make the annual plan in support of the long-range or strategic plan. If done correctly, the projects are in the 20 percent of things to do that will yield 80 percent of the results. This leverage makes the projects "must do." We will review this more as part of the discussion on project selection in Chapter 6.

Once the projects become "must do" high-profile critical, people want to be associated with them, as most people want to have an impact as well as to be able to see the fruits of their labor. This should make the project team selection easier, with the natural leader identified. Further, making this a "must do" ensures that it will get measured on a weekly, if not daily, basis. Finally, it should be the "must do's" that drive the Management Incentive Bonus Plan. Once the projects become this critical, we have put our mouth where our money is. In other words, the projects become what gets talked about, questioned, and challenged when not on track.

Second, it is just as important to know where you are starting from in order to assess what type of trip this will be. This is the opportunity to gather the baseline information as part of the "Measure" portion of problem solving using DMAIC. This phase is where the project team is formed and the schedule for periodic champion reviews is set.

Measure Phase

The Measure phase is the point of gathering the initial information on the current state of the project in finite terms. Usually, the accepted form of measurement is financial. One should always strive to have a financial metric linked to the projects selected, as this is most likely to ensure that the project(s) are linked to the strategy of the company well enough to be sustained. From the baseline, a projected timeline should be established for the project's accomplishment. This schedule should be reviewed weekly. If the project is not important enough to warrant this level of frequency, one should question the project's importance. See Figure 4.5 for the tools used in the Measure phase.

At this phase, the deliverables (including the project plan) must be completed, with the objectives specified and associated timing identified, along with required resources. Tools used in this phase include the project planning Gantt chart, function deployment matrix, critical-to-quality matrix, process mapping, fishbone diagram, measurement system analysis, and initial statistical measures. This phase also includes additional baseline data such as customer complaints, downtime, Cost of Poor Quality, or other financial metrics.

The Measure phase is a critical component of the DMAIC problem-solving methodology, as a significant portion of Six Sigma projects have their solutions

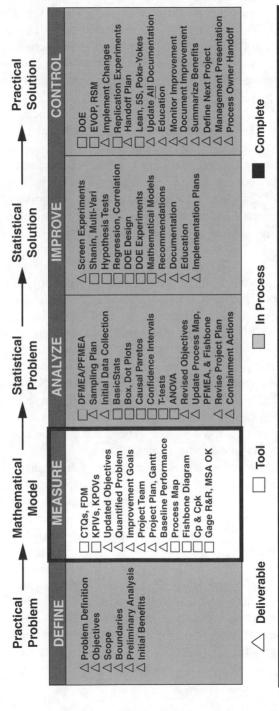

Figure 4.5   Tools used in the Measure phase. Copyright ©2002 by The Center for Excellence in Operations, Inc. (CEO).

linked directly to the measurement system analysis. Further, as the key process input variables (KPIVs) and key process output variables (KPOVs) are identified, all baseline information, as well as projected and actual improvements, will be linked to the accuracy of the measurement system. Lack of attention to detail during this phase can show up as misleading results and costly, incorrect decisions in later phases.

Next, one must assess the most efficient route on the map — the quickest way to close the gap between where we are and where we want to be. There are many possible routes on a journey and taking any of them can lead one to a desired destination, provided enough corrective actions are taken, but there is always a way that seems to be the most logical. This is the "Analyze" portion of the DMAIC. In this phase, we must decide on which tools to use to further understand the problems within the project in order to prioritize our efforts.

Analyze Phase

The Analyze phase is where the project begins to gain some "meat." In other words, this is the point where the tasks required to bring the project to fruition are actually determined. Most often, this phase is where we begin to see just how large the gap is between where the metric is and where we want it to be. This is different from the financial metric as this is where the hidden issues begin to appear. To be sure, there are always hidden trouble spots. This should be intuitive, as the conclusion of this phase would have been implemented if known and completely understood. Once the Analyze phase is initiated, projected improvements can be tested using the more complex tools of Six Sigma such as hypothesis testing and designed experiments. These tests will lead the improvement team into the Improve phase.

Just like the choices of routes on the map, there are many choices when it comes to routes to take or tools to use in order to solve the problem of getting to our desired outcome. All of these tools are not used all the time, but rather only as deemed appropriate for the need. Outside of a training demonstration, using tools for the sake of using them can only lead to mistakes. Training is the only environment where going through the motions of tool use is appropriate. This hands-on training is the means by which the applicability of the tools is derived and misapplication errors are learned. The Analyze phase tools are used to specify the failure modes associated with the process map, in addition to determining a plan for data collection points and data analysis. Again, the tools employed depend on the type of data one has. The most common tools are found in Figure 4.6.

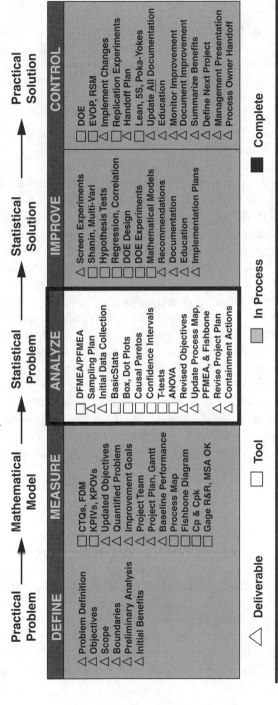

Figure 4.6 Tools used in the Analyze phase. Copyright ©2002 by The Center for Excellence in Operations, Inc. (CEO).

Improve Phase

The Improve phase of DMAIC is where the "rubber meets the road." In other words, after the fancy statistical tests have been completed and the hypothesis proven, the improvement phase is where the test really begins. This is where the power of trusting the data happens. Figure 4.7 shows the tools used during the Improve phase. Even with advances in software to make these tools user friendly, the tools in the improvement phase require a solid foundation in the understanding of their appropriate use and applicability in order to avoid incorrect interpretation and poor decisions.

The key to success in this phase is planning. Since we now trust in the measurement system fixed from the Measure phase, we assess the drivers of the process by monitoring them in an uninterrupted fashion. Once we determine what the drivers (KPIVs that are critical to the KPOVs) are, we can manipulate them in order to optimize the process by using Design of Experiments (DOE). Designed experiments are disruptive and can be costly. The cost of a good DOE is quickly gained back by the improvements that come from the learning associated with it. This only happens if the experiment is properly planned and monitored accurately with a rigid data collection plan. Anything less can lead to confusion in the data collection, mistakes in the process, increased downtime, and a general disenchantment of all associated with it. Planning is critical to avoid wasting time during the DOE. If the data drive the process to operate in new territory, they may require special attention from the team to ensure the parameters are given an opportunity to succeed. This is one of the most difficult phases, as there are usually well-intentioned people who are still accustomed to the previous method. In this case, the team has to be cautious, as any anomalous response will most likely be assigned to the new operating condition, with a rush to return to the comfort zone of the familiar territory. This is why it is critical to have a Control phase.

Control Phase

The Control phase must be implemented immediately following the Improve phase in order to sustain the gains from the improvement phase. The Control phase may also be part of the customer requirement or documented quality management system such as ISO or QS9000. The controls put in place may be mechanical, electrical, or documentation oriented. The bottom line is that the Control phase must be used to implement some form of poka-yoke, or error-proofing mechanism, to prevent the recurrence of the previous condition. We will discuss this more in the section on project management in Chapter 7. Figure 4.8 defines some of the tools most commonly associated with this phase.

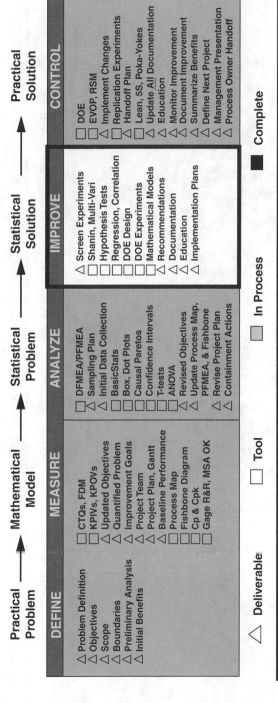

Figure 4.7 Tools used in the Improve phase. Copyright ©2002 by The Center for Excellence in Operations, Inc. (CEO).

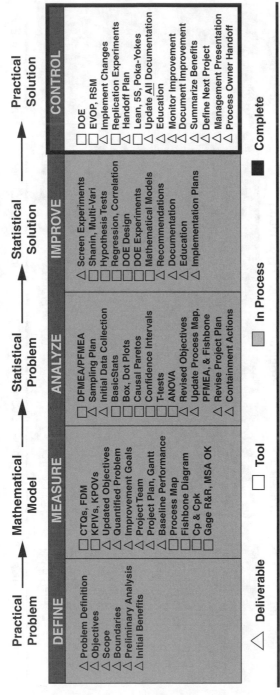

Practical ⟶ Mathematical ⟶ Statistical ⟶ Statistical ⟶ Practical
Problem   Model   Problem   Solution   Solution

DEFINE

△ Problem Definition
△ Objectives
△ Scope
△ Boundaries
△ Preliminary Analysis
△ Initial Benefits

MEASURE

☐ CTQs, FDM
☐ KPIVs, KPOVs
△ Updated Objectives
△ Quantified Problem
△ Improvement Goals
△ Project Team
△ Project Plan, Gantt
△ Baseline Performance
☐ Process Map
☐ Fishbone Diagram
☐ Cp & Cpk
☐ Gage R&R, MSA OK

ANALYZE

☐ DFMEA/PFMEA
△ Sampling Plan
△ Initial Data Collection
☐ BasicStats
☐ Box, Dot Plots
☐ Causal Paretos
☐ Confidence Intervals
☐ T-tests
☐ ANOVA
△ Revised Objectives
△ Update Process Map, PFMEA, & Fishbone
△ Revise Project Plan
△ Containment Actions

IMPROVE

△ Screen Experiments
☐ Shanin, Multi-Vari
☐ Hypothesis Tests
☐ Regression, Correlation
☐ DOE Design
☐ DOE Experiments
☐ Mathematical Models
△ Recommendations
☐ Documentation
△ Education
△ Implementation Plans

CONTROL

☐ DOE
☐ EVOP, RSM
△ Implement Changes
☐ Replication Experiments
☐ Handoff Plan
☐ Lean, 5S, Poka-Yokes
△ Update All Documentation
△ Education
△ Monitor Improvement
△ Document Improvement
△ Summarize Benefits
△ Define Next Project
△ Management Presentation
△ Process Owner Handoff

△ **Deliverable**   ☐ **Tool**   ▨ **In Process**   ▪ **Complete**

Figure 4.8 Tools used in the Control phase. Copyright ©2002 by The Center for Excellence in Operations, Inc. (CEO).

SIX SIGMA IS A JOURNEY, NOT A DESTINATION

In practice, DMAIC is not a true linear process. Black belt and green belt candidates go through an official phase review and sign-off for each phase. However, individuals often find themselves looping back to a previous phase to clarify forward direction or to conduct an additional analysis based on new information. The journey to Six Sigma is more important than the destination itself. The reason for this is the fact that this journey, if taken properly, redefines the culture of the organization. It fundamentally changes the way people work, communicate, and interact with each other as well as customers and suppliers. In other words, it is a complete transformation of the DNA that defines the organization.

This transformation is like giving new life to your organization. The idea of change is usually born from the need. Learning to follow a disciplined approach is like learning to walk; you make lots of mistakes. It is only the relentless persistence that comes from a deeply held belief that walking is better than crawling and that running can be fun that keeps the organization moving forward. Haphazardly trying to track and address fifty problems is a very different world to work in than trying to track and address five critical issues. Even more projects can be worked as long as people can clearly see the link to the critical few. Indeed, when the organization's culture changes to the point that people will not accept mediocrity, running can become racing. This ability is not only a competitive advantage in the marketplace, but a way to keep the culture healthy and vibrant.

Working in an environment where people are sincerely enjoying the process of problem solving is very different than trying to play catch-up. In other words, "working out" only becomes enjoyable after one is addicted to it by seeing the results. Staying in shape is more fun than getting in shape. It would be very difficult to get a bodybuilder to stop working out, and it would be nearly impossible to remove the Six Sigma culture from an organization that has seen its results.

GE is a company that has seen the benefits of Six Sigma. It would be nearly impossible to remove the Six Sigma culture at GE. The lesson here is that if a company as large and old as GE can become as lean and competitive as it is today, then whatever culture, bureaucracy, or other barriers you might face in your organization can certainly be overcome. However, this did not happen overnight at GE. Most overnight successes take time. The good news is that significant improvement can occur quickly if the proper approach is taken.

The same philosophy can be found at Toyota. Consider Toyota and the world-famous Toyota Production System. Toyota has been on this *journey* for sixty years with a destination that is more an ideal than an end — PERFECTION. Its philosophy is not "Is this cost competitive?" or "Can we afford to do this?" but rather one of "If we are not striving for perfection, what are we striving for?" This is an indication that the cultural journey has truly become part of Toyota's DNA. The same culture has to become part of any organization that is serious about pursuing Six Sigma.

Is the destination of Six Sigma the goal? Is it acceptable to think 3.4 airbags in every million cars Toyota sells will not deploy? Is it acceptable to think that 3.4 out of every million operating seconds a GE aircraft engine will not work? Again, the result of Six Sigma must be a culture that strives for perfection by using a disciplined methodology in every aspect of the organization. Anything less is to shortcut the true value of Six Sigma as an operating philosophy.

How do you know when the cultural transformation is beginning to take place? This is something that is easier to determine than most people realize. The same assessment that you would expect at world-class global giants can be made with thoughtful questions posed to any organization. Think of your systems and compare them to your expectation of a world-class global competitor. Some examples of these simple, real-time acid tests are given below.

Points to ponder:
- Are design reviews a formality in your organization?
- Do people really understand the design intent?
- Do people understand the tools that determine design capability?
- Have you measured the process capability to the design requirements?
- How easily could a design review be canceled or postponed at GE?
- How easily would a launch delay be tolerated at Toyota?
- How easily can preventive maintenance yield to production requirements?
- Does your organization understand the mean time to failure in your products and processes?
- Can you show the cost component of the supply base versus the price of the individual components? Do you confuse the two?
- Can you remove the components of our previous improvements?
- How easily can your organization make process changes?
- How well are these documented?
- Do the off shifts have the same capability as first shift?
- Do you know the capability of your forecasting?
- Do your people know what is critical to quality in your products, processes, and services?
- Do they understand the cost consequences of their function? Really?
- Do they measure it? Expectation × Measurement = Results.

These simple points to ponder will provide a real-time measure of the pulse of your organization. It is important to test this several times each day. Using this type of philosophy in your organization is the only way to ensure Six Sigma becomes the way your organization works, not something you are doing in addition to work.

When Six Sigma becomes the way your organization works, you have truly begun the journey. Enjoy using this as a competitive advantage, and test the organization each day to make sure your people are enjoying the journey as well. The right people with the right tools will always take you in the right direction faster than you may have previously thought possible. Figure 4.9 provides a final checklist for the DMAIC methodology.

CHAPTER 4 TAKE-AWAYS

■ The uniqueness of Six Sigma is the DMAIC roadmap of standardization. It is the structure and disciplined approach that makes Six Sigma unique. This approach works to yield knowledge from the unknown every time as long as it is followed accurately.

■ Six Sigma formality is used to address the most critical business issues being faced by an organization. This ensures that it is a respected method and keeps other "more urgent" issues from killing the momentum. If Six Sigma is used to solve critical issues, then problems that do not require Six Sigma are by definition noncritical and should be viewed that way with appropriate resources applied.

■ Determine the right problem to address and the right process will define the right tools to apply. In other words, with an aggressive strategic plan and a gap analysis to assess what barriers stand between where the organization is and where it needs to be, the projects should become obvious. Which process(es), including administrative processes, are holding back the organization and should be elevated in visibility to mission critical and require a formal Six Sigma approach to improvement?

■ The true goal is the journey, not the destination. Once the formal Six Sigma approach is used and the benefits recognized, the logic is to repeat it. As with any other skill, the more it is repeated, the more it becomes second nature. Practice does not make perfect — only perfect practice does. Follow the formality until the organization "thinks" in the language of the formal approach.

■ Test the performance autonomously, like the instrument panel in a car, using points to ponder such as those listed above. It is only with relentless

Phase	Objective	Reality Checks
Define	Demonstrate the project's importance and gain commitment of those who will contribute to its success	■ Is there a link to the strategic plan? ■ Is the project properly scoped to a manageable level? ■ Does the person with responsibility also have appropriate authority? ■ Is the importance of this project publicized? ■ Is the project a daily priority? ■ Can everyone on the management team explain the project's importance?
Measure	Ensure the project is appropriately commissioned with the proper support to be successful	■ Have the baseline data and goals, including timing, been signed off by the champion? ■ Has the appropriate team been selected? ■ Can everyone on the team explain the project's importance? ■ Has a formal evaluation been completed on the measurement system for the KPIVs and KPOVs? ■ Have the sources of measurement variation been addressed?
Analyze	Demonstrate a statistical understanding of the practical problem at hand	■ Have statistical studies been verified to understand the sources of variation in the KPIVs and KPOVs? ■ Is there statistical verification that the project is addressing the highest leverage components of variation?
Improve	Make data-driven irreversible decisions to improve the process	■ Is there a mathematic model to demonstrate statistical understanding of the outcome of proposed improvements? ■ Do the process owners demonstrate a commitment to the new methods? ■ Is there data comparing before and after with the improvements clearly defined?
Control	Sustain the gains	■ Could you convince the process owners to go back to the old method? ■ Has the documentation been updated with the new methods? ■ Have measurements been put in place to monitor the improvements on an ongoing basis to prevent returning to the previous method?

Figure 4.9 Final DMAIC checklist. Copyright ©2002 by The Center for Excellence in Operations, Inc. (CEO).

persistence that the true benefits of Six Sigma will be realized. Anything less will delay the benefits at best. The benefits of Six Sigma are too valuable to put anything less than your best efforts and resources, including your best human resources, on it up front. The benefits will only remain if challenged to do so.

SUGGESTED FURTHER READING

Breyfogle, Forrest, III, *Implementing Six Sigma,* 2nd ed., John Wiley & Sons, 2003.
Eckes, George, *The Six Sigma Revolution,* John Wiley & Sons, 2001.
Kaplan, Robert and Norton, David, *The Balanced Scorecard: Translating Strategy into Action*, Harvard Business School Press, 1996.
Pyzdek, Thomas, *The Six Sigma Handbook,* McGraw-Hill, 2003.
Snee, Ronald and Hoerl, Roger, *Leading Six Sigma*, FT-Prentice-Hall, 2003.

5

TRANSACTIONAL SIX SIGMA AND BEYOND

For many organizations, actual manufacturing represents 15 to 20 percent of their total cost structure. The remaining 80 percent is due to transactional process activity such as sales and marketing, finance, engineering and R&D, customer service, procurement, and distribution. Manufacturing is no longer a competitive weapon; it is just a link in the chain. Optimizing the total value stream is the most critical factor in improving competitiveness, and most of this is comprised of transactional activities. In this total value stream context, most organizations have been focusing their Six Sigma efforts in the middle of the process (production) and on the wrong opportunities. For those who really understand root cause analysis and wish to be honest, ask yourself, "Where do most of the root causes of shop floor problems occur?" The answer to this question is why we now need to focus more attention on things like Design for Six Sigma (DFSS), transactional Six Sigma, and value stream Six Sigma.

WHY IS TRANSACTIONAL SIX SIGMA SO IMPORTANT?

Think about developing a profit-and-loss (P&L) statement and a value stream map for your own enterprise. Guess what you learn? Based on our benchmarking and client experiences, you would find that as much as 70 to 95 percent of product cost is generated outside of your organization. You would find that as much as 75 to 95 percent of lead time is consumed outside of your organization. You would learn that 95+ percent of the key activities of design, supply chain planning, and manufacturing (and the associated employees) are outside of your organization. You would learn that there is a whole stream of conflicting performance measurements in place, creating conflicts between various elements of the total value stream. And hopefully, you will wonder why your organization is not in hot pursuit of this gold mine of collective opportunity.

There is another critical reason to pursue transactional Six Sigma. It has been about ten years since Michael Hammer introduced the business world to Business Process Reengineering. Since that time, organizations have spent billions of dollars in IT investment. During these IT implementations, many organizations focused on implementing hardware and software, with the intention of reengineering business processes at a later date. But many never returned to finish what they said they would do: the tough process reengineering and infrastructure changes required to achieve a return on these IT investments. Many of these key business processes are a mix of patchwork practices and procedures that have evolved over time, and they represent a tremendous *sitting duck* opportunity for most organizations. Areas such as warranty/returns, inventory management, new product development, customer service, advertising effectiveness, product rationalization, absenteeism, and billing errors are just a few of these *soft process* opportunities. Six Sigma is an enabler to translate what are currently enormous sunk costs into significant IT returns on investment.

THE FUTURE OF SIX SIGMA IS HERE

Transactional Six Sigma has grown rapidly during the past few years. This myriad of improvement opportunities is surfacing because executives recognize that transactional processes represent the major component of their businesses from both a cost and activity/resource consumption perspective. As we stated earlier in the book, transactional projects represent 50 percent or more of the scope of our clients' Six Sigma efforts and probably 70 to 90 percent of the potential benefits, particularly for transaction-intensive business environments. To better understand this, Figure 5.1 provides the future of Six Sigma as we see it unfolding. Initially, Six Sigma deployments typically begin with **Stage I: Manufacturing Six Sigma**, where it is easier to observe the process and measure inputs and outputs. In this stage, the deployment is focused around machines and equipment on the shop floor. For the most part, the objectives

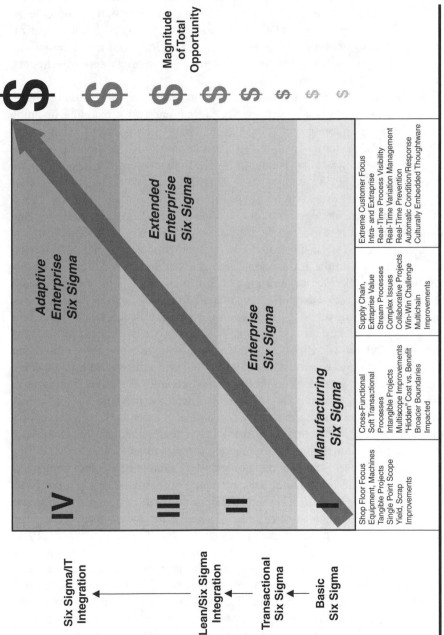

Figure 5.1 The future of Six Sigma.

of these initial Six Sigma efforts are usually centered around scrap reduction, rolled throughput yield improvements, reducing process variation and defects, and centering processes around desired performance targets. Some organizations also conduct analytics around the next tier of localized machine activity such as setups, preventive maintenance, equipment settings and adjustments, tool life, and unplanned downtime.

Sometimes at this stage, the organization has embarked on several improvement initiatives such as kaizen, lean, Six Sigma, enterprise resource planning (ERP), and other enabling technology applications such as supply chain management (SCM), customer relationship management (CRM), supplier relationship management (SRM), product life cycle management (PLM), and other web-enabled IT improvements. At this stage, there are often islands or camps of improvement where each group hypes its initiative as the cure-all and end-all. Rather than working together, these individuals often find themselves working against each other and the organization fails to benefit from every effort.

The next level of sophistication is where organizations recognize the tremendous opportunities in the transactional and support areas, or **Stage II: Enterprise Six Sigma**. Service organizations begin their Six Sigma journey in this stage because they may have little to no manufacturing content in their business. The characteristics of this stage include a high scope of transactional Six Sigma projects focused on key cross-functional business processes. These projects are either totally broken (i.e., it takes five weeks to resolve a customer complaint) or not viewed as being *broken* at all. Individuals do not associate the specific activities of these processes as both defect-free and defective transactional activities. For example, one view may be to reconcile the perpetual inventory to the general ledger and leave it at that, as long as we can make the two match. Another view (the Six Sigma view) is to better understand the root causes of *bad* transactions that may ultimately generate surprise inventory variances during the month-end close. Think about how most organizations solve things like warranty, sales sample accounts, and inventory problems: They *reserve funds to cover the defects in the process* rather than understand variation and eliminate root causes of these defective activities. We make this point because we want you to understand that many of these costs are *hidden*. They are not on the P&L, they are not being measured as a line item on some department's budget, but they are draining cost and resources from doing more productive activities. These projects typically include a broader range of improvement actions ranging from instant containment (kaizen-like events) to process and organizational changes, training, modification of performance measurement systems, process velocity and quality improvements, and IT involvement in system modifications. There are a wide range of potential project opportunities in the enterprise space, including new product development, financial cash-to-cash optimization, sales and marketing, advertising and promotion, customer service/order fulfillment, service/spares management, and procurement. As we mentioned earlier, this may represent 70 to 80 percent of the total Six Sigma opportunity for many organizations. At the Enterprise Six Sigma stage, the organization recognizes that no single-point improvement program or bag of tools by itself is the answer and it is beginning to recognize that integration of kaizen, lean, Six Sigma, ERP, and enabling IT is the key to success, and the first most popular step is lean/ Six Sigma.

The next level of sophistication is where the organization has extended its efforts beyond the four walls of the enterprise. We refer to this as **Stage III: Extended Enterprise Six Sigma**. The characteristics of this stage include a high degree of collaborative problem solving across the total supply chain. The focus is on value stream process improvements that benefit both customers and suppliers (hence increasing the competitiveness of the value chain). These issues are typically complex and require the search for win-win solutions. These projects also require a higher level of IT integration to link customers, suppliers, and other trading partners together in real time. At this stage, IT becomes a more critical enabler of future success. Organizations must now integrate their initial Six Sigma and lean/Six Sigma efforts with ERP and other enabling technology applications such as SCM, CRM, SRM, PLM, and other web-enabled IT improvements. Projects across the extended enterprise require accurate, real-time information, and these IT applications become much more prevalent enablers at this stage.

The final stage of sophistication is **Stage IV: Adaptive Enterprise Six Sigma**. At this stage, the entire value stream has an extreme customer focus. The scope of activities includes internal and external activities of the total value stream. IT adds order to the chaos of activity and enables multiple organizations in the supply chain to collaborate in a matter-of-fact manner about issues. There is instant visibility of issues and process variation is managed in real time. Individuals across the value stream identify, take action, and prevent disruptive activities from happening in the first place. Improvement initiatives are fully integrated and have evolved from a program to a behavioral norm. People live and breathe improvement every minute of every day, rather than viewing it as something to do after something else goes wrong.

Organizations do not move discretely from one stage to the next. Some projects may be local and some may include transactional processes between customers and suppliers, while others may include IT projects. However, Figure 5.1 provides a valid conceptual map that supports the need for more transactional focus with Six Sigma.

THE LARGEST OPPORTUNITIES ARE HIDDEN

A common thread that we see is the *hidden factory* of costs and opportunities when deep diving into these transactional processes. Many of these practices have become institutionalized and accepted, as depicted by comments such as "That is the best we can do" or "These things are going to happen" or "It is just the cost of being in our business." As long as these processes and practices remain in *hidden factory* mode, they cannot be improved and the hidden costs of doing business grow. Not to be cynical, but as outsiders, it is often much easier to see the dilemma of *not having time to change and do my regular job.* It is funny how these individuals and organizations find the time to do things over and over.

One example of this hidden cost dilemma involved an organization that creates mail-order catalogs and web pages as part of its selling strategy. A Six Sigma project was launched to take a fresh look at catalog design and production. Catalog campaigns began as a creative process where management communicated the concept of a catalog and its contents to the advertising organization. The Six Sigma team found that each page of a catalog went through a complex spaghetti flow process and that much of the cycle time was consumed by a page waiting for someone to work on it. The team found that the majority of the work was performed on pages at the tail end of the schedule. The team also found that there were three to four reworks per page, and as pages reached near completion or prepress, the creative process (management) would kick in, make changes, and return a page to the beginning of the process. This process required the hiring of temps to deal with the last-minute spikes in production to meet the printer's schedule. Many organizations have processes like this one, especially if part of their business involves the creation of sales catalogs, documentation, installation instructions, and the like. It is easy to say "So what, it's part of the process." In the above example, the Six Sigma team redesigned the process into a more disciplined and continuous flow. The team also demonstrated with data and facts that the rework component of this process was costing the organization $1 million per year. Further analysis revealed that the organization could either produce X more catalogs and catalog pages per year or do it with 20 percent less resources if it did the right things right the first time. Quantifying the problem grabbed everyone's attention because it was a hidden cost of doing business. Long story short, the process was totally redesigned and this organization saved $500,000 from this one project. But the lesson of this example is that many costs are hidden until you mine for them and present the story with data and facts so that everyone in the organization understands the problem and the need to change. The rework costs of this example were not apparent on the P&L, but they are a real cost of doing business. This is a trend that you will see over and over as you dig into transactional processes.

Another favorite area of opportunity is IT spending. Many organizations add more and more resources to their IT organization only to find that projects grow in scope and require more time to complete. Do you think these professionals come to work every day and make this happen on purpose? Of course not! However, as service organizations, IT groups are hit with a mountain of conflicting IT requests and try to make sense out of all of these user "must haves." Our favorite example is the typical IT help desk. Did you ever wonder how many help desk calls can be solved by a PC restart? Seriously, the analysis of these processes reveals that a good chunk of the requests could be handled locally, but organizations may spend $10 to $20 per call and $50 to $100 per service visit on trivial activities that drain limited IT resources from the more critical activities. Nobody pays much attention until a Six Sigma team quantifies the problem with data and facts and presents its findings: thousands of dollars have been spent on trivia and users have 50 percent of the IT group working on legacy applications that are going away. Another recurring event is the benefits achieved when user requests are evaluated relative to achieving the strategic plan. IT groups can benefit significantly by realigning customer requests and managing to finite capacity.

DESIGN FOR SIX SIGMA

New product development is one of the largest transactional Six Sigma opportunities. This makes sense because we are attacking variation upstream where the process truly begins, not in the middle of the process or further downstream. If a product or process design includes a high level of performance unpredictability and inherent variation in the first place, organizations can only get so far with Six Sigma on the production floor. Six Sigma is a methodology that helps organizations understand and remove variation in a process; in essence, to fix a broken process whether that process is a machine or a quotation process. By contrast, DFSS helps organizations develop products and processes that are flawless; they do not break in the first place, at least as the theory goes. The objective is to achieve breakthroughs in how we identify and select the right new product opportunities, develop superior products faster/better/cheaper, achieve flawless commercialization and release, and capture market opportunities by being the first to market. Figure 5.2 displays the degree of influence that the development process has on total cost. For many companies, they have

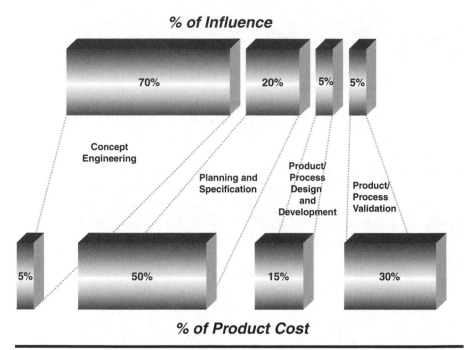

% of Influence

70%	20%	5%	5%

Concept Engineering

Planning and Specification

Product/Process Design and Development

Product/Process Validation

5%	50%	15%	30%

% of Product Cost

Figure 5.2   Design for Six Sigma impact.

committed 80 percent or more to the product's ultimate cost when they write the functional specification. The further you progress in the development process, the less of an impact you have on cost or performance. In a nutshell, this diagram says that you have a higher degree of influence up front in the product development process. While Six Sigma may achieve benefits after launch, the real opportunity is upstream through prevention, robustness, and perfection in product/process design.

Organizations can never achieve Six Sigma if they bypass the development process. Changing the design after a product is introduced is a very costly value proposition. Worse yet, it is too late or cost prohibitive to make many of the changes you would like to make. DFSS is all about eliminating defects and variation before product launch, which results in a tremendous cost savings in the total value stream, a significant reduction in time to market, and superior products in the marketplace. DFSS also employs the voice of the customer and many other statistical tools that result in higher market share and increased profitability. DFSS is all about a flawless design and development process and a flawless rollout.

TRANSACTIONAL SIX SIGMA TARGET OPPORTUNITIES

Sometimes we hear comments like "Six Sigma doesn't apply to finance" or "Six Sigma will kill the creativity in our process." Believe us, there is nothing creative about doing things over and over. Six Sigma is applicable to any process that has problems due to complex, unexplainable variation. While many projects begin with hard processes (i.e., machines and equipment), soft knowledge processes inside and outside the four walls are ripe target areas for Six Sigma projects. The methodology is very appropriate for these end-to-end business processes because it is often the first time someone has looked at these processes with a logical, scientific approach. These processes contain a high level of complex, unexplainable variation. Opportunities such as new product development, inventory pipeline management, logistics and distribution, shipping/billing errors, forecasting and demand management, quick response delivery, packaging, etc. are typically significant pain points and significant wins. Often, the simpler, basic blocking and tackling Six Sigma techniques such as Pareto and graphical analysis, value stream mapping, failure mode and effects analyses, confidence intervals, and basic statistical distributions can reveal a lot about these processes. The more complex tools such as hypothesis tests, ANOVA, Multi-Vari analysis, and Design of Experiments help to understand the critical factors of these processes and to test whether or not the improvements are, in fact, real improvements versus chance. Veteran Six Sigma organizations find that 50 percent or more of their Six Sigma projects are within the transactional process areas. One of our black belt friends summed up his experience: "A Six Sigma project on a welder saves you two to three points of yield; a Six Sigma project in warranty/returns or new product development saves you millions." Below are some suggested areas of opportunity based on our experiences with transactional Six Sigma deployments:

- **New product strategy and creation**: Transition a company from a "me-too" supplier to a market leader; deploy Six Sigma methodologies for market/technology scanning, voice of the customer and requirements definition, business feasibility, pro forma P&L analysis, etc.
- **Sales planning and analysis**: Sales-activity-based value analysis, cross-selling, customer retention attributes, customer and market segmentation, marketing optimization, and customer satisfaction and loyalty analysis.
- **Customer service**: Reduce shipping, credit, invoicing, warranty/returns, invoicing and receivables errors; reduce customer complaint resolution cycle time; and reduce cash-to-cash cycle time.

- **Call center operations**: Reduce customer errors such as wrong product shipped, incorrect configurations, discounts and allowances, billing errors, wrong product ordered for application, wrong color/wrong size, installation errors, and sales service costs.
- **Engineering change**: Reengineer the ECN process into a streamlined, integrated business process (e.g., considering variation reduction, cutover time, obsolescence, commonality, etc.).
- **Forecasting/demand management**: Eliminate mismatches in supply and demand, excessive inventory, poor customer service, premium freight costs, and other supply chain inefficiencies.
- **Inventory rationalization**: Eliminate root causes of poor inventory performance, simplify business processes between multiple ERP platforms, and implement both quick-strike and strategic actions (the "inventory dashboard") to improve asset utilization.
- **Accounting**: Reduce accounts receivable days outstanding, simplify general ledger activity and monthly close process, reduce billing and reconciliation errors, and simplify the process of foreign currency conversion and exchange.
- **Supply chain management**: Improve product management/rationalization, inventory versus service levels, quick response stocking strategies, value stream synchronization, product consolidation and pruning, and large dollar services procurement.
- **New product development**: Reduce time to market, formalize stage/gate process design, design and phase review processes, integrated product/process design, test strategy and reliability engineering, and other DFSS tools.
- **Software development**: Design for value and ease of integration, design for scaleability and ease of configuration, design for high usability (quick, simple, easy to learn, look and feel, assimilates environment, etc.), and analysis of postimplementation debugging activity.

TRANSACTIONAL SIX SIGMA EXAMPLES

Case Study 1: Process Capability Improves Inventory Performance

To improve any process, one must recognize and appreciate the concept of process variation. Some of this variation is natural. It results from the normal expected variations in people, equipment, setups, suppliers, and other types of process variation. However, most variation is unnatural: It can be eliminated by detecting and studying the significant cause and effect relationships. One useful

Six Sigma tool that companies use to support this effort is called *process capability index*, or Cpk.

What Is Cpk?

Cpk is a measure of process capability, which statistically describes how centered or dispersed the variation is in a process. The Cpk goal is expressed as an index of at least 1.33, which equates to a defect rate of 63 parts per million (PPM). However, the actual Cpk will most likely be much lower for organizations that have not used this black belt tool in the past. The Six Sigma equivalent of Cpk is 1.5 long term or 2.0 short term, which means almost zero process shift, which equates to a defect rate of 3.4 PPM. For production runs of 20,000 units or less, normal process defects will make meeting a Cpk of 1.33 challenging. For larger production runs of 300,000 or more, the same level of random defects may make Six Sigma performance more achievable. Whatever your production run or Cpk goal, chances are that your organization will be busy trying to improve processes that are substantially below your Cpk goal.

Organizations should not get hung up on the goal, but just get going on improving process capability. This means making processes very predictable and "centered" around a desired performance goal. Many organizations and their suppliers are not even close to 100 PPM, never mind a Cpk of 1.33 or Six Sigma performance. On the other hand, great organizations are beginning to talk about PPB or parts per billion. The objective of Cpk analysis is to predict and eliminate as many sources of product/process variation as possible via preventive measures, not after something goes wrong.

One of the early pioneers of statistical engineering was Walter Shewhart, whose initial research focused more on product quality, not process quality. He demonstrated that three sigma from the mean is the point where a process requires correction. In the early part of the twentieth century, he viewed quality from the goalpost perspective, where anything inside the specification was acceptable. In the world of Six Sigma, this is no longer true because we are more concerned with variation from a target value. So Shewhart's comment about *"three sigma from the mean is the point where a process requires correction"* is no longer true. Why? As we mentioned in Chapter 1, a one- or two-sigma shift could make a big difference in our stack-up tolerance situation. With Six Sigma, we attempt to understand, quantify, and reduce as much process variation as possible because any deviation from the desired target value has an exponential effect on Cost of Poor Quality.

Figure 5.3 provides an example of using Six Sigma to improve inventory performance. Working through the DMAIC process (Define, Measure, Analyze, Improve, Control), the entire inventory pipeline was mapped and quan-

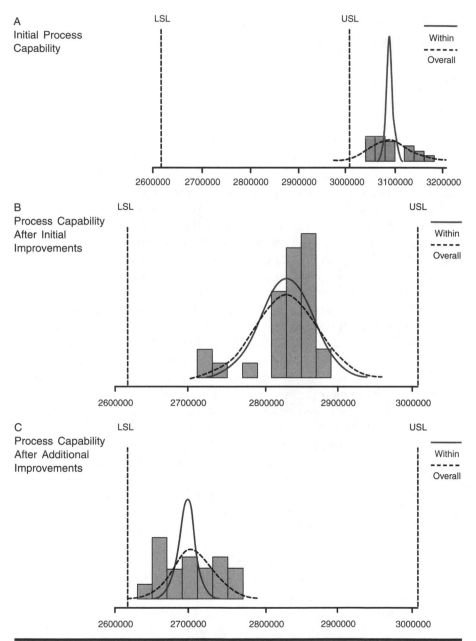

Figure 5.3   Using process capability to improve inventory performance. (A) In the beginning of the project, there is significant variation in the process and a low Cpk; (B) during the project, many improvements are implemented, variation is reduced, and the Cpk improves, validating that our actions are correct; (C) the Cpk improves further as additional improvements are implemented.

tified using current and historical data. One of the objectives was to understand the root causes of inventory performance so preventive measures could be installed to keep inventory within a desired performance bandwidth (turns, days of supply). The Six Sigma team also wanted to quantify the capability of the inventory management process to perform within this bandwidth. The team defined the major and minor inventory drivers with live data and Pareto analysis and could correlate inventory performance to a number of factors including scheduling practices and changes, shortages, supplier defects, late or early deliveries, ECNs, etc. They began implementing improvements to the process and validated that their actions were improving the capability of the inventory management process.

Case Study 2: Gage R&R Provides Error Visibility

Another useful Six Sigma tool is called Gage R&R. This tool helps to distinguish between the variation within the process itself and the variation caused by the measurement system. In any process, the variation is explained by the following formula:

$$Vt = Vp + Vm + Vo$$

The total variation is equal to the part-to-part variation in the process itself (Vp) plus the measurement system variation (Vm) plus the normal noise (Vo for *the other stuff*). Measurement system variation can be broken down further into reproducibility and repeatability. Reproducibility is the variation due to different operators, and repeatability is the variation due to the measurement criterion itself. Why is this an important issue? Because in many cases, we provide measurement systems to people that are bad because they require a lot of discretionary interpretation and guessing. Redesigning the measurement system itself provides additional granularity to identify and solve problems, and sometimes companies such as Allied Signal and New England Business Systems (NEBS) have achieved enormous success by eliminating measurement system variation.

A large telesales organization processed over one million transactions per day. The quality organization developed about fifty different defect codes that representatives were instructed to use when processing orders and customer complaints. There were two problems with the defect codes. First, they did not measure process defects at a level of granularity that allowed the organization to take corrective action. The codes only provided information about what type of problem occurred, but did not provide any other detailed information about the event. Second, several customer complaints resulted in multiple defect codes, but an event could be assigned to just one code. Consequently, many defects were coded based on the reps' best guess about where to slot the complaint. This practice resulted in overstated codes and understated codes and left even more complaints assigned to a miscellaneous category. Some individuals surmised that some code assignments would move the problem and not negatively impact the reps' incentive earnings, which were heavily weighted toward sales volume and light on quality. A Gage R&R analysis validated that the defect code design introduced a significant measurement error in the process.

The defect code list was reengineered to provide very detailed information about the defect and other critical event activity (i.e., product, rep, first-time versus existing customer, etc.). The defects were then segmented and real-time problem resolution measures were implemented on the most likely defect areas. A new Gage R&R validated that the measurement system error was removed and that the organization could now focus on the vital few customer complaint areas. Returns and allowances were reduced by over 50 percent. What is the lesson here? The process was not the source of variation; it was a poor measurement system. Without getting into the statistical details, the measurement system was not allowing the organization to target in on the right actionable information. It was, in effect, hiding the real problems. This is why Gage R&R is important. The measurement system was not capable of doing what it was intended to do. The variation was due to the measurement system, not the process itself. Once the measurement system was reengineered, the organization could harvest the sweet fruit in its telesales process.

Case Study 3: Six Sigma Improves Warranty and Returns

Another Six Sigma team was assigned the task of reducing warranty and returns. The team went through the DMAIC process and conducted multilevel Pareto analysis on the data. Their objective was to isolate the root cause, so they analyzed warranty/return issue by product, by customer, by dollar volume, by quantity, by time period, and many other dimensions. They used many of the other Six Sigma tools like Multi-Vari analysis to categorize root causes and their impact on various warranty/return outcomes and chase down process variation. It was much more difficult for the team than we make it sound. This analysis does not seem technically impressive, but keep in mind that this kind of analysis is a first for many organizations. A major opportunity surfaced when the team isolated warranty/returns to a particular customer and the agreements in place from twenty years ago (i.e., the customer does not have to physically send back the defective return). Further analysis proved with data and facts that the problem was an installation problem, not a product problem. The returns policy was revised, and one of the segments of warranty/returns dropped immediately. The installation process was also revised in much greater detail for the installation techs, and special installation tooling was provided. It was a win-win for everyone. The big lesson here is that most of the time, the perceived problem is not the real problem; the real problem is something else. Think about your incomplete returned material authorizations and field service tags and the wealth of information that they could provide the organization. Only data and facts get you to the real truth.

Case Study 4: Six Sigma Finds the Real Problem

A large distributor of business products was having returns and allowance issues related to imprint errors on checks. This was a very costly problem because the frequency of occurrence was high, there is a lot of information on a check, and an imprint error involves no-charge replacements, often shipped next-day air. Previous efforts centered around measuring the number of imprint errors per week and per month and training and retraining of sales associates. However, the imprint error problem still remained as the number one returns and allowance category. A Six Sigma team was assembled to address the issue. In the Define and Measure phases, the team established the project objective, baseline performance, and improvement goal. The team also developed a detailed value stream map of the process and produced overlays of the order-entry screens used during each step of the process. Next, the team developed its sampling plan and collected data around check imprint errors. Analysis of the defect data revealed that 60 percent of the imprint areas were three data elements (Figure 5.4). The team implemented system recommendations targeted on selective verification and reduced imprint errors by 32 percent.

THERE IS ONLY SO MUCH *SPECIAL PROJECT* CAPACITY

In the past few years, we have stressed the need for capacity regulation, an issue that is critical to Six Sigma success. We have observed many organizations that begin their Six Sigma journey with wave after wave of black belt and green belt training. A week before the wave begins, people are scrambling around the organization looking for a project, any project, so they can attend the first-wave session with a project assignment. Many of these projects are misaligned to the organization's business strategy and many are not good Six Sigma projects (some are kaizen projects, and the answer is obvious without any statistical analysis or even attending training). The goal is to load up the wave because the cost per belt goes down and the supposed return on investment goes up. As

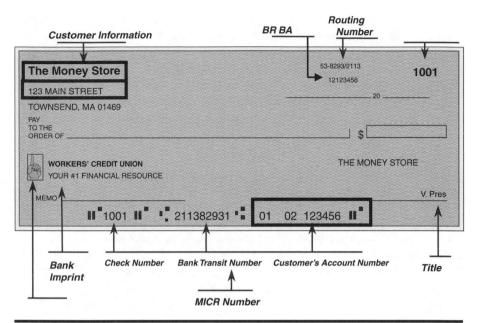

Figure 5.4 Analysis of check imprint errors; 60 percent of check errors occur in the outlined areas.

we mentioned earlier, there is too much emphasis on *belts and motion* and not enough on results.

Every organization has a fixed capacity to conduct special projects, whether lean, Six Sigma, an IT implementation, or a business reengineering initiative. Organizations have the right intentions by trying to *finish their continuous improvement programs* as fast as possible. (We use this statement because a prospect once mentioned that his organization needed Six Sigma because it finished its continuous improvement programs years ago.) However, in the process, they introduce significant inefficiencies to the organization, and the traditional *just make it happen* orders add little to the real solution. We have observed situations where several critical resources are assigned to five or six different teams, some teams include ten to fifteen people and have been meeting for months, and the benefits of several special projects are very questionable. We have experimented with different deployment models and have discovered that smaller and mid-sized organizations can actually accomplish more with less, very targeted efforts. Six Sigma is not about belts and waves and monthly motion reports, it is about improving competitiveness and results!

A preferred deployment that we highly recommend with smaller and mid-sized organizations is to recognize that there is only so much *special project*

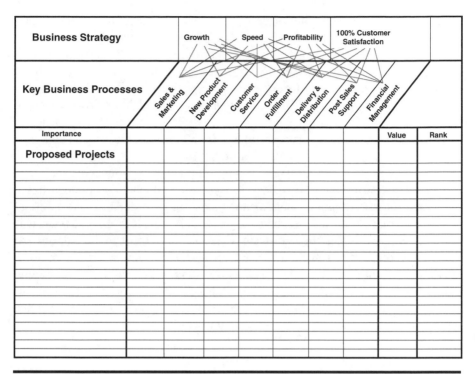

Figure 5.5   Function deployment matrix for project/activity control.

activity available before it disrupts day-to-day operations. Sometimes conditions dictate that we need to turn up the heat beyond this level to put a few changes in place quickly. The goal is to appreciate this limited capacity, regulate the amount of activity, and target the activity toward strategically important requirements. This sounds so "pie in the sky," but take a hard look at your organization and prevent a major mistake: do not allow Six Sigma to take on a life of its own like the other improvement programs that have preceded it. There are plenty of belts and motion cases out there; do not allow yourself to become one of them.

We have used a simple function deployment matrix (FDM) in Figure 5.5 to prioritize and align proposed projects to the organization's strategic plan. This is a subset of our broader Activity-Based Mapping (ABM) methodology, where an organization's budget and actual spending are allocated across the key value-added services it provides to customers. Too much project selection activity tends to focus on negative variance areas of a budget, missing tremendous hidden cost opportunities. The ABM methodology enables organizations to mine for high-impact opportunities regardless of negative or positive budget variances. Once the potential project opportunities are mined, they can be force-ranked against each other in terms of strategic importance using the FDM.

The FDM lists proposed projects and opportunities down the left side. Across the top are the elements of the organization's strategic plan, the key business processes that are engaged to achieve the strategic plan, and each project's relative impact on these key business processes. The FDM removes much of the emotion and politics from the project down-select process. It is better to complete a dozen incredibly successful Six Sigma projects than it is to complete dozens of Six Sigma projects with illusionary savings.

Another characteristic of this process is alignment. Everyone talks about this concept, but few organizations do this well, at least on a continuous basis. Alignment is not a natural phenomenon; it requires leadership and a formal alignment process that links strategy to daily activities in more real time. It is not an alignment module in a software application per se. It is the culmination of people, processes, and enabling technology in synchronization with the business strategy. Without alignment, there is a natural tendency to drift into conflicting objectives throughout the organization, rather than stay focused on mission-critical improvements. Alignment provides a crystal-clear link between the business strategy and the day-to-day improvement activities throughout the organization.

NEXT EVOLUTION: TRANSACTIONAL DESIGN FOR SIX SIGMA

An emerging application of Six Sigma is in the area of Transactional Design for Six Sigma (TDFSS). Some organizations have successfully applied the DFSS concepts to business process redesign. For example, if we are considering a new order-entry process, the Six Sigma methodology can be very useful. If we have historical information about order-entry activity, we can calculate the probability of a defect at each data element of the order-entry screens and across each step of the process. Then we can calculate a cumulative expected process capability of the proposed system design. These techniques have been used to design data input fields for web-based order-entry applications where a customer may attempt to input more information than is physically available (e.g., number of characters). The other use of this information is to establish spot verification practices for certain areas of the order-entry screens to, in effect, mistake-proof the process.

Another useful TDFSS application is the quotation process. Some organizations attempt to quote every single customer request and for every combination of factors requested. If we understand the cost drivers with data and facts, it becomes an easy task to standardize the quotation process and eliminate 80 percent of the drudgery of repetitive number crunching. An interesting exercise is to analyze the relationship between quoted costs, actual costs, and standard costs. It really highlights the need to create a different way of processing customer quotations. One organization developed an Excel application with pull-down menus based on data and analysis from its Six Sigma project. Previously, the quotation process required days of effort to pull the right people together and respond to the customer. In many cases, customers place their orders elsewhere before the organization was able to respond with a quote. The new process was a simple, instant, fill-in-the-blanks process. Approximately 80 percent of quotes could be created and delivered while the sales representatives were on the phone with customers.

Six Sigma is also moving in the direction of what we refer to as *predictive and preventive analytics*. Rather than Six Sigma projects being done in waves or as individually structured projects, some advanced practitioners monitor process data in real time and take proactive measures to predict and/or prevent waste. These activities can also result in residual benefits such as smoother scheduled maintenance and changeovers. Imagine pulling down data in real time, conducting the appropriate Minitab analysis, and then pushing the information out to decision makers via portals (e.g., like their Blackberrys). The future has arrived for a few forward-thinking Six Sigma professionals.

There is no question about the benefits within the transactional Six Sigma arena. A prerequisite to success is getting the organization to recognize that everything has a process. It may be a good process, an ineffective process, a nonstandardized process, or a dozen different processes. However, transactional processes are no different than machines: They have inputs and outputs, cycle times, defects, and ways to measure system performance. Once individuals recognize this fact, the sky is the limit with most transactional processes.

CHAPTER 5 TAKE-AWAYS

- For many organizations, actual manufacturing represents 15 to 20 percent of their total cost structure. The remaining 80 percent is due to transactional process activity such as sales and marketing, finance, engineering and R&D, customer service, procurement, and distribution. Manufacturing is no longer a competitive weapon; it is just a link in the chain. Transactional Six Sigma is a significant enabler of business improvement.
- Transactional Six Sigma is strategically important because as much as 70 to 95 percent of product cost is generated outside of your organization, up to 75 to 95 percent of lead time is consumed outside of your organization,

and about 95+ percent of the key activities of design, supply chain planning, and manufacturing (and the associated employees) are outside of your organization.

■ Transactional Six Sigma has grown rapidly during the past few years. This myriad of improvement opportunities is surfacing because executives recognize that transactional processes represent the major component of their businesses from both a cost and activity/resource consumption perspective. Transactional projects represent 50 percent or more of the scope of many Six Sigma deployments and probably 70 to 90 percent of the potential benefits, particularly for transaction-intensive business environments.

■ A common thread is the *hidden factory* of costs and opportunities when deep diving into transactional processes. Many of these practices have become institutionalized and accepted, as depicted by comments such as "That is the best we can do" or "These things are going to happen" or "It is just the cost of being in our business." As long as these processes and practices remain in *hidden factory* mode, they cannot be improved and the hidden costs of doing business grow.

■ There is only so much *special project* activity available before it disrupts day-to-day operations. Sometimes conditions dictate that we need to turn up the heat beyond this level to put a few changes in place quickly. The goal is to appreciate this limited capacity, regulate the amount of activity, and target the activity toward strategically important requirements.

■ There is no question about the benefits within the transactional Six Sigma arena. A prerequisite to success is getting the organization to recognize that everything has a process. It may be a good process, an ineffective process, a nonstandardized process, or a dozen different processes. However transactional processes are no different than machines: They have inputs and outputs, cycle times, defects, and ways to measure system performance. Once individuals recognize this fact, the sky is the limit with most transactional processes.

SUGGESTED FURTHER READING

George, Michael, *Lean Six Sigma for Service*, McGraw-Hill, 2003.
SAP White Paper, *Building the Lean Extended Enterprise Through Adaptive Supply Chain Networks*, 2004.

6

STRATEGY DEPLOYMENT AND PROJECT SELECTION

So you want to "do" Six Sigma? The first recommendation we could make is to stop and ask yourself as well as your organization why.

Defining why you are doing this is an absolutely essential part of the process of implementing Six Sigma. "Why is that?" you might ask. The answer is because successfully implementing Six Sigma, like any endeavor of value, will not be easy. To be sure, you will meet with problems such as resistance to change or more immediate and more important "priorities" on your road to implementation. For this reason, it is not for the faint of heart. Change is tough business. Implementing Six Sigma can be an expensive proposition if you begin without a clear roadmap.

Defining the strategy deployment vision for the organization takes *time, intelligence, and tools.* We say this not to be insulting, but to get your attention that this is not intuitive. If it were, companies would be doing it and you would not need to read a book about it.

- **Time**: No one has enough of it and yet we all have the same amount. The question is how you will use it. Invest time into this process and it will yield much more in dividends than you may currently realize.
- **Intelligence**: If you have the answers, you should not have the problem any longer. Therefore, it is of paramount importance to recognize what you do not know. As true as it is that the answers to most of your

problems lie within the minds of the people who make up your organization, it is also true that current thinking brought about current problems and therefore cannot solve them.

■ **Tools**: There are specific activities that executive leadership can go through to define a method out of the madness. How many "priorities" do you have? As a leader, you must recognize that you are the pinnacle of the organization and that a small amount of action from you translates into a large amount of activity in the rest of the organization. Therefore, you cannot afford to move from one "priority" to another, as this will keep your organization in a state of chaos. Further, it is also imperative that you quickly recognize that the leaders in your organization will recognize this behavior and its implications and will not tolerate it for long before they will no longer be with you.

DEFINING THE MEASURES

Most companies that have implemented Six Sigma would probably agree that, at a minimum, 25 percent of the projects are solved by fixing the measurement system. This is the same whether in the mail room or the boardroom. People will always respond to how they are measured. This is the level where work becomes personal and ownership evolves. One could probably link the problems you are dealing with today to the measurement system used to assess your people. This may sound harsh, but it is probably true unless your organization actively employs a balanced scorecard approach to performance assessment.

Remember that you get what you inspect (measure), not what you expect. You can improve quality by measuring the quality manager on parts per million (PPM) defective reduction. One way for this to be achieved would be to require end-of-line sorting 300 percent. This is certainly not what one would expect with a metric of PPM reduction, but if you link a person's paycheck to this metric, this will be their focus.

Is the person in quality in your organization measured on customer complaints, PPM defective, or some other traditional quality metric? Is that person also measured on rolled throughput yield or reduced labor cost, scrap cost, obsolescence, etc.? Is the manufacturing person measured against a reduction in quality complaints metric?

What if everyone on the senior staff was measured equally on a balanced scorecard approach to achieving annual objectives that put the strategic plan as a priority over departmental goals? This drives a very different daily behavior. Of course, we are making a bold assumption that the measurement system is in place that links to the strategic initiatives. If not, this is not an initiative, but a pipe dream.

Figure 6.1 Linkage from daily activities to the policy deployment.

LAUNCHING SIX SIGMA

Implementing Six Sigma is so similar to launching a new product that we should take a moment to point out the common pain and pressure points. Have you ever tried to launch a new product or initiative that was clearly doomed from concept design? Of course not, but perhaps you have read about some poor soul that has. What was your first impression? Probably that it hadn't been thought out or hadn't been thought about at all. Maybe there was some pressure to make it work anyway. "These things happen," "We have too much invested in this for it not to work," "We can't turn back, it isn't a perfect world; we'll just have to fix it later" — you know the drill.

To avoid the pitfalls of a poor launch, we must have a mental model of the linkage from our daily activities to the policy deployment or strategic vision of the company. One example of such a model to provide mental guidance is given in Figure 6.1. Again, this is at the conceptual level. We will put some details to this model as we get deeper into the topic of project selection.

PROJECT SELECTION BEGINS WITH THE STRATEGIC PLAN

Six Sigma, in and of itself, is not a strategic initiative; it is how you achieve the strategic initiative. So how do you go about using Six Sigma to implement your strategic initiatives? First, one must note that there are specific tools that can be employed to help determine your priorities for strategy deployment. For example, a prioritization matrix could be used to assess empirical data from your senior staff on the validity and priority of projects to assist with attainment of annual objectives that support the strategic plan. Each departmental manager could use the same tool to roll out the priorities to his or her department.

The key is to create ability to take the vision and link it through the strategic initiatives and annual operating plans into annual improvement objectives for each department. Taken further, each departmental manager would then link each team member's performance review to the department's annual objectives. This provides a direct alignment of the daily activities to the annual plan. The critical-to-quality factor associated with this methodology is the measurement system.

STRATEGY MAPPING AND POLICY DEPLOYMENT

Throughout the year, at a minimum of the monthly reviews, it helps to be able to look at your strategy map or policy deployment matrix for a reference to keep the focus on the projects at hand. Again, these projects must be the critical "go gets" or the "logic" of sidetracking will prevail. An example of the strategy mapping thought process that leads to the policy deployment matrix is included in Figure 6.2. Again, this is a generic high-level map, but it serves as an example to show the process.

Before we can begin to select projects, we have to define what the strategic vision is and how this is linked to the tactical plan. These are usually stated as

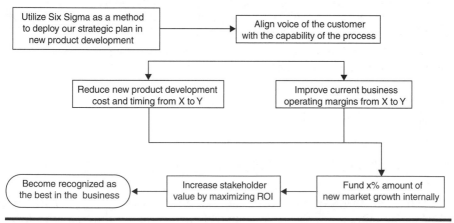

Figure 6.2   Strategy mapping thought process.

financial goals or tactical goals or a combination (i.e., grow market share by 5 percent with two new product platforms launched at 30 percent gross margin). The three- to five-year strategy must be supported by an annual operating plan. This annual operating plan must then be supported by a set of improvement priorities. These critical few priorities create the need for underlying projects. These critical few projects are "must do" to meet the annual operating plan and thus the strategic plan. It is important to separate the *critical few* from the *trivial many* projects than can act as a distraction and dissolve the effectiveness of limited resources.

The Pareto principle (or 80/20 rule) helps define why the above statement is true. In this case, 80 percent of the cost is determined in the first 20 percent of the life of a product. The other 20 percent will be created over the remaining 80 percent of the product's life. Even warranty issues and recalls will follow this rule if traced back to the product or process design. The key is to realize that you have to invest the time up front to recognize that you cannot achieve your strategic goals without using Six Sigma. If you can, then you should do that or revise your goals to something more aggressive. This linkage of Six Sigma to your strategic planning will determine the clarity of your vision in order to better achieve it. A simple example of strategic linkage is provided in Figure 6.3.

BUSINESS UNIT STRATEGY PLAN

Once the linkage is defined and the vision and direction are clear, one can reference this matrix during periodic reviews to reestablish the link of the effort applied to the project with the execution of the strategic initiatives. For example, it serves as a reminder during these reviews of the answer to the original question: "Why do you want to implement Six Sigma?" Further, it can serve as a guiding principle when the tough times mentioned earlier come, and be assured, they will.

Think of the project matrix as a roadmap. When you find out there is a traffic jam, such as an inconvenient time to fund the Six Sigma effort fully during a tough month, quarter etc., look at the map. When there is an accident, such as a customer issue, audit, crisis, etc., look at the map. When you are in the middle of one of those "This isn't a traffic jam or accident — THE BRIDGE IS OUT!" times, look again at the map. Without this strategic link as the anchor of reason, your efforts will be vulnerable to the voices of "reason" of the well-intentioned people directing you to change course "temporarily." These sparks of reason can lead you back into the flames of firefighting.

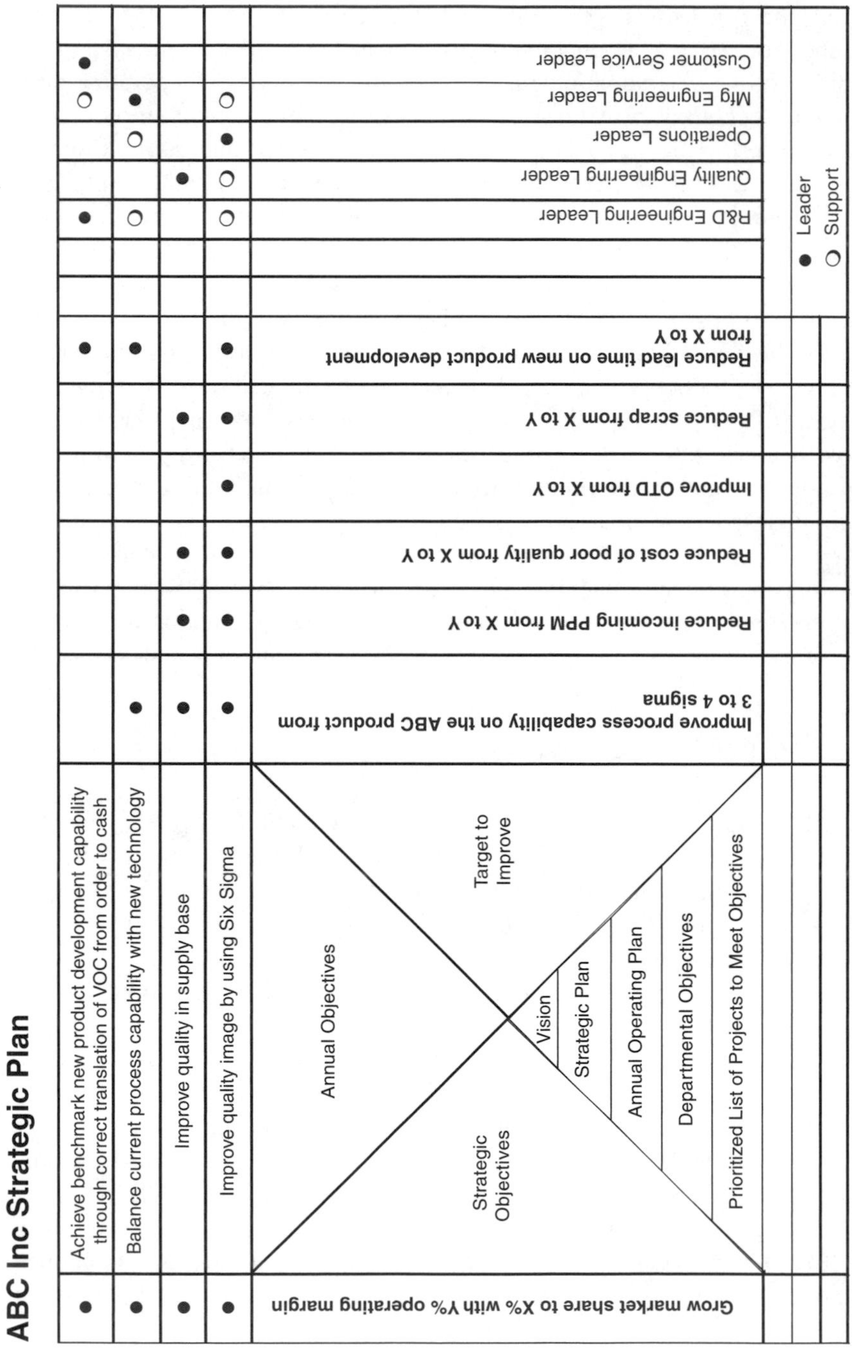

ABC Inc Strategic Plan

Target to Improve:

- Improve process capability on the ABC product from 3 to 4 sigma
- Reduce incoming PPM from X to Y
- Reduce cost of poor quality from X to Y
- Improve OTD from X to Y
- Reduce scrap from X to Y
- Reduce lead time on new product development from X to Y

Annual Objectives:

- Grow market share to X% with Y% operating margin
- Improve quality image by using Six Sigma
- Improve quality in supply base
- Balance current process capability with new technology
- Achieve benchmark new product development capability through correct translation of VOC from order to cash

Strategic Objectives

Vision
Strategic Plan
Annual Operating Plan
Departmental Objectives
Prioritized List of Projects to Meet Objectives

Leaders:

- R&D Engineering Leader
- Quality Engineering Leader
- Operations Leader
- Mfg Engineering Leader
- Customer Service Leader

● Leader
○ Support

Figure 6.3 Strategic linkage example.

If the process map for implementing Six Sigma is done correctly, it invokes the passion of the leaders in your organization. Only then will it become a reference for reasoning for use during those moments of madness. When your best and brightest, who have created your strategic plan, recognize that the time and resources to achieve this vision are truly reduced by using Six Sigma as a competitive advantage, then they will want to stick with it. To reiterate, you must have their buy-in to give up the "departmental" projects for the "company" projects. Invest this time up front.

PRIORITIZING THE PROJECTS TO SUPPORT THE STRATEGIC PLAN

It is a leadership function to define the key projects that will lead to the success of the critical few initiatives. This is also, by definition, gaining the will to refuse the trivial many projects that could come along. This is all a matter of extracting the priorities from the expertise of the senior staff. After all, it is their experience in your industry that has led them to positions of providing direction for the organization. Okay, so how do you prioritize the empirical opinions derived from the experience of your staff? One tool to be used is a prioritization matrix. This matrix, shown in Figure 6.4, is used to build a Pareto chart of the application of resources by project to the project backlog.

The projects from the backlog, a.k.a. list of pet projects, are listed on the left, and their ranking is determined by dividing the sum of the cross-multiplication by the total. The Pareto chart ranks the percentages to allow a visual display of the command of resources. The results can be misleading unless another tool, called the nominal group technique, is employed. This tool is used to silently and individually rank the relationships of the "key" projects as individuals and then collect and tabulate the results as a group average. This removes the "boss's" opinion by giving equal weight to the opinion of each individual staff member. This allows people to address the "elephant in the room" anonymously. You might think you do not need that — maybe *you* are the elephant in the room.

Note that this should be used as a "sanity check" to see if there is agreement among the senior staff on the annual priorities for improvement. If not, this would be the best time for further analysis rather than have people walk out of the meeting with a verbal agreement and head nod but no real belief in the priority. The "rubber meets the road" when the departmental budgets are prioritized to support these projects in the same way.

Project	Importance to Customer Rate 1 to 5 High = 5 Low = 1		Cost to Implement Rate 1 to 5 High = 5 Low = 1		Ease of Implementation Rate 1 to 5 High = 5 Low = 1		Reduces Cost Rate 1 to 5 High = 5 Low = 1		Leverage (Ability to use in similar areas) Rate 1 to 5 High = 5 Low = 1		Cross Multiply Categories	
Uptime on Line A	5	*	4	*	3	*	4	*	3	=	720	64%
Scrap Reduction on Line A	3	*	3	*	4	*	3	*	3	=	324	29%
Labor Reduction Line A	1	*	3	*	4	*	3	*	2	=	72	6%
Redesign the A product	1	*	1	*	2	*	3	*	1	=	6	1%
									Sum		1122	

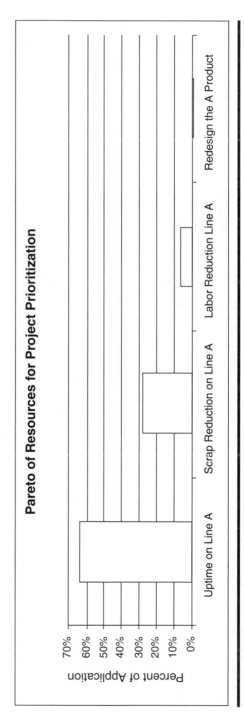

Pareto of Resources for Project Prioritization

Figure 6.4   Prioritization matrix.

The bottom line in prioritizing the project backlog is to avoid implementing Six Sigma on projects that are easy just to enable someone to gain some sort of certification quotient. This mistake truly belittles the whole Six Sigma effort and plants a seed of distrust of the overall process. People need to see that this is serious and that there is a direct link between the projects and the future of the organization. They also need to see that those in the leadership is so serious about this linkage that they have also linked the performance reviews of the organization to the projects.

The correct application is a critical step in the successful utilization of Six Sigma in any organization. The best way to make your efforts fail is to allow someone to sideline the process because they have "real" problems they need to work on. This makes Six Sigma seem trivial and another "flavor of the month." The projects should be such that the solution is not apparent. Again, logic prevailing, you already should have implemented any viable known solution. Further, this sends the message you want and makes a statement that this is not something you do in addition to your "real" work, but that this is how you work.

PROJECT SELECTION MODEL

There are many dimensions to project selection. They include financial, strategic, customer mandated, supply base, safety requirements, environmental issues, etc. The key is not the project itself, but that it is of high importance to the organization and one that will derive the desired benefits if achieved. Of equal importance is the regulation of a project so that it does not take on a life of its own. Projects must be timely and reviewed weekly with the team, if not daily with the champion and the project lead. Daily? Yes. If not, look again at the project. Is it really that critical? If not, you may want to reconsider.

The prioritization matrix mentioned above is meant to leverage limited resources so that the project is completed without adding an army of heads to the organization. This can only be done if the project fits the profile mentioned above. Projects that have an effect on more than one department or facility where there are other processes that are similar can be leveraged to reduce the time associated with the learning curve.

Project migration should be encouraged across similar processes or product lines in multiple facilities by use of statistical comparison. For example, two facilities use similar equipment and make similar products. The performance rates should be similar. If not, the reason should be identified through statistical comparison. It could be that the performance is linked to a difference in suppliers, shifts, tooling used, preventive maintenance plans, etc.

The bottom line is that similar processes should yield variation that is not statistically significant. If so, assignable cause(s) must be identified and removed. These are the hidden factories we live with every day. These hidden factories are accepted in many cases, but they are *NOT* normal.

"Hidden factory" is a term used to describe extra work that is performed unnecessarily to accomplish the tasks at hand. This is not the scrap or reprocessing that you are aware of. If you are aware of something, it is not hidden, and you should already be addressing this waste. A hidden factory is the waste that escapes notice. It may be in front of us all the time, but something we have become so accustomed to that we are blind to it. We accept hidden factories all around us every day in our organizations. Again, just because something is part of our "normal" routine does not make it *NORMAL* and it should not be taken as routine.

Consider this. Imagine sitting in an airplane and hearing the pilot exclaim: "Engine 4 is down again. This always happens right when we need it — Murphy!" This may sound crazy, but it is even crazier to think that we have intelligent people walking past expensive equipment that is performing at a less than optimal level and accepting that fact! You can bet that Southwest Airlines would not accept the fact that one of the planes in its fleet of 737s does not perform as well as the others because "it's always been that way." This may seem intuitively obvious. Airlines are, of course, required by the FAA to maintain maintenance records; however, some airlines take this requirement and utilize it as a strategic advantage by using the data from these records to make tactical advances.

There are strategic and tactical advantages to analyzing such mundane records to address *statistically* significant variation before problems would become *practically* evident. It should start becoming evident that there may be projects that possibly have strategic competitive advantages right in your own organization. This is part of internal benchmarking, but may be just as readily available already by contacting equipment vendors to find out what their other customers experience with similar equipment or processes. This is not revealing proprietary information. Statistically speaking, the average performance would do. What is your vision to reveal the hidden potential in your organization? The waste of potential is the greatest waste of all. It is important to seek out the critical few data points to track the pulse of your organization from the trivial many data that may be available. Figure 6.5 demonstrates conceptually how you must view all the available data points.

Figure 6.5 also demonstrates the logic of the down-selection process whereby the individual members of the senior staff yield up their own pet projects in order to allow the organization to finance the critical few successfully instead

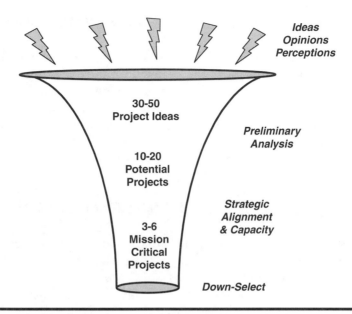

Figure 6.5   Project filtering and selection model.

of trying to accomplish the trivial many unsuccessfully. The senior leadership must supply the organization with the vision of why it is sticking to its plan; this is the strategy matrix. Everyone must be able to clearly link the goals in their own way and recognize that "In order to achieve 'Y', we must have these critical few 'Xs' no matter what." This has to be driven with relentless persistence by the senior leadership and every member of the executive staff. The 80 percent of the desired results you achieve will come from the 20 percent of the activities you engage in; 20 percent of your people, the leadership, will determine 80 percent of the results. This is done by the things they measure and the questions they ask, even when the boss is not around.

Okay, so you have "down-selected" the projects that are to be the priorities this year by using a tool such as the function deployment matrix. You have also created a strategy plan and communicated it via the strategy deployment matrix. Now, how do you measure each project's performance all year long in the face of certain uncertainty and changes that will no doubt occur as you try to implement the best of plans? Further, how do you monitor progress and stay the course in a way that those in the organization can clearly see the direct linkage between their efforts and the company's strategic objectives all year long?

TACTICAL PLANNING AND THE DEPARTMENTAL MATRIX

To ensure the focus is maintained on the areas that will enable the departmental functions to support the business unit strategy, we use a departmental matrix. In this matrix, the strategic goals are replaced with the departmental annual objectives, and the annual objectives are replaced with tactical, departmental objectives. These objectives are assigned a lead person and support persons who have the completion of the objective as part of their performance review. An example of a departmental matrix is provided in Figure 6.6.

DEFINING THE POLICY DEPLOYMENT SCORECARD

Once the critical few have been filtered from the trivial many and a balance achieved, the senior staff members must now be measured on their contribution, with their Management Incentive Bonus Plan linked directly to this. This, in turn, must roll out to a departmental-level scorecard for each member. Each departmental manager must then work with his or her people to determine how they will contribute to the departmental goals, which are linked to the company goals. The two must agree on how the individual's contribution will be measured, with an understanding that this will directly determine financial rewards on the next review.

The policy deployment scorecard is a tool that has been commonly used to monitor the performance to goals for those projects that have been determined to best support the strategic plan. This tool is maintained as a compass to see how well the organization is performing to the expectations, project by project. The goals are set forth with monthly or weekly targets and monitored to demonstrate the linkage between the strategic plan to support the overall vision and the ongoing tactical measures of the supporting projects. An example of the policy deployment scorecard is provided in Figure 6.7.

PERSONALIZING SIX SIGMA

As this departmental plan is established, the contribution of the department is rolled out further to the responsibilities of the select leads in the department. This is the point at which a lead person working as a Six Sigma specialist will be used to drive a project for the department. Now it becomes personal. At this point, it is appropriate to discuss the need to ensure that your organization identifies and selects the right people for these key roles.

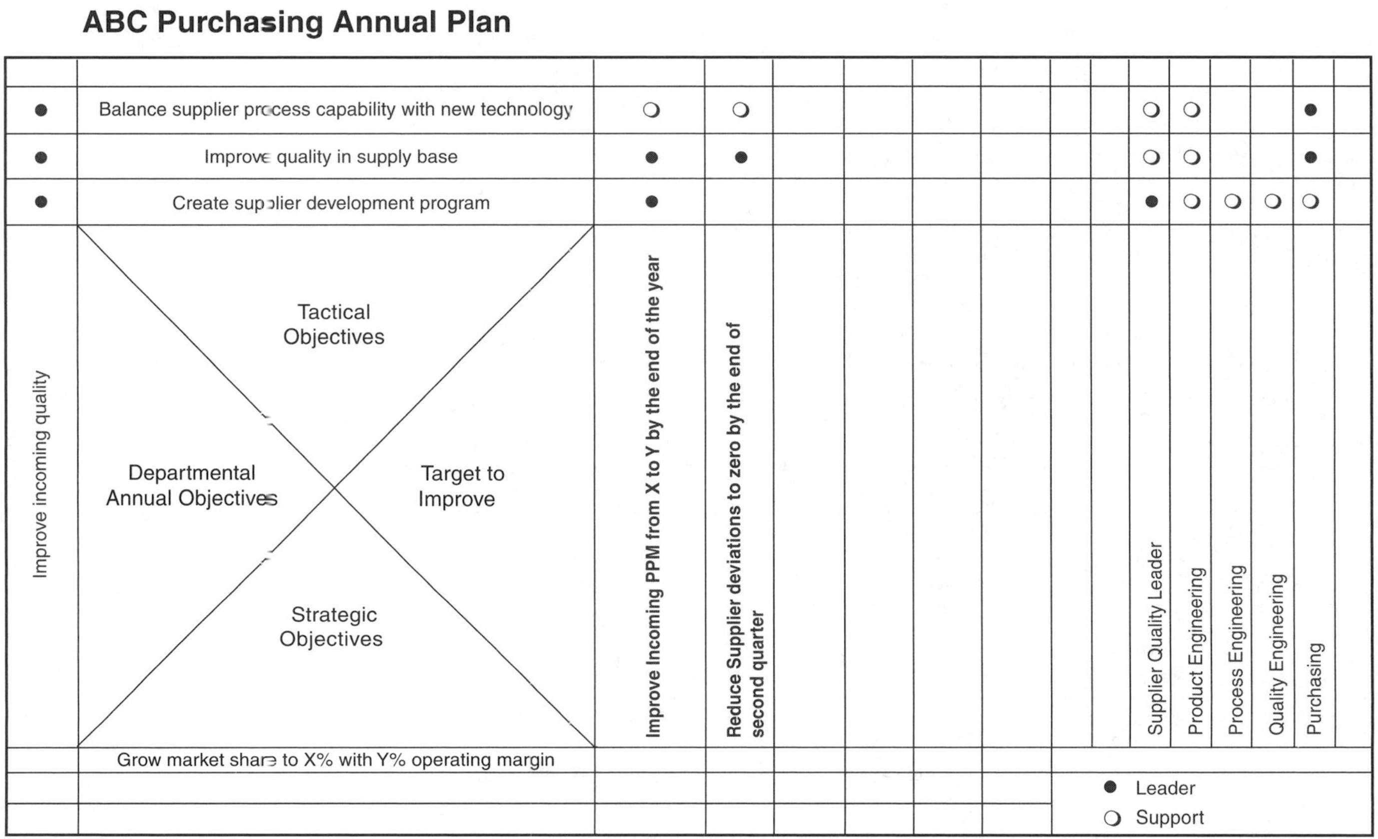

ABC Purchasing Annual Plan

Tactical Objectives
- Balance supplier process capability with new technology
- Improve quality in supply base
- Create supplier development program

Target to Improve

Strategic Objectives

Departmental Annual Objectives
- Improve incoming quality
- Grow market share to X% with Y% operating margin

Improve Incoming PPM from X to Y by the end of the year

Reduce Supplier deviations to zero by the end of second quarter

- Supplier Quality Leader
- Product Engineering
- Process Engineering
- Quality Engineering
- Purchasing

● Leader
○ Support

Figure 6.6 Departmental matrix example.

Metric	Baseline Q4 2003	2004	Q1			Q2			Q3			Q4			Target	YTD
			JAN	FEB	MAR	APR	MAY	JUN	JUL	AUG	SEP	OCT	NOV	DEC		
Incoming PPM	10,000	Plan	9,333	8,667	8,000	7,333	6,667	6,000	5,333	4,667	4,000	3,333	2,667	2,000	2,000	
		Actual														
# Deviations	28	Plan	25	20	15	10	5	-	-	-	-			-	-	
		Actual														

Figure 6.7 Policy deployment scorecard example.

Figure 6.7 is an example of how the departmental-level annual objectives are rolled out to the individual at the scorecard level. It is updated weekly or monthly and may be used to maintain a quarterly and/or year-to-date rolling average.

SELECTING PROJECT LEADERS

Selecting projects really begins with selecting people. The saying "people are our most valuable resource" is not exactly true. That is like saying "practice makes perfect." The reality is that repetition is the mother of skill; practicing a poor method will foster poor skills and yield poor results. Therefore, only perfect practice makes perfect. With this in mind, people are not our most important resource. The right people are.

WHO CAN YOU AFFORD TO TRAIN: DO NOT MAKE THIS MISTAKE!

Be extremely careful here. Fools rush in where the wise proceed with care. The single biggest mistake we see most often is the propensity for organizations to train the people they can "afford" to train. This is just as logical as building a new product that you are going to bet the future of your company on out of extra component inventory that you have laying around. You would never even imagine doing that, yet this is exactly what many leaders do, in effect, when it comes to launching their Six Sigma effort. This results in the "lonely black belt/green belt syndrome" we discussed in Chapter 2.

Who do you count on? If you had a serious problem that had to be fixed right the first time with your boss and customer both watching, who would you put on it? It most likely would not be someone who really was not that busy anyway. The name or names that came to mind when you first read this question would be an appropriate place to start when thinking about the right "who" before implementing the "what" when it comes to launching Six Sigma.

Once the right "who" is selected and you have the right "what" from your project selection, how should your organization work on these? This is a wide-open question. It is just as important to decide what your organization does *not* need to work on. Some things are urgent, and some things are important. Filing your taxes is important, but it is not urgent on January 1. Some things are urgent and important, like filing taxes on April 15. Some are not urgent and are not important. These are obviously a waste of resources. We have to focus on the things that are not urgent, but are important. Planning for market position in three years is obviously not on the "must get done today" list, but it must be done.

Perhaps there are some issues that require immediate attention to "stop the bleeding." What about those? Those projects are urgent and important and usually involve putting out fires. They provide a good exercise for people who need to develop in your organization's process knowledge, but should be "advised" and not led by the person you would count on in a foxhole. This affords those people who do not fit into that category a growth opportunity to rise to the challenge.

Meanwhile, the person(s) who would fit into the "I'd want that person beside me in a foxhole" category should spend 20 percent of their time developing others with their process knowledge, while investing 80 percent of their time on the important but not urgent projects. Notice again the Pareto principle. The 20 percent firefighting will be enough to enable the less experienced to put out the fires. Notice that this time is regarded as time "spent." The other 80 percent of their time is "invested," as it yields longer term payback. Firefighting will only reduce 20 percent of your cost. The 80 percent of hidden cost is determined up front and must be solved *before* becoming an issue.

AVOIDING THE MONEY PITFALL

We have observed organizations that make the determination that no one will get "credit" for cost-avoidance projects as they are "funny money." These organizations want to see "real" dollars hitting the bottom line. Indeed they will. But this thought process makes as much sense as saying you would not pay for an ounce of prevention, but would gladly pay for a pound of cure. It is the *pay me now or pay me later* routine. Now is usually the better investment.

STAYING THE COURSE

So how do you stay focused on the critical few from the trivial many projects? Further, in the heat of the battle, how do you quickly make the decision to distinguish important from urgent? In other words, how do you determine the right activities, select the right objectives, and stay focused on these while juggling multiple priorities all year long?

Our answer to this is to give a quick acid test to each of these "priorities" as they come up. This test for project selection is "If we don't successfully achieve the expected results of this project, can we still make the annual operating plan?" If the answer is yes, this is not the right project for your foxhole personnel. If the answer is "If we miss this, we can kiss the year good-bye," this is a project for your foxhole people.

LESS IS MORE

We have observed that every organization seems to have between three to five critical "must do" initiatives. Each of these usually has a maximum of three projects that will determine the success or failure of the initiative. Mathematically, this puts the mission-critical "foxhole" projects somewhere between nine and fifteen that have to be done per year. The fewer the projects, the easier it should be to focus the limited resources toward a higher probability of success. We suggest using the "acid test" day to day to stay on track. The difficulty of doing this will be reduced proportionately with the amount of time and effort your organization has invested into personalizing Six Sigma by linking the individual performance measurements to the critical few projects.

CHAPTER 6 TAKE-AWAYS

■ Strategic mapping helps conceptualize the direction of the organization and brings clarity to why the emphasis must be on important but not urgent matters. Urgency is firefighting. The important but nonurgent is fire prevention and a sane consideration of where the organization is trying to go.

■ The linkage between the strategic plans, tactical plans, business unit contribution, and departmental goals must be clearly defined. This enables the organization as well as its individual contributors to see each person's contribution. Everyone wants to have a sense of accomplishment. Urgency usually has high visibility and recognition. Remember, rewarding firefighters can promote arson. Recognize fire prevention via the monthly, quarterly, and individual performance reviews.

■ Selecting the right people is just as important as selecting the right projects. Six Sigma is too important not to demand that you put your best and brightest on it. This includes people skills. Michael Jordan owes his success not only to his personal ability to play, but to the fact that others wanted to get the ball to him. Do you have a Michael Jordan who is "smart" but does not play well with others? It is hard to imagine someone actually wasting time on getting a "talented individual" to play well with others when the real goal is to have a talented team. Talented "individuals" are candidates for firefighting and can be arsonists to your Six Sigma efforts.

■ The effort required to gain and sustain momentum is reduced by the amount of time invested in selecting the right project leaders and linking their performance review to the critical few projects. "If I had more time, I would have written a shorter letter" — give Six Sigma implementation planning the time and talent it deserves. If you do not have it, get it. Benchmark, hire, train internally, but make certain you make a wise investment of time up front in order to get the best dividends.

SUGGESTED FURTHER READING

Cowley, Michael and Domb, Ellen, *Beyond Strategic Vision, Effective Corporate Action with Hoshin Planning,* Butterworth-Heinemann, 1997.
Kaplan, Robert and Norton, David, *The Balanced Scorecard: Translating Strategy into Action*, Harvard Business School Press, 1996.
Kaplan, Robert and Norton, David, *The Strategy-Focused Organization*, Harvard Business School Press, 2001.

7

MENTORING AND INDIVIDUAL PROJECT MANAGEMENT

SUCCESSFUL MENTORING BEGINS WITH PERSONAL PREPARATION

Having a successful Six Sigma effort in any organization depends on how it is deployed from the beginning. From the initial rollout communication, the organization is watching to see if this is another "flavor of the month" or if it is really something more. In any organization, people primarily have two basic working desires: to belong to something bigger than what they can be by themselves (something they can believe in) and to be able to have a personal impact with purpose. It is a basic human desire to have significance. It is also something people take very seriously. This is why people will quickly turn cynical if they feel their time and efforts are being taken for granted.

Leaders must be sensitive to the fact stated above. This is one of the greatest failure modes with new initiatives. Consider that technology continues to speed up our perception of time, while the amount of time available continuously seems to decrease. Therefore, with a perceived lack of time, work continues to become a greater portion of our lives. This has relevance and is significant for leaders as it is imperative that we do not waste this time. One indication that an organization has been guilty of wasting time is hearing slogans like "flavor of the month" or other cynical comments.

It is an important consideration and worth *your* time to understand, as the first thing you must know is the type of culture that currently exists within your organization. This is especially true if you *think* you know already what kind of culture exists. Take the time to engage Six Sigma within the organization with well-thought-out and regularly scheduled communication. Show the benefits of Six Sigma in other organizations that people can relate to. If you are not a GE-type company, do not try to compare to that type of organization. If you have examples of improvement from your global competition, use them. If not, take the time to get this type of information. If you think no one in your industry is pursuing Six Sigma, then you may not be the hunter, but the hunted.

This is the "soft" side of Six Sigma, but to underestimate its importance would be a gross error. Keep in mind that you are beginning a project that is meant to create a revolution in your organization. This is how you plan to take your firm to the next level; therefore, this is the new "next generation" design of your organization! We make this linkage intentionally to support the time and consideration needed for the soft side of Six Sigma.

We have all had the experience of working with a product or process that was not clearly thought out. How many times have you been reminded of sins of the past by problems of the present? Have you ever thought "If we'd only had more time" or "If we'd only spent the money up front." This is living out the old adage "There's never enough time to do it right, but there's always time to do it over."

From a Six Sigma standpoint, we know that the Pareto principle holds true on new product and process development efforts. In other words, 80 percent of the cost of the product is determined by the time the design is frozen. Think on that. The remainder of the life of the product or process, even with all the pressure from internal and external customers to reduce cost, can only yield 20 percent. If your breakthrough efforts call for 50 percent cost improvement, you are still only getting 10 percent of the original entitlement. In an environment with as much global competition as we have today, this just does not seem sensible. It is not a leap in logic to realize that this will not compete long term.

THE MOTIVATION

You are aware of the similarity between designing your "next generation" organization and product design. You understand the logic in the cost structure determination. You are concerned with global competition and believe Six Sigma is a competitive advantage. This is obvious by the fact that you have read this far. Hang in there. You must now become dissatisfied with the very thought that the money and time that you are about to invest in Six Sigma could yield results at 10 percent. This dissatisfaction must be great enough to drive you to action. Actually, in this case, it should drive you to inaction.

This may seem counterintuitive, but you should avoid the temptation to jump into Six Sigma and feast on some low-hanging fruit in order to think about the results and the next generation you are about to create. Remember, you will live with this. Anyone can leave an inheritance, but not everyone can leave a heritage. Some leaders have left big benefits to the bottom line during their tenure. Unfortunately, the drive for Six Sigma was *their* drive and limped along after the strength and determination of their personality left the organization.

Other leaders have built the foundation for success so well that the culture for Six Sigma is ingrained in the DNA of the organization. GE's success has outlived Jack Welch. In fact, you could not pry Six Sigma away from GE. What do you want to be a part of? What do you want to create? What is your personal impact on the foundation of the next generation?

Are we trying to motivate you? Well, yes. Why? Because just as the soft side is important for laying the foundation for long-term success of your Six Sigma efforts, it is imperative that you invest the time to get yourself on board personally. You are going to need this stoic commitment during the trying times that will come. If you believe in what you are doing, you can be a leader and a champion of change no matter where you are in the organization. Your personal commitment will prevail if it is solid. Make no mistake: it may prevail someplace else if you do not understand the culture and how to address it properly.

For this reason, you need an organizational motivational map of the cultural change process. This map simplified is the demonstrated linkage of individual efforts to the company strategy using the tools shown in the previous chapters. We will provide an example of how this all ties together in this chapter. For now, accept that all motivation boils down to a simple progression from awareness to understanding. Once understanding has begun, concern for the present state follows. This concern increases until one becomes dissatisfied with the current state. When this dissatisfaction becomes great enough within an individual, it creates the personally driven desire to take action. This is exactly how media commercials work; they take us through this mental model in thirty seconds. Your organizational model will take longer, but you get the idea.

Organizations invest many resources to reach their intended audience in a thirty-second commercial. They do this because they understand the benefits of investing in communication of their message. Have you ever wondered why drug companies and hospitals advertise? If you needed them, wouldn't you be seeking them out already and would you be looking at the TV? The point is this: Even if you have a great product, one that you know people need, you still have to "sell it." Therefore, you must certainly invest time to do research and plan how to reach your target audience. The dividends you realize will be directly related to how you market your Six Sigma effort.

Go back and look for the motivational steps we led you through in the paragraphs above on the organizational map of cultural change. Some companies teach this to their leaders as part of their efforts to create "one convert" at a time. They require their leaders to create a brief sales commercial in the form of an "elevator speech." In other words, when someone asks what you think about this new Six Sigma effort, your response must convey your sincere, passionate belief in the importance of the program as well as demonstrate the direct linkage to your individual efforts, all in the time it would take for an elevator to change floors — theoretically. This can only come after you have first convinced yourself.

How can you possibly know who is going to be asking the question? Good question! The answer is that you must invest the time to research. You must have a vivid image of how critical your personal commitment to Six Sigma is by seeing how it directly links to the success of the organizational goals. This, after all, translates into the success of your teams that make up the organization. GE uses this same type of model to accelerate its change efforts.

So how do you conduct this research? You can begin by asking some profound questions. The answers to these questions will provide guidance to determine your resolve. Questions to answer when defining the compelling purpose for pursuing Six Sigma are:

- What do people in your organization need to be aware of in order to begin to understand the business case of Six Sigma?
- What specific issues, if properly understood, would get people concerned with the current state?
- How can you link this directly to their personal position within the company so that they will be dissatisfied with the cost of doing nothing to the point where they are personally invested into action?

So, what is the answer to the question regarding how you will know who will be asking you the "elevator" questions? Don't worry about that. Instead, be concerned with identifying the core issues facing the organization. These are usually the "elephant-in-the-room"-type issues. In other words, these are the issues everyone knows have to be solved, but no one knows how, so they remain present but not talked about. It is similar to recognizing a chronic illness for which there is no permanent cure. Instead of giving up and feeling doomed, the organization must become motivated to defy the odds of failure in favor of success. The following is a good analogy for this process.

Consider that in order for an alcoholic to get help, the person must become aware of the fact that there is a problem. The person must understand that he or she does not currently possess the ability to solve the problem at hand. Next, the person must become concerned with this fact by recognition of the true personal costs, beyond financial, to the point where dissatisfaction drives action. Obviously, the solution involves a new approach.

Is your organization healthy? Does it have a problem that it does not want to face? How will the current actions impact the future health of your organization? Your dissatisfaction must be personal and strong enough that it is compelling to others by demonstrating the fact that you cannot be successful without their 100 percent commitment. The most successful companies recognize that they cannot afford the cancer of bad cells in their organizations. They align their beliefs with their actions, including rewards and recognition, or lack thereof, to the point that those who do not believe will leave.

Try being successful at GE without believing in Six Sigma; it simply will not happen. This is due to the fact that GE recognizes the importance of good organizational health in order to stimulate growth to the bottom line. You simply cannot afford to have people be successful in your organization without supporting your strategic initiatives. Complacency cannot be safe. Six Sigma must be the way you pursue your most important strategies for the future if you are to be successful. Anything less than this level of resolve is not the type of commitment that will relentlessly drive success.

You must convey the following message as a leader until the momentum of your investment drives you:

If I'd had more time, I would have written a shorter letter.

Time invested up front will make the message crisp and the direction clear and easy to follow, which will save time trying to convince newcomers later on. If you do not believe it is that important, do not pursue Six Sigma further. If you do, make it a priority to define the purpose and the compelling linkage from each person to the critical success factors. Key process input variables (KPIVs) are the causes that effect the key process output variables (KPOVs) in a product or process design. It is the same with the kickoff of this process. For these reasons, it is important to invest the time in careful consideration of what must be managed, what must be minimized, and what must be optimized to effect the desired change.

LAUNCHING SIX SIGMA

As mentioned in Chapter 6, implementing Six Sigma is similar to launching a new product. Here is some food for thought — test it: 80 percent of the cost of a new product is determined by the time the design is frozen. You can try your best to cut cost, improve yield, and smooth the customer issues, but at best you can address the remaining 20 percent. Before you think you have an exception to this rule, consider W. Edwards Deming's statement that the true costs are unknown and unknowable. That may sound like cheating or a cop-out, but if given serious consideration, it quickly becomes evident.

As part of teaching his popular method of designing experiments, Genichi Taguchi called losses generated as the product or process moved from the nominal value of its measured intent a "loss to society." What do you think Taguchi meant by this statement? Consider an example that may be familiar. How do you feel when you are extremely dissatisfied with the service in your favorite restaurant or when the flight you desperately need to leave on time is delayed? Do you take it all in stride and make the most of it? Maybe, but what if it happens repeatedly?

Think of the last time you were personally dissatisfied enough with a product or service that you made the conscious decision to never use it again. Did you inform the decision makers in the company that provided the product or service? If you are like most people, you were probably too busy or just did not take the time to notify the company, no matter how bad you felt. However, if you are like most people, you probably did talk about the incident. Studies show that people who are satisfied with a product or service may purposefully inform a couple of people about it. The danger lies with the other side of these types of studies. If you are dissatisfied, you are likely to tell up to thirteen people! Who do they tell? What is the cost of this form of advertisement for the company being discussed? Taguchi is right! Too many people wasted their time talking about the failure. Deming is also right. The company will never fully understand the true cost of the product or service in its state of inadequacy. Since these cost and customer issues cannot be fully understood, we must seek to avoid them as part of our strategy as well is in our daily work on projects.

INDIVIDUAL PROJECT MANAGEMENT

Once the pathway is clear and the critical success factors have been determined, efficient project management will be the momentum that drives the successful strategy using Six Sigma. Since there is no efficient way to do ineffective things, we must consider how to determine those things that are going to have the greatest effect on the strategic long-range plan. Some organizations would argue that this takes too long and that you should go for some low-hanging fruit in order to "live to fight another day." In other words, "I have to have some 'quick hits' in order to gain organizational buy in to sustain the effort." This may be true if you are tasked with implementing Six Sigma and you are not part of the executive leadership.

If you are part of the executive leadership, then your task is to define what critical success factors, KPIVs, will drive the desired results, KPOVs. This can be done through a cause and effect matrix or functional deployment matrix and strategy deployment chart discussed in the previous chapter. As a reminder, Figures 6.1 through 6.5 provide the key flows from strategic vision to project selection and alignment.

These tools provide a scientific method to model the business mathematically so that the critical few are separated from the trivial many. After using these tools, one should apply the common-sense "acid test" to verify that the input data were valid. The following is such a test. Think of the top ten things you "must" do. If eight are successful and two are failures, which two would still leave you knowing you failed? These are the critical-to-success initiatives. These are the projects that you must use Six Sigma teams to solve because you cannot get there by any other means. If you have the answers already, these are not Six Sigma projects; they are management tasks.

Leadership tasks involve defining the "Big Harry Audacious Goals" (BHAGs) mentioned in the books *Built to Last* and *Good to Great* by James Collins. The result of identifying these goals should be one of those "Aha!" moments that comes from realizing you do not know how to get there. In other words, current thinking created current problems and is therefore limited in its ability to solve them. These are the beginning of your Six Sigma projects. Your task as a leader is to champion the effort by helping to identify the critical-to-success projects using the function deployment matrix and then to define and review the scope of these projects regularly. This is done by using a tool such as a project charter. An example is shown in Figure 7.1.

The project charter links a Six Sigma team, including individual performance review and pay increases, to the strategic goals of the organization. Again, as we discovered in the previous chapter, the relationship between the strategic plan and the critical few "must do" projects must be clearly delineated using the strategy deployment matrix.

The Project Charter

The project charter defines the project champion: the senior staff member whose Management Incentive Bonus Plan (MIBP) is linked directly to the project. In addition, the critical problem statement is part of the project charter. This problem statement should include a direct linkage to the annual improvement priority and the strategic plan. In other words, anyone reviewing the project

Six Sigma Project Charter

Six Sigma Lead		Email	
Champion		Email	
Business Unit		Location	
Department		Charter Revision Date	

Checklist	Supporting Information (attachments)
1. Project Name	
2. Project Leader	
3. Project Description	
4. Team Members	
5. Schedule of Reviews	
6. Budget Information	
7. Critical Considerations	

8. Plan Phase Gate Reviews (update tools project status form for each review)	Date	Status
Define		
Measure		
Analyze		
Improve		
Control		

9. Constraints	
10. Boundaries	

11. Expected Benefits	Benefits require champion sign off	Baseline	Target
	Primary Metric		
	Secondary Metric		

Figure 7.1   Project charter example.

charter should be able to see the critical nature of this project within the strategy of the company.

The project champion is responsible for maintenance of the project charter, including the scope, method of measurement, and performance tracking. This means that the champion will ask the Six Sigma team to bring the charter in for a periodic review and to ensure that the project remains on track, that any issues are being addressed, and, in rare cases, to adjust the scope. Adjusting the scope is an indication that the up-front strategic planning did not accurately identify the correct limits of "must do" projects. Some companies absolutely refuse to adjust the goals or measures once they are set. The thinking here is to drive absolute resolve in goal attainment. Whether or not this rigidity will prove to have long-term success in the rapidly changing global environment remains to be seen.

Regardless, adjustment of the scope can only be done by the champion and therefore usually will not happen if there is a direct linkage back to the strategy as well as the champion's MIBP. By definition, the scope includes not only what is to be addressed but, just as importantly, what will not. Projects can easily get sidetracked as efforts become diluted when the scope has been poorly defined. While the Six Sigma team, under the leadership of a black belt, collectively has responsibility for the project and update of the charter, the champion has the authority to make the resource commitments as well as remove barriers in order to make the project a success.

The champion is responsible for ensuring good project timing by conducting weekly reviews, as well as helping to identify stage gate exit criteria for each of the DMAIC phases (Define, Measure, Analyze, Improve, Control). Further, the champion must have sufficient rank in order to provide the removal of barriers and allocation of resources.

The champion must personally act as mentor. In order to fulfill this role, as well as maintain accountability of the team assigned to the project, the champion must be able to understand the applicability of the various tools of Six Sigma. A good way for champions to be successful in their role is to go through the formal Six Sigma training such as green or black belt certification, including project completion. This also sends the right signal throughout the organization that Six Sigma is being driven from the top and that failure to comply is not an option. It also addresses the most common complaint: "I don't have time to do this in addition to my other work." This method must become the means by which decisions get made and work gets done.

ENSURING TOOL APPLICATION

As stated earlier, the project charter is the key document for the Six Sigma team to use in order to track the progress of their project and report to the leadership. This document acts as no less than a contract of commitment and should be viewed in this way. It should outline the scope of the project as well as identify the resources and support required from the supporting project champion for ultimate success. In turn, the champion also uses this contract to specify the agreed-upon deliverables as well as timing for the project. The project charter document will be the means of control and will manage the projects that are critical to success of the strategic plan.

Once these basic requirements are agreed upon, the Six Sigma team is empowered to pursue the goal of project completion. The instrument used to measure this level of detail is the project status form first introduced in the overview of the Six Sigma DMAIC process in Chapter 4. The success of Six Sigma will be directly proportional to the consideration that has gone into linking the project selection to the strategic direction of the organization. This is the method used to help ensure that the projects do not give way to "urgent" issues, otherwise known as firefighting. Even with careful consideration, it takes proper planning and determination of measurement structure to add to the probability of success for the projects involved with this approach. No matter the type of project, whether lean, value stream, kaizen, etc., the approach should be the same: Define, Measure, Analyze, Improve and Control.

The project status form is the tool to link the champion and the rest of the Six Sigma team to the real power of Six Sigma, the structure. This is the checklist to make sure that the proper tools have been applied in each phase to produce logical, statistically valid conclusions to that phase *before* moving on to the next phase. In a sense, it slows us to sanity. Beware of the "intuitive." In our experience, the experts who have this level of intuition are usually confounded by the facts based on data that interfere with their theoretical intuition.

Take time to review some of the detail in each of these phases. If you have gone through Six Sigma training, the "regimentation" of a project status form such as the one in Figure 7.2 seems second nature. If you have not gone through the training, it looks as complicated as first observing someone drive a vehicle with a manual transmission. In much the same way, all the steps become almost subconscious in terms of what has to happen next in order to progress to the desired end.

While reviewing the form, ask yourself a couple of questions. First, which problems are you facing that are truly new versus those that are repeats? Second, if you employed the scientific method outlined in Figure 7.2, based on valid data, would you still have the repeat problems? Obviously, the point is that the temptation to avoid such "regimentation" and skip to the "logical" or "intuitive" answer must be avoided during project management. This failure mode in project management is called slot machining. That is, trying one idea after another, hoping something works, but mostly resulting in wasted resources by confusing activity with accomplishment. Follow the map to success.

CHAPTER 7 TAKE AWAYS

■ Mentoring is personal. It is part of value-added leadership. Therefore, Six Sigma mentoring must begin with each person in a leadership role iden-

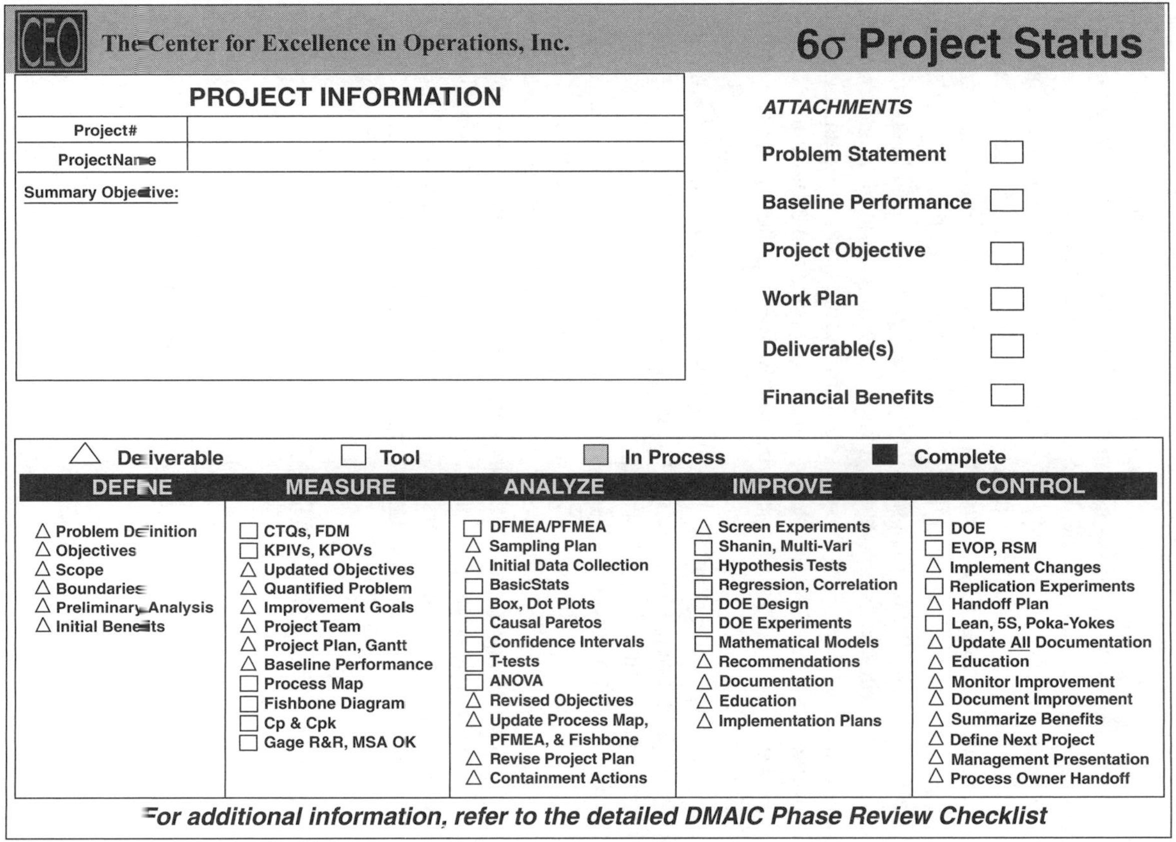

CEO | The Center for Excellence in Operations, Inc.

6σ Project Status

PROJECT INFORMATION

Project#

ProjectName

Summary Objective:

ATTACHMENTS

☐ Problem Statement

☐ Baseline Performance

☐ Project Objective

☐ Work Plan

☐ Deliverable(s)

☐ Financial Benefits

△ Deliverable   ☐ Tool   ☐ In Process   ■ Complete

DEFINE	MEASURE	ANALYZE	IMPROVE	CONTROL
△ Problem Definition	☐☐ CTQs, FDM	☐ DFMEA/PFMEA	△ Screen Experiments	☐☐ DOE
△ Objectives	☐☐ KPIVs, KPOVs	△ Sampling Plan	☐☐ Shanin, Multi-Vari	☐☐ EVOP, RSM
△ Scope	△ Updated Objectives	☐ Initial Data Collection	☐☐ Hypothesis Tests	△ Implement Changes
△ Boundaries	△ Quantified Problem	☐☐ BasicStats	☐☐ Regression, Correlation	☐☐ Replication Experiments
△ Preliminary Analysis	△ Improvement Goals	☐☐ Box, Dot Plots	☐☐ DOE Design	△ Handoff Plan
△ Initial Benefits	△ Project Team	☐☐ Causal Paretos	☐☐ DOE Experiments	△ Lean, 5S, Poka-Yokes
	△ Project Plan, Gantt	☐☐ Confidence Intervals	☐☐ Mathematical Models	△ Update All Documentation
	△ Baseline Performance	☐☐ T-tests	△ Recommendations	△ Education
	☐ Process Map	☐☐ ANOVA	△ Documentation	△ Monitor Improvement
	☐ Fishbone Diagram	△ Revised Objectives	△ Education	△ Document Improvement
	☐☐ Cp & Cpk	△ Update Process Map,	△ Implementation Plans	△ Summarize Benefits
	☐☐ Gage R&R, MSA OK	PFMEA, & Fishbone		△ Define Next Project
		△ Revise Project Plan		△ Management Presentation
		△ Containment Actions		△ Process Owner Handoff

For additional information, refer to the detailed DMAIC Phase Review Checklist

Figure 7.2 Six Sigma project tracker.

tifying the benefits to him or her personally of having ownership and commitment to the Six Sigma process.

■ Successful Six Sigma is directly proportional to personal commitment. High personal commitment means a higher probability of success with Six Sigma — *if* this personal commitment is shared by *all* leadership. It is not what is said, but what is done. How do you know? One method is to reflect on what questions are asked and what is measured, recognized, and rewarded. One quality manager refused a bonus based on a 50 percent reduction in parts per million defective. His logic was that he could easily achieve the goal by sacrificing the productivity, cost, and on-time delivery goals simply by sorting the product multiple times. That is personal commitment.

■ Investing the time to establish the linkage pays long-term dividends. People need to be able to see their personal contribution in order to sustain personal commitment. When a person has one of those days when everything "seems" to get worse, it helps give hope to be able to see that the critical-to-success area(s) still got better.

■ The executive tools must be used to demonstrate and "sell" the linkage between departmental and individual contribution and the overall strategy of the organization.

■ The project status form is used to ensure that the Six Sigma team follows the map to success by using the structured approach. The product status form must be employed to ensure the organization continues to walk the walk instead of talking the talk. Once people become fluent in the tools of Six Sigma, it becomes quite easy to spot someone who is talking instead of walking. Inappropriate tool use is the evidence. If the tools are used, the form becomes a mode to acknowledge the efforts of the team.

SUGGESTED FURTHER READING

Collins, James, *Good to Great,* HarperCollins, 2001.
Lowenthal, Jeffrey, *Six Sigma Project Management,* ASQ Press, 2001.
Pyzdek, Thomas, *The Six Sigma Project Planner,* McGraw-Hill, 2003.

8

SIX SIGMA BEGINS AND ENDS WITH PERFORMANCE MEASUREMENT

We could not possibly write a book on Six Sigma and leave out the topic of performance measurement. Executives fully understand how to gauge the enterprise's financial performance. They have a strategic plan and know what needs to be done. The financials provide periodic information about profitability, cash flow, return on investment, dividends and equity, asset utilization ratios, market value, revenue growth, margins, market penetration, and a host of other critical business metrics. Performance measurement is the needle and thread that sews strategy and execution together and turns the Six Sigma strategy into results. It enables organizations to achieve alignment and integration throughout the organization. More importantly, it allows people to measure the right things so everyone can tell if things are getting better. The all-too-familiar disconnects occur in the details of the organization because there is poor alignment at the operational level. We have observed celebrations for hitting a particular performance target that was totally meaningless, like variances or IL/DL ratios. Sure, the target was hit, but there is no clear rhyme or reason between the target and people's actions. Was it deliberate or was it an accounting adjustment? People do not set these disconnects up on purpose; they just happen because of a lack of understanding about the importance of measurement and alignment. Why? Because it is a lot more difficult than it looks on the surface.

Performance measurement is not only concerned with measuring the right metrics; it includes many levels and must be designed to link and align the organization and drive the right behaviors. It must create that hard-wired spiral between the organization's strategy and its daily improvement activities. Otherwise, initiatives tend to wander away from the original objectives. In this chapter, we will discuss some of the common performance measurement issues that relate to Six Sigma and strategic improvement. It is not our intent to write a measurement textbook because there are other references that cover this subject very well. Later in the chapter, we provide our detailed Six Sigma assessment process.

LEVELS OF PERFORMANCE MEASUREMENT

With a Six Sigma deployment, there are multiple levels of performance that we must address (Figure 8.1). First there is the Extended Enterprise level, where we focus on more aggregate critical-to-SIPOC (Supplier, Input, Process, Output, Customer) needs. At this level, we need to be concerned with the success of every player in the total value stream community. The second level is the Enterprise level, where we must maximize the value propositions of stakeholders, shareholders, and customers and focus on strategic services that build brand image and customer loyalty. At this level, we focus on critical-to-strategy (CTS) needs. Shareholder value, market share, growth, revenue from new products, and brand image are a few of the key measures of this level. The third level is the Business Process level, where we must focus on external and internal

LEVEL	CUSTOMER	MISSION
Extended Enterprise	The Total Value Stream Community	Maximize Total Value Stream Performance
Enterprise	Stakeholders, Shareholders	Maximize Enterprise Performance
Core Business Process	External Customers	Maximize Individual Customer Requirements
Operational/Event	Internal Customers	Maximize and Align Process Performance

Figure 8.1   Levels of performance measurement integration.

customer synchronization, flexibility, and quick response to existing product demand/supply issues. At this level, we focus on specific critical-to-quality (CTQ) requirements in every aspect of what we do as an organization. On-time delivery performance, target cost, warranty/returns, profitability, and customer satisfaction are a few key measures of this level. The fourth level is the Operational level, where the focus is primarily on internal process steps with attention to *next customer* requirements. At this level, we focus on critical-to-value-proposition (CTVP) requirements along specific steps in our processes. Cycle times, productivity, quality, cost, and other traditional cost accounting measures are part of this level. A successful Six Sigma deployment strives for performance measurement and alignment between each of these levels.

There are specific practices that best-in-class organizations follow to ensure alignment between the business strategy and the daily activities of improvement throughout the organization. They require time, effort, and the right information and require constant attention because the world changes quickly, organizations drift, and individuals oscillate around perceived expectations. First, we need to make sure that there is alignment between Six Sigma projects and the strategic plan so we avoid the common trap of motion in the absence of progress. Project selection is critical, and process characterization and measurement is the first step. Without baseline performance, we cannot determine with data and facts that our actions are improving the process. Results just do not happen; they just do not fall out of the sky after a lot of motion and activity. Results are the product of a deliberate, well-executed improvement process that focuses on eliminating root causes of poor performance, one project at a time. Second, we need to structure performance measurement in a manner that enables true enterprise performance and fosters the right behaviors at every level of the organization. A familiar saying about this topic is "Be careful what you measure, you might just get it." A final consideration is the right measurement. Sure, there are conflicts between traditional cost accounting practices and strategic improvement, but the key to success is moving beyond the debates and building connections. For example, metrics such as overhead absorption, variances, purchase price variances, and efficiency or utilization measures tend to drive organizations in a direction contradictory to what is important strategically. One approach is to point fingers, but a more proactive approach is to put the right performance measures in place with solid data and facts. In many cases, there is a direct correlation between financial performance and operational performance. You just need to find it and educate others. In one great Six Sigma project, a black belt candidate quantified the cause and effect relationships of inventory performance and their impact on days of supply. Most intelligent people are willing to reconsider and compromise their position when you show them the real data and facts behind a situation. Many of the traditional cost accounting measures are a *pay now or pay later* proposition. Balance is critical, and you will not get anywhere in business by calling your financial organization public enemy #1 or recommending that the organization throw out its cost accounting system or keep multiple sets of books. Rather than treat the financial resources in the organization as adversaries, get them deeply involved in kaizen, lean, and Six Sigma efforts, particularly in the project selection and baseline performance efforts. Validate operational improvements and any other financial or operational data that you can with these people. Try to relate collective Six Sigma activity to return on assets or return on capital. Financial organizations with Six Sigma expertise can provide useful inputs about strategic alignment and pegging operational performance to financial performance.

THE CRITICAL IMPLEMENTATION STAGES: PLAN-DEPLOY-EXECUTE

The remainder of this chapter provides the detailed Six Sigma Assessment Process. In Chapter 3, we discussed the Sixteen Requirements for Six Sigma Success. Figure 8.2 provides CEO's PLAN-DEPLOY-EXECUTE model of improvement and displays how these Sixteen Key Requirements for Six Sigma Success fit together.

The three stages in the model have overlapping paths and directions. In other words, it is not a discrete, sequential, left-to-right, or single-cycle model with an end. Organizations need to move continuously from stage to stage to sustain success and transform culture. If an organization is in the EXECUTE stage and

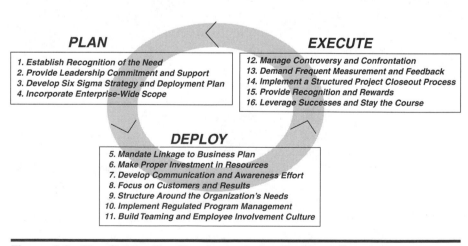

Figure 8.2 The Sixteen Key Requirements for Six Sigma Success.

is either having implementation difficulties or running out of steam, it needs to go back into the DEPLOY and PLAN stages to sustain momentum and then work its way back to the EXECUTE stage. This is the characteristic of the model that makes it interactive and continuous, as in continuous improvement. These cycles also enable the organization ultimately to transition from a Six Sigma program to culturally anchored, subconscious Six Sigma thinking.

Many executives are not happy with the results versus investments from their previous improvement initiatives. In fact, many are skeptical about Six Sigma based on previous experiences. The most frequently discussed reasons for previous improvement failures include lack of leadership, the wrong measures, and failure to communicate change, among others. However, a missing ingredient that is not discussed enough is the improvement strategy. Many organizations skip this step and jump right into applying the tools and techniques. They may not realize it, but they are viewing the tools and techniques as the *ends* rather than the *means*. As a result, there is no formal linkage between the customer, the company's business plan, the day-to-day improvement activities, and financial objectives. At best, many organizations see only symptomatic fixes (firefighting) versus prevention and elimination of root causes.

Plan

The most important stage of Six Sigma is the PLAN stage. This is the foundation of Six Sigma or any other strategic improvement initiative. It provides a working roadmap to focus on the most significant opportunities with limited resources. The PLAN stage does the up-front, deep-core drilling to the organization's key strategic and operations issues. The PLAN stage of the implementation panel includes:

- Benchmarking best-in-class performance
- Conducting a self-assessment to understand current performance
- Defining gaps between current and desired performance
- Developing a Six Sigma strategy and implementation approach
- Establishing the need for Six Sigma

The PLAN stage lays out the vision, goals, and all of the details on how to implement Six Sigma. The specific Six Sigma tools and methodologies are the enablers, determined only after an organization defines its specific requirements, actions, and barriers for improvement. The focus is on facts and results, not on random application of Six Sigma tools and techniques. Too many organizations jump right into black belt training and find themselves frantically looking for projects. We are no longer taking the *bag of tricks looking for a problem* approach. Rather, we are carefully sizing up key opportunities and then realizing those opportunities via deployment of the correct Six Sigma projects and methodologies.

The following is a quick snapshot of each of the elements of the **PLAN** stage:

- **Current Business Performance**
  - □ What is your current performance?
  - □ Have you characterized current performance with data and facts?
  - □ What are the key customer service issues?
  - □ What improvements have been made?
  - □ What is working well, what is okay, and what is severely "broken"?
  - □ Where are the most significant "pain points"?
- **Best-in-Class Performance**
  - □ How are you doing vis-à-vis your strongest competitors in the areas of profitability, cost, delivery, quality, flexibility, responsiveness, innovation, new products, customer intimacy, leadership, stakeholder development, and benchmark industry performance?
- **Gaps Between Current and Best-in-Class Performance**
  - □ Do you understand current performance?
  - □ Do you understand best-in-class performance?
  - □ Do you understand the gaps between current and best-in-class performance as they relate to business strategy, CTQ, leadership and culture, organization structure, key business processes, customer/supplier links, and customer satisfaction?
  - □ What needs to change?
- **Integrated Business Improvement Strategy**
  - □ What is your Six Sigma improvement strategy?
  - □ What are the priorities and plans for improvement?
  - □ How will the organization change and take care of day-to-day activities?
  - □ Do you have all the skill sets internally?
  - □ What do you expect to achieve and by when?
  - □ Is there a shared vision of change?
  - □ Are there any barriers to success?

The **PLAN** stage is critical to success because:

- Implementation of Six Sigma is based on quantified facts, not perceptions or opinions of what needs to change.

- The Six Sigma approach is integrated, focused, and addresses root causes of current performance. The methodology targets improvements in both "hard" and "soft" processes and both "inside" and "outside" of the bricks.
- The Six Sigma strategy and implementation plan is directly linked to gaps between current and desired performance, the business plan, and financial performance. Measurement is a critical element of implementation and results.
- The tools of change (e.g., Six Sigma, lean, kaizen, ERP, etc.) are determined after defining what needs to be done. These various techniques are the tools, the enablers of improvement. Six Sigma is powerful, but it does not apply to every improvement opportunity.
- The Six Sigma strategy includes a clear roadmap for change (e.g., the vision, improvement goals, implementation plan, expected deliverables and timetable, teaming and deployment plan, and education/skill set needs). It provides a communication vehicle to deliver a uniform message to the organization.
- The improvement opportunities and expected benefits are realistically calibrated and linked to financial performance.
- The barriers to success are identified and dealt with up front.

Developing a well-structured Six Sigma strategy may not seem like such a big deal, but this deliberate, up-front planning process is missing in about 80 percent of the companies we walk into that are pursuing Six Sigma, lean, kaizen, supply chain, ERP, new product development, and other strategic improvement initiatives. During one meeting, an anxious executive commented, "We don't need a plan. We already know what we need and we're moving ahead." Two years later, when his company had been in the red for months, this same executive said, "We're going to continue on our same track because we know it's the right thing to do." Sorry, but there *is* a big difference between motion and progress, activity and results. If you want tangible progress, measurable results, and permanent cultural improvement in your Six Sigma initiative, then do not skip the PLAN stage. And do not accept the plain vanilla, one-size-fits-all implementation approach. This advice makes a significant difference in your ultimate Six Sigma success.

Deploy

The second stage of our implementation model is the DEPLOY stage. The objective of DEPLOY is to translate the activities of our PLAN stage into initial actions and pilot successes. Sometimes there is some confusion between DE-PLOY and EXECUTE. Think of DEPLOY as the initial pilot successes and prove-outs, the winning over of the skeptics, and think of DEPLOY as a larger scale migration of activities through cultural transformation.

The DEPLOY stage of our implementation model includes both deployment and validation and typically includes the following activities:

- Formalizing the executive leadership/sponsorship, project management, and individual task teaming infrastructure.
- Developing and delivering Six Sigma education and training on the various methodologies, tools, and enabling technologies.
- Detailed implementation planning by project and at the task/responsibility/due date/deliverable level.
- Quick-strike containment actions. Remember, every improvement does not require a study or lengthy Six Sigma analysis. If the work area is a mess, clean it up. Do not do a Design of Experiments (DOE) on the operators so you can get your black belt. Wrong tool!
- Contingency planning (e.g., having the right people on the right teams, having a realistic plan and timetable, regulating activity and implementing change without disrupting day-to-day activities, etc.).
- Chunking, which means the "Pareto-izing" of opportunities (e.g., how to prevent boiling the ocean, solving world hunger, or setting up a Six Sigma team for failure). Chunking implies slicing off manageable pieces of improvement that a team can get its hands around and achieve quick successes.
- Retrofitting the Six Sigma practices, principles, methodologies, tools, and enabling technologies to the realities and unique requirements of the business.
- Quick Six Sigma successes, validation of initial improvements as real, linking of operational improvement to financial improvement.
- Internal selling, showcasing, and "show-me" efforts to the skeptics so it is no longer necessary to deal with the brainfog comments mentioned in Chapter 2.

Execute

The third and final stage of our implementation model is the EXECUTE stage. The objective of EXECUTE is to transform the Six Sigma activities of our PLAN and DEPLOY stages into broader migration opportunities and ultimately into subconscious everyday actions. Ideally, an organization would like a large critical mass of its organization to make improvements every day without even thinking about DMAIC (Define, Measure, Analyze, Improve, Control), a fishbone diagram or t-test, a DOE, or Multi-Vari chart. The essence of EXECUTE is transformation from a Six Sigma program to a way of life, thus institutionalizing the common Six Sigma language and approach to problem solving.

The EXECUTE stage of our implementation model includes implementation, measurement, and migration. This stage typically includes the following activities:

- Continuing to manage Six Sigma implementation efforts around focused hits that are directly related to the strategic plan. Over time, any improvement initiative becomes derailed without proper reinforcement and alignment.
- Establishing very structured Six Sigma review processes so that the right projects are selected and improvement efforts do not break down into just activity for activity's sake.
- Maintaining a formal project closeout process. Six Sigma projects go through DMAI, but C is the most important point where we implement improvements, turn things over to process owners, and put the money on the table.
- Holding periodic celebrations, awareness and communication activities, and reinforcement of the Six Sigma philosophy as the standard of daily conduct.
- Realignment of performance and rewards systems.

The remainder of this chapter will expand on this implementation model and provide a methodology for assessing Six Sigma performance.

THE SIX SIGMA ASSESSMENT PROCESS

The ultimate measure of Six Sigma or any other improvement initiative's success is financial performance. If there is not a measurable improvement in financial performance, we need to return to the drawing board and figure out what we can do differently with our Six Sigma deployment. Financial performance is an outcome. We cannot order improvements in financial performance with Six Sigma. However, we can deep dive into the potential root causes of our current performance and hopefully move our Six Sigma deployment toward a more positive direction. We have developed a Six Sigma Assessment Process based on our PLAN-DEPLOY-EXECUTE implementation model and the Sixteen Key Requirements for Six Sigma Success. The remainder of this chapter provides this assessment process.

THE SIX SIGMA ASSESSMENT PROCESS

PLAN	0	2	4	6	8	10	Actions Required	Responsibility
1. Establish Recognition of the Need								
The organization understands CTSIPOC, CTS, CTQ, CTVP, and gaps between current and desired performance								
The strategic plan addresses mandatory improvement expectations								
The executive leadership team has developed a clear vision for improvement								
Executives understand how to deploy Six Sigma as an enabler of improvement								
The competitive landscape and consequences of not changing are well understood and ready to be communicated to the organization								
Subtotal								
2. Provide Leadership Commitment and Support								
The executive team is passionate and has an unwavering commitment about implementing Six Sigma; the executive team is in it for the long term								
The executive team has articulated clearly the organization's challenges, improvement goals, and how Six Sigma will enable success								

THE SIX SIGMA ASSESSMENT PROCESS (continued)

PLAN	0	2	4	6	8	10	Actions Required	Responsibility
The Six Sigma improvement vision has been communicated and embraced by the entire organization								
Senior management has a clear vision of Six Sigma and can reinforce the strategy verbatim to others in the organization								
The barriers to improvement are identified and addressed promptly								
Subtotal								
3. Develop Six Sigma Strategy and Deployment Plan								
The organization has developed a formal Six Sigma strategy and implementation approach								
The executive team has established an implementation infrastructure (e.g., steering group, Six Sigma core team, etc.)								
The Six Sigma strategy presents goals and objectives that are aligned to the business plan, financial plan, and competitive needs								
The improvement goals are concise, targeted, quantified, baselined, and physically measurable								

THE SIX SIGMA ASSESSMENT PROCESS (continued)

PLAN	0	2	4	6	8	10	Actions Required	Responsibility
The Six Sigma strategy is not "top-down," but tailored to the organization's specific needs to ensure a quick return on investment								
Subtotal								
4. Incorporate Enterprise-Wide Scope								
The organization views Six Sigma as an enterprise-wide enabler of improvement, not a manufacturing quality effort								
The improvement goals encompass the entire organization (e.g., manufacturing, engineering, product development, sales, finance, supply chain, etc.)								
The improvement goals include selected joint projects between the organization and its customers and suppliers								
Beyond the Six Sigma black and green belts, the organization has included process owners, project sponsors, and candidate managers in the deployment effort								
The executive leadership team has established expectations of Six Sigma and manages cross-functional issues and resource constraints								
Subtotal								

THE SIX SIGMA ASSESSMENT PROCESS (continued)

DEPLOY	0	2	4	6	8	10	Actions Required	Responsibility
5. Mandate Linkage to Business Plan								
There is a formal project prioritization and selection process to evaluate, prioritize, align, and launch the highest impact opportunities								
The project selection process evaluates benefits, risks, time, resource requirements, and likelihood of success								
There is a formal process to align all Six Sigma activities to the business plan								
Projects are qualified by preliminary analysis prior to assignment and broken into manageable implementation "chunks"								
There is a formal process to prevent resource overload and total organizational involvement								
Subtotal								
6. Make Proper Investment in Resources								
The executive leadership team has made it clear to the organization that they will allocate resources to support Six Sigma deployment								
Six Sigma black belt/green belt candidates are allowed the time for education and completion of their mandatory projects								

THE SIX SIGMA ASSESSMENT PROCESS (continued)

DEPLOY	0	2	4	6	8	10	Actions Required	Responsibility
Education includes a well-thought-out approach to develop a critical mass of resources at various technical levels (e.g., black belts, green belts, and yellow belts across the total organization)								
Education includes the entire spectrum of executive, middle management, supervisory, and hourly employees								
A significant percentage of the employee population has been developed into deployable Six Sigma resources so that there is a "bench" of organizational talent								
Subtotal								
7. Develop Communication and Awareness Effort								
There is a formal Six Sigma communication plan for building awareness, reporting on current progress, and keeping the need to change in front of people								
The organization is fully aware of the need to change and people understand and accept their roles in the change process								
The executive leadership team leads by example and encourages everyone to become involved in Six Sigma								
The communication plan sets down the expectations for the right enabling behaviors and standards of conduct								

THE SIX SIGMA ASSESSMENT PROCESS (continued)

DEPLOY	0	2	4	6	8	10	Actions Required	Responsibility
The organization encourages multidirectional communication (top down, bottom up, horizontal, and lateral) throughout the organization								
Subtotal								
8. Focus on Customers and Results								
All Six Sigma projects begin with a clear problem statement that includes current performance versus internal/external customer requirements								
Every project initially focuses on defining the objectives, scope, baseline performance, improvement goal, and dollarized anticipated benefits								
The organization continuously quantifies and updates CTSIPOC, CTS, CTQ, and CTVP and understands the gaps between current performance and these requirements								
Six Sigma projects incorporate financial validation in the DMAIC process and use financial resources to help peg operational performance to financial performance								
The executive leadership team has established, and everything begins and ends with, a financial performance mind-set								
Subtotal								

THE SIX SIGMA ASSESSMENT PROCESS (continued)

DEPLOY	0	2	4	6	8	10	Actions Required	Responsibility
9. Structure Around the Organization's Needs								
The Six Sigma strategy and implementation plan is custom tailored to fit the organization's specific needs								
The Six Sigma strategy and deployment has been retrofitted to the particular uniqueness of the organization, its markets, and industry characteristics								
The Six Sigma deployment is generating significant benefits, although it does not emulate a traditional top-down textbook deployment								
Six Sigma education plans and candidate selection occur after the strategy and project selection process								
Black, green, and yellow belt education has been modified to include company-specific applications and examples								
Subtotal								
10. Implement Regulated Program Management								
The executive leadership team regulates how many Six Sigma, lean, kaizen, or other improvement activities are in progress at any given time								
Six Sigma projects have regularly scheduled reviews with sponsors, managers, and process owners								

THE SIX SIGMA ASSESSMENT PROCESS (continued)

DEPLOY	0	2	4	6	8	10	Actions Required	Responsibility
Six Sigma projects and team leaders use a structured project management process to define tasks, responsibilities, timelines, and deliverables								
There is a formal cross-check between projects and resources to prevent individual involvement on multiple teams and using the same go-to resources								
Six Sigma is deliberately managed as an enabler of strategic improvement versus allowing Six Sigma to take on a life of its own								
Subtotal								
11. Build a Teaming and Employee Involvement Culture								
Employees embrace cross-functional teaming as the organizational norm and it is also considered a normal responsibility of everyone's job								
The organization provides formal education on basic teaming skills, facilitation, group dynamics, conflict resolution, and meeting discipline								
Teams complete projects and are unplugged or redeployed on other teams (versus teams that stay together for long periods of time)								

THE SIX SIGMA ASSESSMENT PROCESS (continued)

DEPLOY	0	2	4	6	8	10	Actions Required	Responsibility
Individuals on teams are empowered to make decisions and improvements because they are totally supported by the executive leadership team								
The organization encourages risk taking, entrepreneurial thinking, and out-of-the-box approaches to improvement								
Subtotal								

EXECUTE	0	2	4	6	8	10	Actions Required	Responsibility
12. Manage Controversy and Confrontation								
Potential issues and barriers to change are proactively identified and evaluated in terms of potential responses								
Executives send a clear, frequent, and consistent message that "You're either part of the solution or part of the problem"								
Executives have identified the expectations for behavior, values, and professional standards of conduct								
The leadership approach promotes a positive, mentoring style; however, it also deals with and removes barriers to change								

THE SIX SIGMA ASSESSMENT PROCESS (continued)

EXECUTE	0	2	4	6	8	10	Actions Required	Responsibility
The organization endorses the way that senior leadership handles controversy and confrontation honestly, up front, and by example								
Subtotal								
13. Demand Frequent Measurement and Feedback								
There is a balanced scorecard approach to measuring Six Sigma performance, one project at a time and at a more aggregate, continuous level								
There is a formal process to link project, operational, and financial performance; all projects go through a validation process before initiation and after completion								
Improvement goals are part of the individual's performance and education/professional development plan								
Individual Six Sigma teams are required to provide frequent updates of their progress and the sense of urgency is reinforced by this review practice								
Measurement data are visible and directly linked to the organization's business plan and Six Sigma strategy; there is a clear understanding about how all projects correlate to these plans								
Subtotal								

THE SIX SIGMA ASSESSMENT PROCESS (continued)

EXECUTE	0	2	4	6	8	10	Actions Required	Responsibility
14. Implement a Structured Project Closeout Process								
For every project, each phase of DMAIC includes a formal review and sign-off by a black belt and/or core Six Sigma project team								
There is a formal project completion process to ensure correct process owner handoffs and to create a sustaining capability with the improved process								
The project completion process ensures that all "C" activities of DMAIC have been met, particularly implementation and the achievement of results								
Project completion includes a financial validation step to determine if a team should remain intact or dismantle because the goals/maximum benefits have been reached								
Project completion includes adding all project information into a project repository for use by future lean/Six Sigma teams or others in the organization								
Subtotal								

THE SIX SIGMA ASSESSMENT PROCESS (continued)

EXECUTE	0	2	4	6	8	10	Actions Required	Responsibility
15. Provide Recognition and Rewards								
Recognition and rewards are viewed as both a means of reinforcing desired organizational behaviors and a celebratory event for individuals who champion change via Six Sigma								
A formal awareness process includes recognition of star performers (on a company communication board or video board)								
Recognition follows performance and meaningless "up-front" recognition items (e.g., coffee mugs, T-shirts, etc.) are avoided								
Recognition and rewards set employees apart based on their contributions								
Recognition and rewards include some financial element beyond just recognition for superior performance (e.g., gainsharing, stock options, gift certificates, etc.)								
Subtotal								

THE SIX SIGMA ASSESSMENT PROCESS (continued)

EXECUTE	0	2	4	6	8	10	Actions Required	Responsibility
16. Leverage Successes and Stay the Course								
Six Sigma successes are highly publicized and used as an interest-generating and recruiting tool for others in the organization (e.g., project fairs, regularly scheduled information and knowledge exchanges, etc.)								
The organization provides professional development opportunities for its people so they are equipped with the right tools and skills for change								
The steering group leverages the benefits of every Six Sigma project across the entire organization (e.g., multiplant opportunities)								
There is a constant monitoring of integration opportunities (i.e., kaizen, lean, Six Sigma, IT, etc.) to ensure that the right approaches are applied to the highest impact opportunities								
The steering group keeps expectations high, celebrations short, and sends a repeating message to the organization that it can do even better								
Subtotal								

CHAPTER 8 TAKE-AWAYS

- Performance measurement is the needle and thread that sews strategy and execution together and turns the Six Sigma strategy into results. It enables organizations to achieve alignment and integration throughout the organization. More importantly, it allows people to measure the right things so everyone can tell if things are getting better.
- Performance measurement is not only concerned with measuring the right metrics; it includes many levels and must be designed to link and align the organization and drive the right behaviors. It must create that hard-wired spiral between the organization's strategy and its daily improvement activities. Otherwise, initiatives tend to wander away from the original objectives.
- Rather than treating the financial resources in the organization as adversaries, get them deeply involved in kaizen, lean, and Six Sigma efforts, particularly in the project selection and baseline performance efforts. Validate operational improvements and any other financial or operational data that you can with these people. Try to relate collective Six Sigma activity to return on assets or return on capital. Financial organizations with Six Sigma expertise can provide useful inputs about strategic alignment and pegging operational performance to financial performance.

SUGGESTED FURTHER READING

Kaplan, Robert and Norton, David, *The Balanced Scorecard: Translating Strategy into Action*, Harvard Business School Press, 1996.

9

INTEGRATING LEAN/SIX SIGMA AND MORE

We have covered a lot of ground about Six Sigma and alternative deployment strategies for smaller and mid-sized organizations. However, it is important to realize that Six Sigma is not the cure-all and end-all for every organizational challenge. It is merely a methodology and set of comprehensive tools for certain types of improvement opportunities, particularly for more complex processes where there are many unknowns about the details. Many of the basic Six Sigma tools and Minitab analyses are not only applicable to other improvement initiatives like kaizen and lean, but they can actually increase implementation robustness and financial results. We have found the DMAIC (Define, Measure, Analyze, Improve, Control) thoughtware to be very useful in providing a single, structured, problem-solving approach for all of these improvement initiatives. DMAIC prevents the confusion caused by feeding people six different versions of the same thing because it is presented as a common, structured, problem-solving methodology. This uniform approach to business improvement presents Six Sigma as another drawer of tools in the DMAIC tool chest. Keep in mind that there are other drawers of improvement tools (e.g., kaizen, lean, reengineering, enterprise resource planning (ERP), enabling IT applications such as supply chain management [SCM], customer relationship management [CRM], product life cycle management [PLM], etc.) that may or may not serve you better than Six Sigma in certain situations. Put these tools together and apply them correctly, and your organization will achieve breakthroughs in

163

operational and financial performance. Use them incorrectly and you will end up with window dressing improvements.

The major message of this chapter is that no single improvement methodology or set of tools will make an organization world class. The largest opportunities are derived from understanding and integrating all of the tools available — teaming and soft skills development, kaizen, lean, Six Sigma, ERP, and enabling IT — into a unified, lasting powerhouse improvement initiative.

CONSISTENCY OF INTEGRATION

As we have mentioned several times, many organizations have consumed a lot of time flitting from buzzword program to buzzword program. Blindly following a guru's latest buzzword fad reduces an organization's creativity to a rigid set of commoditized improvement actions. We visited one organization that was very anti–Six Sigma as a result of being conned into believing that kaizen and lean are much faster than Six Sigma for improving quality problems in its complex welding lines. Not surprisingly, the consulting firm the organization had hired provided just lean services. The outcome: a lot of fast motion and promises, but no results! Wrong problem definition and wrong tools equals wrong results. Ultimately this kind of advice creates a tremendous amount of confusion as the organization moves from fad to fad, and it also destroys leadership credibility when these "flavor-of-the-month" programs fail. When you walk into an organization that is antichange, leadership usually has a lot to do with it. We have visited many organizations that did total quality management in 1994, reengineering from 1995 to 1997, ERP from 1999 to 2000, lean from 2001 to 2002, and Six Sigma in 2003 and have failed miserably at all of these efforts. What is the appetite for another improvement program for these organizations? The larger challenge is getting organizations like this to change once they have been through the disappointing spin zone of improvement programs. These organizations must step out of their *paintball and smorgasbord* approaches and learn quickly how to benefit from improvement before they become victims of their competitors' improvements.

Consistency of the message and focus are important; that is why the "flavor-of-the-month" programs fail. Consistency avoids feeding people fifty different versions of the same thing and confusing them. Unfortunately, this is the current situation for many organizations that have dabbled in business improvement programs. Management is often impatient when it comes to improvement, and there is a tendency to launch more activity than the organization can physically digest and apply. The employees become totally distracted and confused as another glossary of buzzword terms is introduced. Consistency and focus lay down the right set of priorities, expectations, and thought processes to drive the right actions. Consistency of the message must be followed by consistency in actions and behaviors; otherwise people will become very cynical if they *hear* one message but *observe* a different action. Organizations must adopt the philosophy that they only have one chance to get these things right, and then pour in the leadership, commitment, improvement infrastructure, and measurements to ensure success. With the right unwavering leadership, strategy, and successful execution, we can make changes at clockwork speed because we have the methodologies and IT enabling technologies. Those organizations that do this right will make giant-step improvements before their competitors know what hit them.

THE DIMENSIONS OF LEAN/SIX SIGMA INTEGRATION

Integration is a critical factor in maximizing business improvement results. Figure 9.1 displays this graphically. First, organizations must expand their focus *vertically* and get beyond the production operations. We have beat the shop floor to death with previous quality improvement programs and that is not where the large opportunities exist. In many cases, manufacturing groups are ahead of the improvement power curve, and we can learn several good lessons

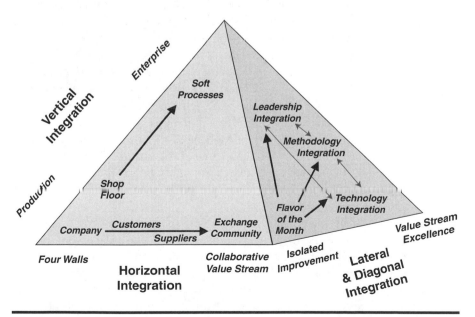

Figure 9.1 Total business integration.

from their experiences. The largest opportunities in most organizations now lie in the transactional process areas. Many of these transactional processes are untouched territory and ripe for improvement, and organizations can make dramatic improvements rapidly. Opportunities in the warranty/returns, invoicing, quotations, customer service, purchasing, sales and marketing, new product development, and human resource areas are in the millions of dollars. Over the past few years, we have seen the scope of our lean and Six Sigma projects grow to over 50 percent transactional process content. Organizations can get at these opportunities by applying many of the improvement methodologies familiar to their manufacturing groups, such as structured quick-strike kaizen events, lean assessments (e.g., value stream mapping and waste elimination, cycle time reduction, simplification and standardization, flow synchronization, basic quality improvement, etc.), and Six Sigma for situations that have more complex process variation. We will discuss this particular topic in more detail later in this chapter.

Migrating into the transactional process areas requires strong leadership with a consistent message about improvement. In too many organizations, it is easy to point fingers at the manufacturing group and take the status quo or automation route in the transactional process areas. It is easy to blame the ERP monster when business processes fail, but the reality is that improvement is 95 percent process and 5 percent system. One of the most rewarding experiences is watching people conduct Six Sigma projects in their backyard. The education changes their perspective, but they are required to deep dive into causals and follow the methodology. They discover that *the problem is me,* and then they make the necessary changes and *live* the improvements. Humbling experiences turn transactional process employees around, and they are much more effective than lectures and improvement edicts. The best way to develop change agents is by encouragement and letting people discover their own "Eureka!" moments.

To gain the full benefits of Six Sigma, we need to get everyone in the organization thinking about process improvement, root cause analysis, and solving problems. We discussed many of these areas and examples of tremendous benefits in Chapter 5. People's employee status may be exempt, but no one is exempt from business improvement. Everyone in the organization is part of one or many processes that include unexplainable variation and that can be dissected and improved. As we mentioned earlier, think *root causes* for the issues in manufacturing because the majority of root causes in the production area are "hidden factory" defects in the transactional processes. Take a hard look at these transactional process areas and their potential impact on the enterprise's *cash-to-cash* position, design or delivery performance, life cycle costs, and customer satisfaction. Process improvement, simplification, and defect reduction in the transactional areas also have a positive residual impact on the IT world. If you are willing to step back and look at your transactional areas objectively, you will see many wasteful situations, along with many attempts to automate and support ineffective processes. Enough said; we must move beyond the production floor to the high-impact transactional process areas. We need to go *vertical* with our Six Sigma efforts.

Another aspect of integration involves transforming our Six Sigma thinking *horizontally* beyond the four walls to the total value stream. The opportunities beyond the four walls are enormous because 70 to 95 percent of the customer-impacted activities, cycle times, and costs is generated in these segments of the supply chain. The benefits of instantaneous demand and supply adjustment, business collaboration, and information exchange are pretty obvious. Part of this horizontal integration includes building the value stream community. This may also include looking again at core competencies and deciding to outsource activities or keep them in-house. It may include rationalization of product offerings, customer satisfaction performance, new product development, supplier management, manufacturing locations, distribution/logistics redesign, third-party service providers, aggregate load balancing, and the like. These activities are focused on simplifying link paths in the total value stream to facilitate speed and collaboration. Some people are referring to these efforts as spiral or fractal collaboration structures. The most challenging effort in this stage is connecting the links electronically to facilitate collaboration and instantaneous upstream/downstream activities. This is where the focus on ERP, SCM, PLM, SRM (supplier relationship management), networks exchanges and portals, and other enabling technology comes into play. Keep all of the methodologies and tools in mind as you seek improvements to these transactional processes. Applying kaizen, lean, or Six Sigma may provide various levels of improvement, but obliterating the process via automation might remove the need to apply these other improvement tools. Keep the options open and always strive to select the best option. The bottom line here is that we need to step outside of the four walls, focus our Six Sigma efforts *horizontally*, integrate Six Sigma with other appropriate methodologies and tools, and harvest these new opportunities across the total value stream.

The other focus of Six Sigma is *lateral* and *diagonal* integration. This includes success through empowered people and teams, through soft problem-solving skills development, through creative leadership and cultural transformation, and through the integration of Six Sigma with kaizen, lean, ERP, and other enabling technologies. The total value stream encompasses the full spectrum of process opportunities. Lateral and diagonal integration broadens our toolbox and our knowledge about applying the right tools to the right situations. It helps us to move away from our preoccupation with the methodologies and tools themselves and focus on solving critical business problems. Lateral and diagonal integration also replaces functional silos and rigid chains of command with person-to-person knowledge networks.

We need to let go of our old binary choice practices about improvement because it is not a matter of kaizen *or* lean *or* Six Sigma. We need to expand our business toolbox because the total value stream includes the full array of problems and opportunities. Like your toolbox at home, you are very limited with just a hammer, a wrench, and a few screwdrivers. Pretty soon every problem starts to look like a nail or a screw. We need to stop the debates about kaizen, lean, Six Sigma, ERP, SCM, CRM, PLM, and other improvement enablers and recognize that they all have their place in total enterprise improvement. The methodologies and tools are not magic mantras; they are simply *tools of the trade* that work well when integrated and deployed correctly and to the right opportunities. We need to provide new injections of skills so that people understand how all of the improvement methodologies fit together. We need to focus on integrating processes, people, and information across the total value stream. We need to stay with a common, organizational approach for analyzing and solving business problems, and the DMAIC methodology provides a uniform problem-solving structure. Finally, we need to close the loop with real-time performance measurement. Everything begins and ends with performance measurement. This is what *lateral* and *diagonal* integration is all about.

INTEGRATION OF IMPROVEMENT METHODOLOGIES

In the Enterprise, the Extended Enterprise, and in the realities of business improvement in general, there is a continuum of problems. If we blindfold ourselves and randomly select touchpoints in the total value stream (i.e., the production floor, purchasing, customer service, sales and marketing, finance, engineering, IT, suppliers, customers, logistics, third-party distributors, etc.), this continuum of issues is a reality. In our experience, the improvement objective and the complexity of execution are the two major drivers of which tools to apply to the improvement opportunity. Figure 9.2 displays this graphically.

Organizations that attempt to implement all of these methodologies at the same time often end up with an alphabet soup of short-lived improvements. Many organizations begin with basic improvement activities in the kaizen and lean areas, and this approach is very effective in getting at the organization's low-hanging fruit. Eventually, the organization must go after fruit further up the tree with more comprehensive improvement tools, and that is where Six Sigma works best. This is not necessarily the rule of thumb for your organization. We visited a company that had spent a year on kaizen blitzes and was puzzled about why it could not make any headway in its complex welding lines. The company

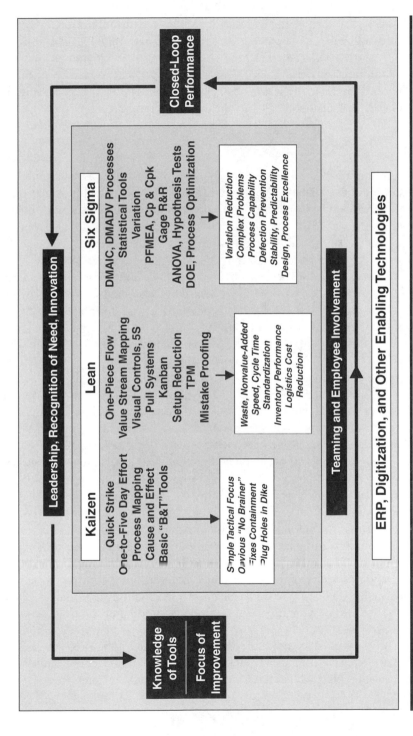

Figure 9.2 Integrating methodologies, tools, and enabling technologies.

was deploying the wrong improvements. Many organizations recognize the complexities of their operations and the need for new thinking and new approaches right up front. They make the commitment to Six Sigma and achieve new breakthroughs in performance. The most important point here is that it takes organizations years to become competent at integrating and deploying the right improvement methodologies to the right opportunities.

Kaizen

On the left side of this continuum are the *no-brainer* improvement situations that require little to no analysis to resolve. Many of these may not even require a team. Some require just action: "We know what needs to be done, so let's lock ourselves away for a few hours or a day and get it done." The roots of kaizen are derived from the Japanese word *kai,* meaning "to take apart," and *zen,* meaning "to make good." Kaizen is the gradual, incremental, and continual "improvement" of activities so as to create more value and less nonvalue-adding waste. Kaizen should be used as a process that is applied to achieve event-specific continuous improvement that is focused across several levels of the organization. Thus, the process of kaizen events is used as a basis for application of lean and Six Sigma activities such as setup reduction, 5S, daily corrective action activities, Design of Experiments, one-piece flow, visuals controls, housekeeping, and other lean tools. Kaizen is a low-cost, common-sense approach of incremental improvement and is a low-risk approach for value stream improvements. Kaizen is about going after the obvious low-hanging fruit or the fruit on the ground. Within the soft process areas and support activities, there is enormous potential for improvement with the simple kaizen approach. In many cases, this is the first structured "look-see" at these business processes.

Another good example of kaizen is housekeeping and the general physical organization and appearance of a work area. Kaizen-like events and the 5S principles (sort, straighten, scrub, systematize, standardize) are the best tools of choice. Sometimes the answer is not so obvious and may require further analysis. While we may still be in the realm of quick-strike improvement, the basic blocking and tackling tools (e.g., Pareto analysis, checksheeting and charting, fishbone diagrams, spreadsheet analysis, etc.) are best suited for these structured problem-solving situations. A solid kaizen effort should also be data and fact driven, and the use of Minitab and these tools should be encouraged. In summary, kaizen is best suited to *quick-strike opportunities* and *quick containment measures* in a process. In our experience, many Six Sigma projects identify dozens of these "make-it-happen" quick fixes. Granted, it may not be the optimal solution, but the situation is incrementally better than we found it.

Lean

As we continue across this continuum, we move into the realm of lean. Lean includes tools such as 5S, visual management, value stream mapping, work cells, kanban and pull systems, quick changeover, total preventive maintenance, and the like. Lean tools are best suited for projects seeking to simplify and standardize processes, compress cycle times, eliminate unnecessary process steps or waste, or synchronize individual processes into a more continuous flow. The driving force for waste elimination is based on the Five Basic Principles of lean:

1. Accurately **specify value** from the customer's perspective for both products and services
2. Identify the **value stream** for products and services and remove nonvalue-adding waste along the value stream
3. Make the product and services **flow** without interruption across the value stream
4. Authorize production of products and services based on the **pull** by the customer
5. Strive for **perfection** by constantly removing layers of waste (e.g., overproduction, waiting, transportation, processing, inventory, motion, defects, and human potential)

These principles are fundamental to the elimination of waste and must be embraced across all functions within the organization and also applied up and down the value chain by suppliers and customers. It is important to get the entire organization focused on understanding the value streams so that waste can be identified and eliminated from them. Many lean efforts are more *compensating improvements* in practice because people use the lean tools in a way that compensates for deep-rooted process variation. Techniques such as kanban, buffer inventories, and scheduling practices definitely improve flow, but we can get even better if we understand the system constraints and drive toward perfection.

Again, lean improvements are best when they are data and fact driven. We have used many of the Six Sigma tools and Minitab for simulating kanbans and pull system capabilities, balancing and realigning stations in work cells, analyzing downtime, machine setups and standardization, and the like.

Six Sigma

On the right side, we discover situations that are totally unexplainable — processes that contain very complex variation. Why does the molding machine produce scrap? What are the factors that contribute to excess/obsolete inventory or warranty and returns? Why is there so much unplanned maintenance? Why is there so much variation in productivity and quality across fifty operators running the same equipment? Why does every operator change tools and reset equipment at the beginning of each shift? How can we improve the manufacturability and reliability of new products? What practices have the greatest impact on cash position? Six Sigma is a more *perfection-driven improvement* because we make the effort with data and facts to understand and reduce/eliminate complex process variation. Six Sigma drives processes to a new level of performance and capability. These are more complex problems that lend themselves to the Six Sigma methodology and tools. Hopefully, this book has provided a more comprehensive guide on the when's and how-to's of Six Sigma.

Beyond Lean/Six Sigma

Information technology such as ERP, SCM, CRM, SRM, PLM, networks and portals, and all of the other enabling technologies also plays a critical role in this improvement continuum. These are referred to as *instantaneous improvements* because we can often eliminate or replace a bad process with a real-time process. We need accurate information to solve any kind of problem in the continuum. More importantly, we need accurate real-time information to prevent problems from occurring in the first place. Some may argue that ERP and other enabling technologies are also tools to improve processes. In some earlier implementations, these technologies forced a discipline on organizations that was previously missing. In other cases, they added complexity and confusion, particularly when the organization began with bad processes and practices, and there was a lack of both business process education and application user education. One of the problems with many ERP implementations was the compression of education. In the interests of budgets and schedules, we rounded people up and gave them the abbreviated user manuals and the ERP crash course, and then we told them to go out and do great things. Many people understandably forgot what they learned almost immediately and began pushing buttons without understanding the implications up and down the total value stream. Others are still searching for the functionality or module that enables lean/Six Sigma and many other things they are trying to do. Implementation time and budgets are certainly reasonable constraints, and we must learn how to improve and operate within these constraints. If the constraints are unreasonable, we must change them or pay the consequences.

In summary, integration of the various improvement methodologies and tools is critical to success. Although organizations cannot pursue everything at the same time, they need to keep developing their improvement skills and making more and more progress. Organizations will never see *best in class* with a single "flavor-of-the-month" improvement program. You cannot blitz yourself there in the next two to three months. You cannot get there with the "back-to-basics" of lean or 5S and kanban. You cannot get there solely with complex statistical tools, and you certainly cannot get there by relying on IT. But you can get there with all of the above, deployed deliberately and correctly to the right value stream opportunities. *All* means a solid strategy of improvement, unwavering and relentless leadership, and integration of *all* the improvement methodologies and enabling technologies discussed in this section.

MISSION-CRITICAL SIX SIGMA EDUCATION

The need for education and knowledge development is obvious. Without education, knowledge, and new skills, people and organizations cannot develop the core competency of strategic improvement. People in the organization need various levels of education to support a strategic improvement effort. They need to understand the need to change, the strategy of change, and their roles in the process. They need to understand and feel the organization's challenges and the consequences of doing nothing. They need a uniform deployment and implementation approach. We have already discussed how confusing it can be when people are flying different banners of improvement. Without the right investment in education and skills development, we end up with the *same people, same process, same thinking = same results* syndrome.

Another enabler of success with small and mid-sized organizations is in how the education is designed and delivered. Personally, we see too much infatuation with Six Sigma belts and status and not enough attention on Six Sigma results. Small and mid-sized organizations simply cannot afford the investment in time and capital to implement Six Sigma using the traditional top-down model. The Scaleable Six Sigma™ model also addresses how to develop and educate these organizations in a practical manner. The organization first identifies the strategic improvement infrastructure where education follows the improvement strategy, implementation plan, definition of specific projects, and identification of opportunities. Next the Six Sigma education is customized around the organization's specific operations issues, opportunities, and implementation constraints. The education includes the Six Sigma strategy and mission-critical opportunities that we need to improve. This strategy is the major determinant of Six Sigma requirements. Rather than calculating the number of black and green belts needed based on some fictitious standard without knowing anything about the organization, the requirements are based on the individual organization's needs and operating constraints. How about that for a novel idea! Although the Six Sigma education covers all of the areas that make it a Motorola-, GE-, or Caterpillar-equivalent program, the education stresses the areas that are most applicable to the client's operations issues and opportunities. (One of these organizations refers to our green belt program as a *very dark green* green belt.) Beyond the formal Six Sigma classroom sessions, several short, targeted sessions are held around specific candidate projects. The education also includes real-life examples of how to apply the methodologies and tools to specific improvement areas using client data and examples. People walk away with a connection between the Six Sigma concepts and reality and get right to work on their assigned projects. The usual debates about applicability and whether or not we should change do not occur. Further, the usual "I need a project for certification" activities do not occur because the assigned projects are defined up front and are linked to the organization's business plan.

There is so much groundwork that should be laid before an organization thinks about education. Education without a strategy is like a mathematical vector with magnitude but no direction. For the past decade, we have adopted a real-world approach to education that we refer to as Achievement-Based Education. It has taken years of experimenting with various alternatives to improve education effectiveness, and the Achievement-Based Education model works well. We have adopted this approach for all kaizen, lean, and Six Sigma education. During the classroom component, participants understand the strategy and implementation plans for change. They learn both the concepts and the nuts-and-bolts methodology of how to apply these concepts to their projects and operating environment. We also incorporate several client-specific simulation exercises designed to demonstrate that they can apply the tools over and over and see continued improvements. Small and mid-sized organizations are interested in making something happen quickly, and the way that education is delivered makes a big difference in the speed of results.

IMPROVEMENT IS ALWAYS NECESSARY

A mind-set that best-in-class organizations embrace is that no matter where your current performance lies, it simply is not good enough beyond today. The world is moving at clock speed, technology and product life cycles are very short, and everyone is involved in business improvement. The diagonal vector and bandwidths in our Kano diagram (Figure 9.3) are rising at a much faster speed than many organizations can keep up with. However, this also provides the opportunity to leapfrog and surprise the competition with the right strategy. The Kano

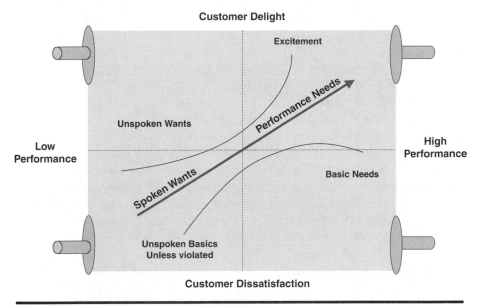

Figure 9.3 "Demand-Slide" Kano diagram.

diagram represents this phenomenon graphically. For example, let's say you want a $299 notebook PC. You call up HP Computer and learn that the price is $2,199. You are in the lower right quadrant; you are looking for performance, but you are disappointed in the quoted price. Next you call Hell Computer and learn that it just introduced a notebook with everything you are looking for and the price is $99.95. Now you are elated and in the upper right quadrant of the Kano diagram. You are excited and place the order. When you receive your new notebook, the display is 1" × 1", the hard drive is 40KB, not MB (a typo on the web site), and it does not come with a power cord. Now you are in the lower left quadrant of the Kano diagram because your assumed expectations were violated. Finally, you open the rest of the contents of the box and find three extra batteries, a bunch of CDs for AOL, QuickTime, CD Creator, game subscriptions, another catalog, a Hell umbrella, and a few other things that are not relevant to your needs. Now you are in the upper left quadrant of the Kano diagram. You return the box with all of its contents to Hell. In the process, you learn that Dell Computer has just introduced a notebook for $799. You compromise your price expectations, order the notebook, and are very happy with your decision. Now you are back in the top right quadrant and everyone else has slipped down and to the left. We are spending time on the Kano diagram because the combined actions of your customers, the organization, and your competitors are continually moving relative positions around on this model. In addition, customer and market needs, and the combined responses to these dynamic requirements, are causing the model to scroll up to higher expectation levels. Great organizations execute strategies that delight customers and keep themselves in the top right quadrant of the Kano diagram in the process. Organizations that do nothing will see their relative position slip quickly in the new Demand-Slide economy.

The best time to change is now. Great leaders recognize opportunities for improvement and the challenges faced by the people around them. They also find the time to initiate and lead improvement initiatives even though it may look like the last thing they need to worry about. They have an overwhelming and unwavering resolve to prevail, no matter what may jump out at them. They have the faith and confidence that the organization can change without compromising current customer obligations. Finally, they create an open culture and problem-solving environment where improvement and celebrations replace blame and substandard performance.

Each improvement methodology discussed in this chapter by itself can provide some gains, but there is a danger of going overboard. It is like the *hammer looking for a nail* analogy. If you are a big believer in just kaizen, then you will subconsciously believe that everything can be solved with a blitz. If you are a narrow-minded lean disciple, then you will try to fix everything with 5S, kanbans, and cells. We can hang up signage and shadow boards, purchase color-coded totes, and label everything in the place. We have seen organizations literally tie their business in knots with the various buzzword tools. Then they become so infatuated with trying to make their tools work that they forget about the original objective. One organization became a bit obsessive with its 5S program. It labeled every file cabinet and piece of equipment labeled in the office — as if people needed help identifying payroll records, the copy machine, the water fountain, the paper cutter, and the paper shredder. To our amazement, everything in the men's room was also labeled: sink, urinal, toilet, paper towels, trash. Do you think people would be lost without this 5S signage?

Whether it is kaizen, lean, Six Sigma, or enabling IT, we can end up in the same situations if we are not careful. The most significant benefits are achieved by combining and integrating tools and deploying the right tools correctly to the highest impact opportunities. We need to ask ourselves these questions constantly because sheer motion is not improvement.

Another factor that an organization should prepare itself for is failure. Mistakes are part of learning unless you fail to learn from your mistakes. Improvements are not always successful on the first try either. Remember that the passion for learning and improvement is never wasted. Learning is a lot like improvement: For some, it is a passion; for others, it is a knee-jerk reaction to a particular need. People are most successful when they develop a passion for both, because one feeds the other. Learning is not always vital to the task at hand, but it rounds out and enhances careers and life in general. Knowing how to integrate kaizen, lean, Six Sigma, and enabling IT will provide a total powerhouse improvement initiative, especially once the organization understands how to deploy the right improvement methodologies to the right opportunities.

CHAPTER 9 TAKE-AWAYS

■ Many of the basic Six Sigma tools and Minitab analyses are not only applicable to other improvement initiatives like kaizen and lean, but can also actually increase implementation robustness and financial results. We have found the DMAIC thoughtware to be very useful in providing a single, structured, problem-solving approach for all of these improvement initiatives.

■ DMAIC prevents the confusion caused by feeding people six different versions of the same thing because it is presented as a common, structured, problem-solving methodology. This uniform approach to business improvement presents Six Sigma as another drawer of tools in the DMAIC tool chest.

■ The largest opportunities in most organizations now lie in the transactional process areas. Many of these transactional processes are untouched territory and ripe for improvement, and organizations can make dramatic improvements rapidly. Opportunities in the warranty/returns, invoicing, quotations, customer service, purchasing, sales and marketing, new product development, and human resource areas are in the millions of dollars. Over the past few years, we have seen the scope of our lean and Six Sigma projects grow to over 50 percent transactional process content.

■ Another aspect of integration involves transforming our Six Sigma thinking *horizontally* beyond the four walls to the total value stream. The opportunities beyond the four walls are enormous because 70 to 95 percent of the customer-impacted activities, cycle times, and costs are generated in these segments of the supply chain. The benefits of instantaneous demand and supply adjustment, business collaboration, and information exchange are pretty obvious.

■ Kaizen, lean, Six Sigma, ERP, SCM, CRM, PLM, and enabling IT are all compatible improvement methodologies. The methodologies and tools are not magic mantras; they are simply *tools of the trade* that work well when integrated and deployed correctly and to the right opportunities.

■ Kaizen is best suited to *quick-strike opportunities* and *quick containment measures* in a process.

■ Many lean efforts are more *compensating improvements* in practice because people use the lean tools in a way that compensates for deep-rooted process variation. Techniques such as kanban, buffer inventories, and scheduling practices definitely improve flow, but we can get even better if we understand the system constraints and drive toward perfection.

■ Six Sigma is a more *perfection-driven improvement* because we make the effort with data and facts to understand and reduce/eliminate complex process variation. Six Sigma drives processes to a new level of performance and capability.

■ Information technology such as ERP, SCM, CRM, SRM, PLM, and networks and portals is referred to as *instantaneous improvements* because we can often eliminate or replace a bad process with a real-time process.

SUGGESTED FURTHER READING

Burton, Terence and Boeder, Steve, *The Lean Extended Enterprise: Moving Beyond the Four Walls to Value Stream Excellence,* J. Ross Publishing, 2003.

Devenport, Thomas, *Mission Critical: Realizing the Promise of Enterprise Systems,* Harvard Business School Press, 2002.

George, Michael, *Lean Six Sigma: Combining Six Sigma Quality with Lean Production Speed,* McGraw-Hill, 2002.

George, Michael, *Lean Six Sigma for Service,* McGraw-Hill, 2003.

Godwin, Malcolm, *Who Are You: 101 Ways of Seeing Yourself,* Penguin Publications, 2000.

Waterman, Thomas, *Adhocracy,* Whittle Books, 1990.

Wheat, Barbara, Mills, Chuck, and Carnell, Mike, *Leaning into Six Sigma,* McGraw-Hill, 2003.

10

DELIVERING
THE GOODS

This chapter was appropriately named by borrowing a favorite saying of an executive and friend. During our projects, we always talked about the need to achieve results — fast, measureable, and validated by the financial organization. It became known as *delivering the goods*. This chapter provides a few final thoughts about achieving success with your Six Sigma deployment and ultimately — *delivering your goods*.

Six Sigma presents an enormous improvement opportunity for every organization. The upside potential is almost unbelievable; some organizations are reporting savings in the millions of dollars to hundreds of millions to billions. The downside risk is manageable with great leadership and an implementation approach directly linked to the strategic plan. Earlier in the book, we discussed the origins of Six Sigma, some of which date back to before we were all born. We presented a new model for small and mid-sized organizations called *Scaleable Six Sigma™,* and in Chapter 3, we stressed the need to pay attention to the most important, nonstatistical implementation issues: leadership, strategy, and infrastructure (PLAN, DEPLOY, EXECUTE). The remainder of this chapter provides final ideas on how to make your Six Sigma deployment successful.

LEADERSHIP: THE FIRST NINETY DAYS

Six Sigma leadership represents 80 percent of the success factor, while the statistical tools and belts themselves represent the other 20 percent. Leadership is the turbo-charged engine that drives a successful Six Sigma deployment. It

179

comes from all directions and also from beyond the four walls. After reading this book, you may feel overwhelmed about where to begin your Six Sigma journey. We suggest that you begin with the following steps:

1. Build the courage and openness to see reality as it is. Every organization is involved in strategic improvement, and it needs to become a daily business practice like processing orders, checking e-mail, and sending out invoices. Establish the break points and push the organization into a transition state of mind. In today's fast-paced economy, you are either gaining ground or falling behind your competition. There is no such thing as staying the same anymore, and close enough is no longer good enough.

2. Take the initiative to begin your Six Sigma journey NOW! Regardless of what has been done in the past or what any of the critics claim, Six Sigma works if you do the right things from a leadership standpoint. Six Sigma or any strategic improvement is not dependent on industries, revenues, or statistical tools; it resides within you as a leader. Take the bold road and you will find it to be one of the most rewarding experiences of your executive career. Hit the ground running and never stop.

3. Conduct the right due diligence and understand gaps between current and best-in-class performance. Understand the largest challenges the organization is facing and will face in the near future. Create a bold vision of where you would like the organization to be in the next twelve to thirty-six months. Do not be afraid to go for levels beyond what any other competitor has achieved; it is called breakthrough improvement, and the only limits are those you place on yourself and the organization.

4. Revisit the organization's value system and cultural norms. Understand the current organizational practices and missing skill sets. Identify what needs to change, and then begin by setting the example for others. Realigning the organization means redirecting resources and activities, abandoning current activities for new opportunities, and changing organizational structure. Begin developing and mentoring the leadership talent in others and assembling the champion change agents.

5. Develop a solid Six Sigma strategy and send a uniform message to the rest of the organization about the challenges, need to change, expectations, and what is in it for all stakeholders. Avoid any Six Sigma programs that begin with belts, waves, and training before you understand what the organization *needs*. Deal with the barriers up front. Go for the early wins via pilot projects to establish Six Sigma believers and build momentum. Then execute, execute, and execute through everyone in the organization.

Leadership is not clustered at the top of the organization and it can spawn from many directions. Leadership is within an individual, not within an office or a title. CEOs and executives must take the initiative personally to point their organization in the right direction because leadership, vision, and the strategy of improvement are the most critical elements of change. Managers and individual contributors must also lead by pointing out the inequities in business processes rather than tolerating them. Brainstorm and share your thinking with others; make the ground move. Lead and help the executive team think through where and how the organization needs to change. Stop tolerating waste and mediocrity in your business processes. One individual recently said: "That's easy for you to say because you do not work here. It's better not to make waves and let the chips fall where they may in this economy because it's difficult to find another job." In our opinion, this is a very career-limiting perspective. Some of these folks are the people who call us weekly asking for information about how they can become black belt certified for their resume. These people wake up one day and wonder what happened to their career, their personal values, and their life. It is a fundamental career decision: Do you want to be a *champion* of change or a *victim* of change? It is that simple, and the risks of speaking out are imaginary if you use data and facts, professionalism, and logical analysis of current conditions. Six Sigma provides everyone with all of the skill sets to become very successful at this mode of operation.

CULTURE IS THE FOUNDATION

Another topic we wish to stress is culture — the foundation of Six Sigma where ordinary people grow to do extraordinary things. Everyone may be at a different starting point. If your organization has the demonstrated core competency of strategic improvement in place, then hit the starting line. It is an anomaly that the best organizations use outside assistance because there is tremendous power, focus, and velocity with the injection of new thinking coupled with internal knowledge and experience. If you are new to strategic improvement and the concepts of Six Sigma presented in this book, the first thing you should consider is getting outside assistance. Keep in mind that many organizations have been working on these principles for a decade, and outside assistance will help you to accelerate the improvement process. On the surface, these things look easy to implement, but the devil is in the details, especially if you are a small or mid-sized organization. If you are an organization with a track record of "flavor-of-the-month" programs, this is probably the toughest starting point to overcome. How do you convince an organization with a string of failed improvement programs that *this time we are really serious about Six Sigma.* It is about as difficult as trying to convince a herd of goats that they need quantum physics. You cannot do it with a speech. It is a slow process based on demonstrated leadership, commitment, and results. It requires many hits of consistent communication, awareness, and dialogue and sometimes an admission that we screwed up! It also requires extreme levels of patience and perseverance, and it may feel like you are turning the Queen Mary around in Boston Harbor. Trying to move quickly into another set of improvement frameworks and tools will only add to the confusion of mixed messages and the barriers will be raised. Maybe you built this culture and maybe you did not, but recognize that this type of culture will eat your Six Sigma strategy for breakfast if you do not recognize it and deal with it. Communication, awareness, rebuilding confidence, and change management are all critical to avoid another failed fad improvement program. Because we are dealing with humans with human frailties, constant reinforcement of the Six Sigma message is critical. Six Sigma will manifest itself in direct proportion to the organization's collective leadership and passion to succeed.

Cultural transformation is not geography or industry or market or product or program or local culture dependent. We have heard so many excuses why organizations cannot change. They run the gamut from "we're located in Europe" to "we're out in the middle of Nowheresville, USA" to "we have a union" to thinking that "our employees are not smart enough to implement lean or Six Sigma." We like to simplify business and life into two categories: performances and excuses. The right leadership does not let the excuses get in its way. The leaders develop and grow ordinary people to do extraordinary things in their organization regardless of the particular characteristics of geography, markets, or products.

EUREKA MOMENTS TRANSFORM CULTURE

Scientists use the term "Eureka!" moment to describe the point at which we have enough context to understand a new fact. At Tufts University, they believe they can now tell exactly when a "Eureka!" moment happens through measurements of the electrical activity in the brain. An intriguing result of the Tufts research is the notion that confusion is an essential part of remembering things. The activity of trying to make sense of information leads us to understand and remember the result.

The ability to sustain improvement is directly associated with culture. In our Six Sigma practice, we coined the term *Personal Discovery Moments* (our version of "Eureka!" moments) to describe the personal experience of feeling project success. In the past, too many improvement programs have attempted to change behaviors and culture directly. The fact is that nothing really changes in an organization until people change. We cannot order it, we cannot do it by threats, we cannot do it with posters and mugs, and we cannot hope it. Personal Discovery Moments occur in the context of individual experience with change, particularly when individuals feel inner success and personal growth. Improvement programs that stress this context of personal discovery are much more successful at promoting learning and behavioral change.

Personal Discovery Moments can be very rewarding and they can be very disappointing. The outcome shapes a particular individual's behavior and response to more change. As we said earlier, project selection is critical to a positive outcome. We mentioned an example of a Six Sigma black belt candidate who was assigned a kaizen-like mandatory project for certification. He solved the problem in a few days, but he went through the full four-month certification process, literally creating make-work demonstrations of the methodology and tools. His efforts were nonvalue-added, except to satisfy an academic need — education for education's sake, with no learning opportunities on his assigned project. Every step of the DMAIC (Define, Measure, Analyze, Improve, Control) process after the first few days was a big waste of his time. He received his black belt certification, but is he a believer? Absolutely not. At the end of the day, will he speak positively about his experience to others? Absolutely not. Can an organization be successful with Six Sigma when it produces hundreds of people with this experience? Absolutely not.

Positive personal discovery experiences create a positive spiraling effect on the organization. They set the stage for creating believers in improvement and change. They transcend Six Sigma to a level of meaningful reality by achieving results. They raise individual confidence and commitment to new levels where these people begin mentoring others. This, in turn, leads to more positive personal discovery experiences and more behavioral change. After we cultivate hundreds of believers and accumulate thousands of positive personal discovery experiences, the organization begins to transform culture.

The inverse is also true. People with negative personal discovery experiences are not believers. They will complain and discourage others about improvement. The rumor mill will carry this message just like the one unhappy customer who tells his or her friends, who tell their friends, and suddenly three hundred people know about the bad experience. Bad news always travels faster than good news. The e-mail cartoons start flying around. People become standoffish and reluctant to join in, and pretty soon the improvement initiative loses momentum. Behavior and culture never change. Soon the initiative fades away as if it never existed.

Personal discovery experiences shape our thinking, our beliefs, and our careers. If you live and breathe business improvement long enough, you will be involved in hundreds and thousands of these experiences. In the process, you will also discover that helping the organization reach its next level of improvement has a residual effect of helping you reach your next level of growth. It is a two-way street of professional development when done correctly, and it is also extremely rewarding to help organizations and people reach new planes of improvement and accomplishment together.

TARGET AND FOCUS SIX SIGMA

Six Sigma may seem like an enormously overwhelming initiative to take on. It is a major strategic undertaking, and it will take years to achieve. Developing a solid implementation strategy and approach is critical to the success of Six Sigma. Organizations that short-circuit this important step end up with a significant disconnect between means and ends. They fail to establish a dynamic process for defining new opportunities, establishing priorities, aligning and managing critical resources, and judging success. They embark on another "flavor-of-the-month" program destined for failure because there is too much focus on statistical tools and belts and not enough focus on results. There is no alignment between the strategic needs of the organization and the specific Six Sigma activities that people are involved in, and it also fosters a false sense of improvement. The goal is to understand core-value-creating processes, identify gaps and opportunities, calibrate pain points and opportunities, think through the implementation approach, and begin communication and awareness efforts. Tangible and significant business improvement comes from understanding and improving the core business processes in the total value stream. Failure to develop a solid Six Sigma strategy is analogous to a balloon full of hot air. We can blow it up and let it go and it will fly around the room, but quickly it will fall to the floor — just like "flavor-of-the-month" programs do.

Early on in a Six Sigma effort, it is often helpful to conduct executive brainstorming sessions and create a high-level, enterprise business map. This identifies the core business processes in the value stream, their interdependencies and interrelationships, and key performance issues that need to be addressed. The enterprise business map should also be populated with descriptive data such as value add, cost, waste, cycle time, and pain points. We can take this down a level of detail and conduct preliminary data analysis to validate our collective insights. The enterprise business map usually provides excellent insights about where to focus initial efforts. Next, we need focus, and the best and easiest

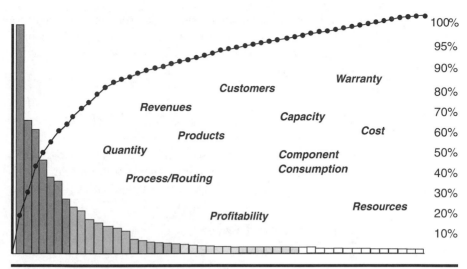

Figure 10.1   Multilevel Pareto analysis.

way to accomplish this is by using multilevel Pareto analysis (Figure 10.1). When you consider all of the content in this book, Six Sigma is overwhelming. Multilevel Pareto analysis enables us to analyze various factors of our business in relation to each other. In essence, the objective of focus is to answer questions such as:

- What 20 percent of our customers generate 80 percent of revenues?
- What 20 percent of our products generate 80 percent of revenues?
- What 20 percent of our products generate 80 percent of profits?
- What 20 percent of our inventory items represent 80 percent of our inventory investment?
- What products flow through what process steps or routings?
- What 20 percent of our products consume 80 percent of capacity?
- What products consume what raw materials?
- What elements consume 80 percent of our cash-to-cash cycle time?
- What are the stratified expenditures by supplier and commodity?
- What is the distribution of root causes for unplanned downtime?
- What are the warranty costs by product and by customer?

What insight does this type of analysis provide to us? It helps us to focus on the critical 20 percent of the problems that will generate 80 percent of the results. If we try to focus on everything, we will spread our resources too thin and end up working on the other trivial 80 percent of the problems. As you deep dive into the relationships between these critical factors, Six Sigma becomes a lot less overwhelming. Multilevel Pareto analysis is also very useful for the chunking and project selection activities covered earlier.

TEN MOST VALUABLE SIX SIGMA LESSONS LEARNED

As we approach the end of our last chapter, we would like to summarize what we believe are the ten most valuable points presented in the book. Small and mid-sized organizations have a unique challenge when implementing Six Sigma.

Lesson #1: Six Sigma Is About Results, Not Belts and Statistical Tools

The business community has been bombarded with advice from consultants, trade publications, web sites, and assorted gurus about Six Sigma. A lot of this advice is valuable, but much of it is an inconsistent, ambiguous generalization of what it takes to be successful in your own environment, especially a small and mid-sized company environment.

Six Sigma is not a business strategy; it is a powerful enabler of executing on business strategy. Six Sigma is not about belts or how many black and green belts an organization needs. It is all about business improvement and whatever it takes to make it happen. Six Sigma does not require millions of dollars in investment, dedication of full-time resources, and training of the masses. The traditional top-down Six Sigma deployment structure and approach is not only inappropriate, but is totally unrealistic for smaller and mid-sized organizations.

Lesson #2: Scaleable Six Sigma™ Is the Right Deployment Approach for Smaller and Mid-Sized Organizations

Scaleable Six Sigma™ works well in these environments because the strategy and deployment plan, scope, and focus of Six Sigma are designed around the organization's requirements, learning/digestion capabilities, financial constraints, and timing with other critical business events. This program and building-block approach is modularized so that the organization can quickly transition its Six Sigma resources to the next highest level of achievement. Additionally, it can accomplish its Six Sigma implementation at a more manageable pace and scope. The number of projects, the levels of education, and the whole deployment and execution approach occur at a digestible pace, with a direct link to strategy and results. Unlike the traditional top-down deployment, black belts are, in effect, outsourced resources. This scaleable Six Sigma approach is much more practical for our smaller and mid-sized clients because it becomes self-funding much more quickly.

Lesson #3: Strategic Improvement Is a Core Competency

It all looks so easy and logical, but the ability to define, organize, and lead a major initiative like Six Sigma is a skill that most organizations do not have internally by osmosis, and they underestimate the difficulty of launching and deploying a strategic improvement initiative of this magnitude. If these initiatives are launched incorrectly, it becomes very difficult to turn them around and make them a way of life. Organizations must learn how to define, lead, and execute strategic improvement. You do not get there by developing a grand strategy and then delegating it to a powerless organization. You do not go to a Six Sigma seminar and become an instant change master. You do not wake up one day, flip a switch, and have these competencies in place throughout your organization. It takes a huge, long-term commitment to define and organize a strategic improvement initiative and then integrate strategy, leadership, execution, the right methodologies, and permanent culture change. Those organizations that have achieved impressive results from their improvement programs do so because they understand this fact. Although most improvement methodologies such as Six Sigma offer steps and tools that are necessary to achieve success, they are neither sufficient nor exhaustive. Further, improvement methodologies are ineffective without the right improvement strategy and infrastructure bundled around them. Six Sigma methodologies, tools, and enabling technologies are only the *means*, not the *ends*.

Lesson #4: Leadership, Strategy, Infrastructure, and Deployment Are Most Critical

Six Sigma leadership represents 80 percent of the success factor, while the statistical tools and belts themselves represent the other 20 percent. Leadership is the turbo-charged engine that drives a successful Six Sigma deployment. Although many of the Six Sigma statistical tools are based on chance, a successful Six Sigma deployment is a matter of choice. Many organizations skip the most important element of improvement: the Six Sigma Strategy and Deployment Plan. Organizations tend to skim over this process and dive into the methodologies and tools. People select and implement tools and techniques in an effort to get quick results. Their intentions are good because they are trying to make a quick impact, but their actions are bad because they end up chasing down outcomes and symptoms because they do not have a solid improvement plan. The anxiety of jumping in leaves the rest of the organization in initial confusion and doubt. In the absence of a well-defined Six Sigma Strategy and Deployment Plan, activities are "perception driven" versus "fact driven" and not focused on strategic gaps and root causes of poor performance.

Most successful Six Sigma efforts are led by an executive steering group that reconciles strategic needs and Six Sigma activity. This executive steering group typically provides broad Six Sigma direction in the organization on critical areas of improvement. Most also have a formal process of putting potential projects through a litmus test for prioritizing strategic importance. Some even regulate the amount of activity in progress at any given time, so Six Sigma does not take on a life of its own, like previous improvement programs. A few even maintain a rolling, project-by-project Six Sigma return on investment.

Lesson #5: DMAIC Is the Roadmap to Individual Six Sigma Project Success

DMAIC is a standardized, disciplined approach to problem solving, no matter what type of problem you are facing. DMAIC provides a common, problem-solving language for the organization and weaves together the specific statistical tools and deliverables used at each stage of the process. The purpose of the DMAIC roadmap is to take a practical problem, translate this problem into a statistical problem, form and test a hypothesis until a statistically sound solution is discovered, and then translate that statistical solution back into a practical solution for the original problem. In order to accomplish this end, several tools within each phase are employed, and a checklist is used to verify the application of the tools for each phase in order to exit that portion of the project and move to the next stage of problem solving. DMAIC prevents the confusion caused by feeding people six different versions of the same thing because it is presented as a common, structured, problem-solving methodology. This uniform approach to business improvement presents Six Sigma as another drawer of tools in the DMAIC tool chest.

Lesson #6: Transactional Six Sigma Presents High-Impact Opportunities

For many organizations, actual manufacturing represents 15 to 20 percent of their total cost structure. The remaining 80 percent is due to transactional process activity such as sales and marketing, finance, engineering and R&D, customer service, procurement, and distribution. Transactional Six Sigma is strategically important because as much as 70 to 95 percent of product cost is generated outside of your organization, up to 75 to 95 percent of lead time is consumed outside of your organization, and about 95+ percent of the key activities of design, supply chain planning, and manufacturing is outside of your organization. A common thread is the *hidden factory* of costs and opportunities when deep diving into transactional processes. Many of these practices have become institutionalized and accepted as the norm in many organizations. As long as these processes and practices remain in *hidden factory* mode, they cannot be improved and the hidden costs of doing business grow. This myriad of improvement opportunities is surfacing because executives recognize that transactional processes represent the major component of their businesses from both a cost and activity/resource consumption perspective.

Lesson #7: Project Selection Is a Critical Element of Six Sigma Success

A prerequisite to project prioritization and selection is the Six Sigma strategy and how this is linked to the tactical plan. This annual operating plan must then be supported by a set of critical few improvement priorities. These priorities create the need for underlying projects. These critical few projects are "must do" to meet the annual operating plan and, thus, the strategic plan. It is important to separate the *critical few* from the *trivial many* projects that can act as a distraction and dissolve the effectiveness of limited resources. Another critical element of this process is alignment — the culmination of people, processes, and enabling technology in synchronization with the business strategy. Without alignment, there is a natural tendency to drift into conflicting objectives throughout the organization, rather than stay focused on mission-critical improvements. Alignment provides a crystal-clear link between the business strategy and the day-to-day improvement activities throughout the organization.

There is only so much *special project* activity available before day-to-day operations are disrupted. Sometimes conditions dictate that we need to turn up the heat beyond this level to put a few changes in place quickly. The goal is to appreciate this limited capacity, regulate the amount of activity, and target the activity toward strategically important requirements. It is better to complete a dozen incredibly successful Six Sigma projects than it is to complete dozens of Six Sigma projects with illusionary savings.

Lesson #8: Performance Measurement Is the Only True Gauge of Six Sigma Success

Performance measurement is the needle and thread that sews strategy and execution together and turns the Six Sigma strategy into results. It enables organizations to achieve alignment and integration throughout the organization.

More importantly, it allows people to measure the right things so everyone can tell if things are getting better. The all-too-familiar disconnects occur in the details of the organization because there is poor alignment at the operational level. People do not set up these disconnects on purpose; they just happen because of a lack of understanding about the importance of measurement, alignment, and resulting behaviors. Performance measurement is not only concerned with measuring the right metrics, but includes many levels and must be designed to link and align the organization and drive the right behaviors. It must create that hard-wired spiral between the organization's strategy and its daily Six Sigma improvement activities. Everything begins and ends with performance measurement.

Lesson #9: Integration of Six Sigma with Other Improvement Initiatives Equals a Powerhouse Improvement Initiative

The entire spectrum of enterprise activity and business processes includes the full array of problems and opportunities. Any methodology like Six Sigma, lean, kaizen and new IT applications by itself is suboptimizing and will not make an organization world class. Each improvement methodology by itself can provide some gains, but there is a danger of going overboard. It is like the *hammer looking for a nail* analogy. If you are a big believer in just kaizen, then you will subconsciously believe that everything can be solved with a blitz. If you are a narrow-minded lean disciple, then you will try to fix everything with 5S, kanbans, and cells. We can hang up signage and shadow boards, purchase color-coded totes, and label everything in the place. Like your toolbox at home, you are very limited with just a hammer, a wrench, and a few screwdrivers. Pretty soon every problem starts to look like a nail or a screw. If you attempt to solve a problem with the wrong tools, you will probably get the wrong answer. We have observed the misuse of improvement methodologies over and over. Some blindly follow DMAIC and make quick-strike molehills into complex Six Sigma mountains. Others try to reduce very complex process variation with an opinion-driven blitz effort. Some believe that 5S-ing and kanban-ing the universe and rearranging equipment into cells is the answer. Some believe that everything must be web-enabled and real time. They are all partially right and partially wrong. Sticking to a single-point improvement and discounting the other methodologies is very limiting on the realm of improvement potential. We need to stop the debates about kaizen, lean, Six Sigma, ERP, SCM, CRM, PLM, and other IT enablers and recognize that they all have their place in total enterprise improvement. The methodologies and tools are not magic mantras, but are simply *tools of the trade* that work well when integrated and deployed correctly and to the right opportunities. We need to provide new injections of skills so that people understand how all of the improvement methodologies fit together. We need to focus on integrating processes, people, and information across the total value stream. We need to stay with a common, organizational approach for analyzing and solving business problems, and the DMAIC methodology provides a uniform problem-solving structure.

Lesson #10: Six Sigma Is Powerful Stuff, Especially for Small and Mid-Sized Organizations

Six Sigma is not the silver bullet, nor is it the panacea for all of management's challenges. But make no mistake about it — Six Sigma is here to stay because its demonstrated success is proven in the numbers. Six Sigma is a highly "customer-centric" improvement process that focuses on tangible results, one project at a time. Many organizations are well into Six Sigma and are migrating the methodology upstream to new product development and suppliers. Many smaller and mid-sized companies that are suppliers to these larger organizations recognize this trend and are proactively implementing Six Sigma before they are told to do so. These organizations are the early beneficiaries from Six Sigma.

If you are implementing Six Sigma, there is a good chance that you will see millions of dollars added to your company's bottom line this year. Congratulations to you, your employees, and your stakeholders! If you are not currently implementing Six Sigma or have not heard about it yet, chances are that you will — especially if you do business with any Fortune 1000 company. If you wait until one of these organizations mandates Six Sigma as a condition for doing business in the future, you have given away a lot of ground to your competition.

SLEEPLESS IN SIX SIGMA

The Six Sigma revolution is well under way in the Fortune 1000 arena. These organizations have been pressuring the next tiers of suppliers to get with the program and begin implementing Six Sigma. For executives in small and mid-sized organizations, the dilemma of how to implement Six Sigma for their customers and themselves is just another mounting issue that keeps them up every night, joined by slow economic recovery, foreign competition, the movement of more and more business to China and other third-world countries, and dozens of other shorter term challenges. There are no big bumps in sight to put small and mid-sized companies over the top, and it is difficult to think about a longer term strategic initiative like Six Sigma. By now we hope that you understand enough about variation to recognize that the economy is an uncontrollable factor anyway. Bulls, bears, terrorist threats, and Fed monetary policy are totally irrelevant to the potential improvement opportunities in any organization.

On the other hand, most executives recognize the benefits of Six Sigma, but have been struggling with how to deploy Six Sigma in their environments without tying up their star performers and breaking the organization's bank account. It is a catch-22: Executives cannot afford to hold off on Six Sigma because waiting will put you behind, but acting has been financially impractical and will introduce additional commitments and constraints on the organization.

We were having dinner recently with the executive group of one of our clients. We were discussing why some organizations are more successful than others with Six Sigma. The conversation drifted to something like the following: "Some organizations are great and some are mediocre. There are strong leaders and weak leaders. Some organizations get it and are quick to change, and others don't get it and operate in the slow lane. Some organizations are market leaders and others are followers. Some have better and brighter people than others. Culture is different in Boston than it is in Austin, San Jose, Appleton, London, or Kuala Lumpur. It's that 80/20 thing at play. That's what creates competition and makes the world go round." One executive finally said, "If you look inwardly at our own Six Sigma successes, I don't buy any of this discussion. It all comes down to choices. There's nothing special about our organization except the choices we've made to become market leaders and build the right infrastructure to support this strategy. It's the choices we've made to become the best at everything we do. We're just ordinary people doing extraordinary things." When you think critically about strategic change, it really comes down to choices. We all have the choice of leading change or hanging around and becoming victims of someone else's change. We all have the opportunity to learn, apply new knowledge, and grow professionally or sit around and become stagnant thinkers. We all have the choice of operating in the slow lane or displacing our competition in the upper 20 percent echelon. Six Sigma represents a strategic change of choice, and the *choice* and the *outcome* are directly in your control. As we mentioned earlier in the book, it is deciding whether to be the hunter or the hunted. You have the opportunity to lead and benefit from change or hang around and become the victim of your competitors' change.

As we were writing this book, a colleague sent an e-mail that is very appropriate for this chapter:

> In Africa there is a daily challenge for zebras. Zebras are a unique animal because when they are together, individual zebras are

camouflaged from predators. Predators attempt to single them out so they can see, attack, and kill them for food. Together, the zebras find a source of security and safety, but on their own they are susceptible to fatal attack.

Lions face a similar daily challenge. Every morning when the lions awake, they must run like hell for the zebras or they will starve. Every morning when the zebras awake, they must run like hell from the lions or they will be killed. Moral of the story: It doesn't matter if you're a lion or a zebra — you better stick together and run like hell every morning when you awake.

The same holds true in business: Organizations need a well-defined Six Sigma strategy and a deployment and execution plan, and the entire organization needs to pursue it relentlessly every day.

Scaleable Six Sigma™ and the contents of this book provide new and more practical approaches for small and mid-sized organizations to now take advantage of Six Sigma. These proven approaches now make Six Sigma deployable and affordable for small and mid-sized organizations. There is no mystery or magic to Six Sigma's success. For small and mid-sized organizations, we hope that we have removed some of the mystery of and barriers to successfully deploying Six Sigma in your organization. Six Sigma is not magic, but it requires a strong commitment, unwavering leadership, persistence, focus and targeting in on the issues that really matter, chasing down and reducing process variation and root causes, and then starting all over, throughout the entire enterprise. Now that you have reached this point, the rest is up to you. Doing nothing or waiting for the economy to turn around or for the next election is much more risky than deploying Six Sigma, especially now that you have new approaches that are more suited to your company environment. So *hit the ground running,* and best of luck on your Six Sigma deployment.

CHAPTER 10 TAKE-AWAYS

■ Six Sigma leadership represents 80 percent of the success factor, while the statistical tools and belts themselves represent the other 20 percent. Leadership is the turbo-charged engine that drives a successful Six Sigma deployment. It comes from all directions and also from beyond the four walls. Regardless of what has been done in the past or what any of the critics claim, Six Sigma works if you do the right things from a leadership standpoint. Six Sigma or any strategic improvement is not dependent on industries, revenues, or statistical tools. It resides within you as a leader.

- Culture is the foundation of Six Sigma where ordinary people grow to do extraordinary things. Everyone may be at a different starting point. If your organization has the demonstrated core competency of strategic improvement in place, then hit the starting line. It is an anomaly that the best organizations use outside assistance because there is tremendous power, focus, and velocity with the injection of new thinking coupled with internal knowledge and experience.

- In the past, too many improvement programs have attempted to change behaviors and culture directly. The fact is that nothing really changes in an organization until people change. We cannot order it, we cannot do it by threats, we cannot do it with posters and mugs, and we cannot hope it. Personal Discovery Moments occur in the context of individual experience with change, particularly when individuals feel inner success and personal growth. Improvement programs that stress this context of personal discovery are much more successful in promoting learning and behavioral change.

- Developing a solid implementation strategy and approach is critical to the success of Six Sigma. Organizations that short-circuit this important step end up with a significant disconnect between means and ends. There is no alignment between the strategic needs of the organization and the specific Six Sigma activities that people are involved in, and it also fosters a false sense of improvement. The goal is to understand core-value-creating processes, identify gaps and opportunities, calibrate pain points and opportunities, think through the implementation approach, and begin communication and awareness efforts. Tangible and significant business improvement comes from understanding and improving the core business processes in the total value stream.

- Focusing and targeting in on critical opportunities is critical to Six Sigma success. If we try to focus on everything, we will spread our resources too thin and end up working on the other trivial 80 percent of the problems. As you deep dive into the relationships between these critical factors, Six Sigma becomes a lot less overwhelming. Multilevel Pareto analysis is also very useful for the chunking and project selection activities covered earlier.

- Scaleable Six Sigma™ is the right deployment approach for smaller and mid-sized companies because it allows these organizations to deploy, learn, digest, and benefit at a much faster and more manageable rate. The strategy and deployment plan, scope, and focus of Six Sigma are designed around the organization's requirements, learning/digestion capabilities, financial constraints, and timing with other critical business events. Additionally, the organization can accomplish its Six Sigma implementation at a more manageable pace and scope.

■ Transactional Six Sigma presents high-impact opportunities. For many organizations, actual manufacturing represents 15 to 20 percent of their total cost structure. The remaining 80 percent is due to transactional process activity such as sales and marketing, finance, engineering and R&D, customer service, procurement, and distribution. Transactional Six Sigma is strategically important because as much as 70 to 95 percent of product cost is generated outside of your organization, up to 75 to 95 percent of lead time is consumed outside of your organization, and about 95+ percent of the key activities of design, supply chain planning, and manufacturing is outside of your organization.

■ Integration of Six Sigma with other improvement initiatives equals a powerhouse improvement initiative. Any methodology like Six Sigma, lean, kaizen, and new IT applications by itself is suboptimizing and will not make an organization world class. Sticking to a single-point improvement and discounting the other methodologies is very limiting on the realm of improvement potential. The methodologies and tools are not magic mantras, but are simply *tools of the trade* that work well when integrated and deployed correctly and to the right opportunities. People must understand how all of the improvement methodologies fit together.

APPENDIX: SCALEABLE SIX SIGMA™ GENERIC IMPLEMENTATION PLAN

	Month							
Phase I: Implementation Planning	1	2	3	4	5	6	7	8
1.1 Review organization, products, markets, customers, competition	■							
1.2 Establish the Six Sigma executive leadership team	■							
1.3 Conduct a detailed assessment of the business (e.g., customers, products, markets, operations, key business processes, enabling IT, etc.)	■							
1.4 Evaluate current conditions against benchmarking and best practices data	■							
1.5 Define critical-to-customer requirements for superior industry performance	■							
1.6 Understand gaps between current and desired business performance	■							
1.7 Develop the Six Sigma vision, strategy, and deployment plan	■							
1.8 Review findings with the Six Sigma executive leadership team and "internalize" a deployment approach based on leadership, organizational, resource, and cultural characteristics	■							
1.9 Define and down-select the critical strategic initiatives and stakeholders, and scope out further into individual projects	■							
1.10 Select and assign candidates and team members to projects and hold the initial kickoff meetings	■							
1.11 Define specific Six Sigma skill set requirements and develop the green belt/ yellow belt education wave plan	■							

APPENDIX: SCALEABLE SIX SIGMA™ GENERIC IMPLEMENTATION PLAN (continued)

	Month							
	1	2	3	4	5	6	7	8
Phase I: Implementation Planning								
1.12 Deliver Six Sigma leadership and overview education to the executive leadership team	■							
1.13 Develop the Six Sigma awareness and communication plan	■							
1.14 Develop the detailed green belt wave schedule and program plan	■							
Phase II: Six Sigma Quick-Strike Pilots								
2.1 Select two to three pilot areas to demonstrate the power of Six Sigma	■							
2.2 Define and assemble pilot implementation teams and launch pilots	■							
2.3 Provide four-hour Six Sigma education module focused on pilot project needs	■							
2.4 Provide Six Sigma facilitation and lead technical help for the pilot teams		■						
2.5 Direct the pilot teams through the DMAIC process		■						
2.6 Complete the two to three pilot projects successfully and demonstrate how Six Sigma has enabled new improvement opportunities not previously possible		■						
2.7 Showcase Six Sigma pilots to the executive leadership team, middle managers, and process owners			■					

APPENDIX: SCALEABLE SIX SIGMA™ GENERIC IMPLEMENTATION PLAN (continued)

				Month				
	1	2	3	4	5	6	7	8
Phase II: Six Sigma Quick-Strike Pilots								
2.8 Gain support and consensus on Six Sigma as a strategic improvement initiative and critical enabler of business strategy			▪					
2.9 Revise the Six Sigma strategy, deployment plan, and areas of focus based on pilot lessons learned			▪					
2.10 Deliver Six Sigma champion certification workshop to the executive leadership team and management group		▪						
2.11 Develop the Six Sigma Strategy and Deployment Plan, next level of detail based on pilot lessons learned		▮						
Phase III: Deployment and Implementation								
3.1 Further develop the Six Sigma strategy and policy deployment process with the executive leadership team			▮					
3.2 Integrate the Six Sigma strategy into the business unit strategic plan			▮					
3.3 Develop potential 1 st of projects that enable the achievement of the business unit strategic plan based on actual sales and marketing, operations, and financial data			▮					
3.4 Establish a formal project selection criteria and methodology and select the critical few strategic projects				▮				

APPENDIX: SCALEABLE SIX SIGMA™ GENERIC IMPLEMENTATION PLAN (continued)

	Month							
Phase III: Deployment and Implementation	1	2	3	4	5	6	7	8
3.5 Work with Six Sigma teams to create detailed charters (problem statement, project objectives, scope and boundaries, improvement goal, baseline performance, savings when goal achieved)			■	■				
3.6 Handle deployment logistics (e.g., ordering books, Minitab software, production of education materials, scheduling education, etc.)			■					
3.7 Conduct Six Sigma yellow belt training session for team members (one day) ■ Introduction to Six Sigma and DMAIC ■ Basic statistics/data analysis ■ Minitab basics ■ Value stream mapping ■ Process capability ■ MSA and Gage R&R studies ■ Teaming fundamentals ■ Kaizen quick-strike improvement ■ Lean and lean/Six Sigma ■ Catapult laboratory			■					
3.8 Conduct Six Sigma green belt training session, days one and two ■ Introduction to Six Sigma and DMAIC ■ Project requirements and deliverables ■ Basic statistics and analytical tools				■				

APPENDIX: SCALEABLE SIX SIGMA™ GENERIC IMPLEMENTATION PLAN (continued)

		Month							
	Phase III: Deployment and Implementation	**1**	**2**	**3**	**4**	**5**	**6**	**7**	**8**
	■ Minitab overview ■ Minitab analytical exercises: basic "B&T" tools ■ Value stream mapping ■ Function deployment matrix (FDM) ■ Cost of Poor Quality (COPQ) ■ Failure mode and effects analysis (FMEA) ■ Process capability (Cp & Cpk) ■ Catapult laboratory								
3.9	Provide facilitation, mentoring, and Six Sigma technical support to the implementation teams (DEFINE, MEASURE)				■	■			
3.10	Conduct Six Sigma green belt training session, days three and four				■	■			
	■ Refresher/review exercises ■ MSA, Gage R&R analysis ■ Lean manufacturing/lean enterprise ■ Kaizen and quick-strike improvement ■ Six Sigma leadership ■ Teaming fundamentals ■ Project management ■ Catapult laboratory ■ Peer review #1 ■ Book review #1								

APPENDIX: SCALEABLE SIX SIGMA™ GENERIC IMPLEMENTATION PLAN (continued)

		Month							
		1	2	3	4	5	6	7	8
Phase III: Deployment and Implementation									
3.11	Provide facilitation, mentoring, and Six Sigma technical support to the implementation teams (ANALYZE, IMPROVE)				■	■	■		
3.12	Provide facilitation, mentoring, and Six Sigma technical support to the implementation teams					■	■		
3.13	Conduct Six Sigma green belt training session, days five and six					■			
	■ Confidence intervals ■ t-tests, f-tests ■ Screening experiments (Multi-Vari) ■ Hypothesis testing ■ Analysis of variance (ANOVA) ■ Design of Experiments (full factorial designs) ■ Catapult laboratory ■ Peer review #2 ■ Book review #2								
3.14	Conduct Six Sigma green belt training session, day seven						■		
	■ Advanced DOE (fractional factorial designs) ■ Catapult laboratory ■ Peer review #3 ■ Book review #3								

APPENDIX: SCALEABLE SIX SIGMA™ GENERIC IMPLEMENTATION PLAN (continued)

Phase III: Deployment and Implementation	Month 1	2	3	4	5	6	7	8
3.15 Provide facilitation mentoring, and Six Sigma technical support to the implementation teams (IMPROVE, CONTROL)						■	■	■
3.16 Wrap up first wave of green belt projects and bring to a successful closure							■	
3.17 Hand off projects to process owners and monitor final implementation efforts							■	■
3.18 Establish knowledge repository and load all project information into a searchable Livelink-like application for future use							■	■
3.19 Executive and management project fair, certification ceremony for green and yellow belts								■
3.20 Define next steps in the deployment process (e.g., more green and yellow belt waves, elevation of selected green belts to black belts, horizontal/divisional deployment, etc.)						■	■	
3.21 Develop remaining Six Sigma deployment plan, schedule, expected benefits, etc.								■
3.22 Plan and launch the next waves of Six Sigma activities (ongoing)								■

Copyright ©2004 by The Center for Excellence in Operations, Inc. (CEO).

INDEX

A

Accounting, 98
Achievement-Based Education, 174
Activity-Based Mapping, 105
Adaptive Enterprise Six Sigma, 91, 93
Alignment, 106, 112, 141, 147
Allied Signal, 101
American Society for Quality, 8
Analyze phase, 14, 78–79, 86
   measurement criteria, 58
Annual operating plan, 111, 112
ANOVA, 97
Assembly line, 5
Average, 9, 10, 11
Awareness, 38, 46, 54–55, 147, 152–153

B

Balance, 55
Balanced scorecard, 110
Baseline performance, 141, 142
Bell curve, 9, 11, 12
Benchmarking, 8, 143
Best-in-class organizations, 141
Best-in-class performance, 143, 144
Black belt, 16, 29, 30, 37, 39, 41, 83
   certification, 38, 135
   outsourced mode, 40
   training, 36
Blocking and tackling tools, 39, 97, 170,
   see also specific tools

Brainstorming, 6
   executive sessions, 184
Brand image, 140
Business plan, linkage to, 53, 151
Business Process level, 140–141
Business Process Reengineering, 90
Business strategy, alignment of projects to,
   103
Business unit strategy plan, 113, 115

C

Call center operations, 98
Capacity regulation, 103–106
Caterpillar, 1
Cause and effect relationships, 6, 98, 141
Celebrations, 147
Certification, 39
Champion, 36, 38, 41, 74, 133, 134, 135
   education, 39
Change, 48–49, 54
   culture, see Culture change
Checksheeting, 170
Chunking, 146
Closeout process, 57, 58–59, 60, 147, 158
Collaboration, 55
Collins, James, 133
Commitment, 41, 46, 49–50, 54
Communication, 38, 46, 54–55, 128, 147,
   152–153
Confidence intervals, 97